PAUL DOWSWELL

Aliens

The Chequered History of Britain's Wartime Refugees

Biteback Publishing

First published in Great Britain in 2023 by
Biteback Publishing Ltd, London
Copyright © Paul Dowswell 2023

ISBN 978-1-78590-793-7

10 9 8 7 6 5 4 3 2 1

A CIP catalogue record for this book is available from the British Library.

Set in Adobe Caslon Pro

Printed and bound in Great Britain by
CPI Group (UK) Ltd, Croydon CR0 4YY

FSC
www.fsc.org
MIX
Paper | Supporting
responsible forestry
FSC® C171272

To Ilse Gray
and
Jenny and Josie Dowswell

Contents

Introduction

A Proud Tradition?

Refugee, *n*.: Someone driven from his home by war or the
fear of attack or persecution; a displaced person.
OXFORD ENGLISH DICTIONARY

The welcome given to refugees from fascist Europe is part of our fond nostalgia for Britain's role in the Second World War, nestling in our imagination next to images of tiny evacuees clutching teddy bears, and milkmen stoically picking their way through bomb rubble during the Blitz. But there is a darker side to this story.

Today, we are frequently told our country has a long, proud tradition of helping refugees – not least by our government. On 14 April 2022, Boris Johnson told an audience in Kent: 'For centuries, our United Kingdom has had a proud history of welcoming people from overseas, including many fleeing persecution.'

However, then, as now, refugees were seen as an unwanted burden. Then, as now, government used bureaucratic barriers and obfuscation to prevent their arrival. Then, as now, newspapers demonised them and created a climate of fear and resentment. Our attitude towards refugees has not substantially changed in eighty years,* and neither has the government's method of approaching the problem.

That's not to deny that we, as a country, have done useful and humanitarian things to help refugees. Many elderly Jews, for example, have fond memories of the kindness they received in Britain, when they came here as children before the war closed borders and prevented Jews from leaving the Nazi realm. 'To my dying day, I will be grateful to this country,' suggested one *Kindertransport* veteran in an article in the *Times of Israel*.

Many other refugees were not so lucky. In March 1939, a passenger ship named the *St Louis* sailed from Hamburg with 900 Jews on board. All the passengers carried visas permitting them entry to the ship's destination, Cuba. These they had bought at the Cuban Embassy in Berlin for between $200 and $300 ($3,000 to $5,000 at today's prices). When they arrived, the Cuban authorities had changed their minds about admitting them and they were refused entry. The captain sought permission to bring his human cargo to the United States and then Canada, both of which refused to take them. Returning across the Atlantic, the captain asked the British government if they would take his passengers. The refugees were told their applications would be considered if they returned to Hamburg and reapplied from there. It was now June and what seemed to be an inevitable war was less than three months away. But here, at last, events turned in their favour. The American Jewish Joint Distribution Committee – a Jewish refugee charity – agreed to pay a guarantee of $500,000 (around $8 million today) towards

---

* Although, today, refugees have become confused with asylum seekers (people claiming to be refugees whose status is determined by an often lengthy and complicated process) and 'economic migrants'.

the financial cost of accommodating these desperate people. So, when the ship arrived in Antwerp en route to Hamburg, Britain, Belgium, France and the Netherlands agreed to take the passengers. Britain took 288. Of the other 600 or so, who went to mainland European countries, 250 were murdered by the Nazis in the years following the fall of Western Europe.

*   *   *

So, what is our 'long and proud tradition'? Britain has been offering refuge, and assimilating other cultures from overseas, for centuries. In the previous millennium, Jews, Huguenots and Roman Catholics all arrived fresh from continental persecution. How much up-heaval and resentment this caused it is difficult to gauge, but of all these groups, the Jews faced the greatest difficulties, not least with their expulsion en masse in the late thirteenth century. Manuscripts from the medieval era also show both defamatory depictions and the promulgation of the bizarre belief that Jews sacrificed Christian children in rituals.

Another bunch of newcomers, Flemish weavers – who arrived in fourteenth-century London as economic migrants rather than refugees – were set upon and massacred during the upheaval of the Peasants' Revolt.

The first modern-day stirrings of unease with refugees fleeing to Britain occurred when 150,000 Jews arrived from Russia and other parts of Eastern Europe during the pogroms of 1881 to 1921. This particular influx marked the first attempt to restrict refugees and led to the 1905 Aliens Act, which introduced immigration controls and registration for the first time.* From then on, who was allowed to come into this country became a matter for the Home Secretary. The newly created tabloid press also seized on the unease these new arrivals generated. On 3 February 1900, for example, the *Daily Mail* described Jewish refugees arriving in a British port thus: 'When the Relief Committee passed by they hid their gold and fawned and whined, and, in broken English, asked for money for their train fare.'

A Conservative politician at the time, William Evans-Gordon, was a prominent anti-immigration campaigner who railed against the admission of 'destitute foreigners', claiming dramatically and without evidence in 1902 that 'not a day passes but English families are ruthlessly turned out to make room for the foreign invaders'.

The beginning of the Great War brought a further influx of refugees, with 250,000 Belgians arriving when the German Army occupied their country. To this day, this remains the greatest single influx of refugees at one time. Newspapers, now under the stern control of the Defence of the Realm Act, were instructed to write favourably about these newcomers from 'gallant little Belgium'. British assistance was seen as a necessary part in the propaganda campaign to justify fighting the war. Ninety per cent of these new arrivals returned to Belgium when the war ended.†

In the 1930s, alongside the German and Austrian Jews fleeing from the Nazis, there was a further influx of refugees from the Spanish Civil War. The Second World War would also add a quarter

---

* An article in the online magazine INVERSE from May 2016 notes that the word 'alien' is Latin in origin, meaning, initially, a slave, and then more widely, a stranger or foreigner. In medieval times, monks used the word to mean something unnatural within the context of society or the environment. The word was first used to mean something not of this earth in 1920. It has always had sinister undertones, and in Britain, the term 'alien' was frequently seen by many to be interchangeable with 'refugee' or 'immigrant' for much of the nineteenth and twentieth centuries.

† Ruth Ellis, the last woman to be hanged in Britain, was the daughter of one of the Belgian refugees who chose to stay.

of a million Poles to the population, both during and afterwards, as well as 50,000 refugees from the Soviet Union.

Though *Aliens* will look at the many types of refugees who came to Britain to escape from fascism, much of its attention will focus on that most persecuted group, the Jews.

Germany's Jews suffered the iniquities of Nazi rule in incremental steps. But for those who cared to take an interest, right from the start it was immediately plain that Germany would not be a safe place to live, even for the long-assimilated, many of whom had fought for their country in the First World War. Following Hitler's electoral triumph in January 1933, the Nazis were swift to set up concentration camps and wasted no time passing laws to exclude Jews from the civil service and state schools. Out in the streets, Jews were subjected to physical attacks, business boycotts and book burnings. In the Nazi state, laws protecting citizens from such behaviour were no longer applicable to Jews.

So, the 1930s saw a gradual influx of increasingly desperate German Jews to other countries. But would-be arrivals to Britain faced a government anxious to exclude them, not least because the Great Depression had created millions of unemployed workers and they feared stoking antisemitism. Then, as now, there was a fear that immigrants of any persuasion would be taking jobs that should belong to British people. But the Nazi pogrom of Kristallnacht in November 1938 marked a change in attitude among the government and many British people. Restrictions were relaxed and more visas were made available. The *Kindertransports* were arranged for children under seventeen, who were mostly taken in by kindly souls or charities who had agreed to guarantee that their charges would not become a 'burden to the state'. By the time war broke out on

3 September 1939, around 80,000 Jews had arrived in the UK. Many of them came on transmigration visas, granting them a temporary stay on condition they moved on to another country.

Having already endured several years of high anxiety, the Jewish arrivals, alongside other refugees, faced further concerns. Today, it is difficult to imagine the extent of antisemitism in Britain in the early part of the twentieth century. Certainly, it was far more widespread and out in the open than it is now. It's also well to bear in mind that attitudes that are now considered unspeakable were more generally acceptable at the time. From the present, the Nazi T4 programme, with its determination to rid Hitler's Reich of its physically and mentally disabled citizens, is rightly considered one of their more significant atrocities. But while German eugenicists, or racial scientists as they were known within the Third Reich, spoke of 'life unworthy of life', British civil servants could employ similarly disparaging terms in their professional language. In January 1939, the Home Office's medical inspector complained to the Visa Office that a Polish child with cerebral palsy had been granted an entry visa. He was especially outraged because this boy was 'a physical defective who [would] never be able to support himself'.*

It is sobering to realise that the Third Reich was not, as we might like to think, an outlier in how it considered Jewish or disabled people. Rather, what distinguished it was the length it was prepared to go in service of those ideas.

But – overriding everything – when war broke out, there was every expectation that the Nazis would invade Britain, and the establishment reacted to this threat by rounding up many of the recently

---

* The Nazis were not alone in their clammy embrace of eugenics. The ideology was popular in Western democracies too. In America, for example, compulsory sterilisation of those deemed 'unfit to breed' was practised throughout the twentieth century and still is in some states and circumstances.

arrived refugees and interning them in prisons and then larger camps in the Isle of Man and elsewhere. Some were even placed on passenger ships to Australia and Canada. With an extraordinary lack of empathy on behalf of the authorities, German and Austrian Jews were placed on the same ships as British fascists, who had also been interned. But if there was trouble between the two groups, it paled into insignificance next to the danger of U-boat attack.

Others fleeing European fascism, such as Spanish refugees, had also arrived in Britain during this time. And there was a small but notable Italian community, many of whom had been here for decades. Once Mussolini joined Hitler to fight against Britain, they too became 'enemy aliens'. Although they did not provoke quite the suspicion and enmity incurred by Austrian and German Jews, they faced hardships and hostilities, and their experiences are also considered in later chapters. The war brought further arrivals – hundreds of thousands of German and Italian prisoners of war and millions of Americans and other Commonwealth and empire soldiers. The effect of this huge influx is considered in Chapter 10 and it is instructive to compare the treatment of these further enemy and friendly 'aliens' with attitudes towards Jewish refugees.

Although it is a myth that Britain did all it could to help fleeing Jews, the truth is that British assistance was often more generous than other European nations. For example, the UK took nearly 10,000 *Kindertransport* children – a large share compared with 1,850 to the Netherlands, 800 to France, 700 to Belgium and 250 to Sweden. Figures for overall Jewish refugees before and during the war also look impressive. Between 1939 and 1945, Canada took 5,000, Australia 10,000, South Africa 6,000 and America 157,000. The UK took up to 80,000 Jews in all, although Home Office visa application records show that at least 500,000 further applications were rejected. We took approximately 16 per cent of the Jews who had wanted to come to Britain. It is safe to assume that many of those 84 per cent who were refused entry went on to perish in the Holocaust.

* * *

The final chapter of *Aliens* looks at our current attitude towards refugees and compares wartime experiences with now. Though I've been cautious about delving too deeply into the immediate present, for fear of being overtaken by events, the stories of Ukrainian families settling in Britain as a result of the Russian invasion, and the Afghani British Army interpreters and their families left behind in their Taliban-controlled country, provide powerful illustrations of our often conflicting attitudes to immigration in the 2020s.

Eighty years on from the Nazi era, 21st-century Britain still has an ambiguous approach to refugees, and it is instructive to consider how little attitudes and government behaviour have changed, not least in the maintenance of labyrinthine bureaucratic hurdles. Creating fear and suspicion will always sell newspapers, and politicians such as the former Home Secretary Priti Patel (herself a first-generation child of immigrants) can be sure to find support among their natural constituency by painting refugees in an unsympathetic light. For example, Patel justified the extremely stringent visa restrictions on families fleeing from Ukraine in early spring 2022 by making reference to the Russian chemical weapon attack in Salisbury.*

---

* In March 2018, two Russian agents tried to poison a former Russian double agent living in Salisbury with a nerve agent known as novichok. It failed to kill him or his daughter, but later in the year it did kill a British woman who accidentally came into contact with the substance, which had been carelessly discarded.

Today, 'the Jews' have long been replaced by 'the Blacks' and 'the Muslims' as hate figures for some conservative-minded people and their newspapers of choice.* Correspondingly, in the first two decades of the twenty-first century, the majority of refugees to Britain have been from the Middle East or Africa, and debate rages over the legitimacy of their 'refugee' status.

Tabloid newspapers understand this is a subject that both interests and incenses their readership, so frequent news stories have stoked the topic to fever pitch. This has been the case for many years. Research carried out twenty years ago showed that the *Daily Express* featured asylum seekers on its front page at least once a week over 2002. In that same period, the *Daily Mail* ran over 200 stories about asylum seekers. According to the House of Commons Library, asylum applications in 2002 were 84,132. Granted, this is not an insignificant number, but for a population of 60 million (in that year), it was obviously not such a pressing issue to merit this weekly coverage. And, as so often happens with the tabloid news agenda, its very ubiquity made the subject far more of an issue than it actually was.

Twenty years on, this still makes the news almost every day. The impression this gives is that Britain is a magnet for refugees. In the early years of the twenty-first century, tabloid stories were so hostile that none other than the Association of Chief Police Officers called upon tabloid editors to moderate their reporting, since they feared it would create trouble within the communities where refugees settled ('ill-informed, adverse media coverage has contributed to heightened local tensions and resentment of asylum seekers').

---

* To give just one example, on 18 July 2016, the former editor of the then best-selling *Sun* would suggest in that paper that it was inappropriate for the Channel 4 newsreader Fatima Manji to wear a hijab to report on an Islamist terrorist attack in Nice in 2016. ('Was it appropriate for her to be on camera when there had been yet another shocking slaughter by a Muslim?')

The sad fact is that tabloid newspapers never lose money by pandering to their readers' fears and prejudices. It was so in 1900 and is still true today. This has led to a serious distortion in perceptions. A survey carried out in 2002 showed that the British public thought the UK hosted around 25 per cent of the world's refugees – the actual figure was less than 2 per cent. Curiously, exactly the same misapprehensions existed during the Second World War, when a survey showed that British people thought there were millions of refugees living in Britain, rather than tens of thousands (see Chapter 7).

The April 2022 government plan for dealing with the current refugee crisis by sending asylum seekers to Rwanda to have their claims processed saw the British Prime Minister denigrating opponents of the scheme as 'a formidable army of politically motivated lawyers who for years have made it their business to thwart removals and frustrate the government'. This did not stop him also describing Britain's refugee policy in the same speech as 'a beacon of openness and generosity'. This is classic Johnson 'cakeism', but his popularity with some sections of the population, even after his removal from office, does illustrate this disparity between the British image of ourselves as a welcoming, generous people and the actual reality – both now and during the Nazi era.

In 1947, the United Nations declared that the failure of the world community to act on behalf of the Jews in the Nazi realm had been a catastrophic mistake. What help they did get often depended on the kindness and generosity of individuals and non-governmental organisations. This still seems to be very much the case today.

Chapter 1

A Catalogue of Calamities: Britain in the 1930s

'Everyone that isn't scared stiff of losing his job is scared
stiff of war, or fascism, or communism, or something.
Jews sweating when they think of Hitler.'

GEORGE BOWLING IN *COMING UP FOR AIR* BY GEORGE ORWELL

To understand Britain's treatment of its wartime refugees, it is useful to shed light on the interwar years, especially the decade that preceded the Second World War and how it shaped the attitudes of the government and the British people towards foreigners, refugees and Germany as a whole.

At the start of the 1930s, anyone over twenty would have memories of the Great War. Way before the second global conflict began, the events of 1914–18 were already being referred to as the *First World War.** Here, barely a household in the country had escaped the death or life-changing injury of a direct family member or other

---

* The phrase was coined by *Times* and *Telegraph* journalist Charles à Court Repington, who published a book with that title in 1920. The French supreme commander Marshal Ferdinand Foch was no less pessimistic about the inevitability of another global conflict and correctly predicted another war in twenty years' time. Prime Minister David Lloyd George agreed and told him that the peace treaty they were negotiating was merely a ceasefire and 'we shall have to do the same thing again in twenty-five years at three times the cost'. He was five years out and underestimated the casualties by 25 per cent at the very least.

close relative. As the decade wore on, the inevitability of another great war loomed like a giant spectre in the night sky.

So, the 1930s were a time of great anxiety in Britain. The name of the decade brings an unquiet feeling, perhaps because we know what followed but also because those ten years held a catalogue of calamities all of their own. Devastating economic collapse, fascism rampant in Germany, Italy and Spain, the grotesque spectacle of Stalin's Bolshevik Russia, Japan's descent into barbarity... all promised something far worse than the carnage of the Great War that preceded and then ultimately engendered these further catastrophes. It was almost fitting that the decade would end with the beginning of the greatest war humanity had ever seen.

At the end of the First World War, Lloyd George promised his electorate 'a fit country for heroes to live in' (often misquoted as 'homes fit for heroes'), but the reality of providing such a utopia quickly fizzled out in an economy which had been hit desperately hard by the cost of waging the war.

The discontent this provoked culminated in the General Strike of 1926, where those who had most to fear from destitution took industrial action in May, most particularly in the coal and transport sectors. The strike petered out after nine days, having caused much disruption.

Circumstances conspired to visit further trouble on Britain's post-war population at the end of the decade. The 1929 Wall Street Crash, and the subsequent Great Depression of the next decade, swept the world. The effects were selective. The 1930s were an age where suburbia came into its own, promising a middle-class idyll of owner-occupiers with their own car, smartly turned-out children and, perhaps, a Scottie dog.* The architecture of the period, most evident today in the art deco cinemas, concert halls and seaside arcades still visible on our high streets and promenades, reflected surplus income and the opportunity of greater leisure time. And this was true for the more prosperous parts of the United Kingdom, especially in the south-east.

But for those living in Wales, northern England, the Midlands and Scotland – the parts of the country that had previously been hailed as the 'workshop of the world' – it was a very different story. The statistics alone paint an extraordinary picture of how Britain was affected by the Great Depression. In the textile-producing areas either side of the Pennines, production fell by two-thirds between 1929 and 1931. Coal production shrank by a fifth. The hitherto highly successful shipyards of the Tyne and Clyde, where 60 per cent of the world's shipping had once been built, saw demand for new vessels drop to 7 per cent of 1914 levels. The industry, described by academic Anthony Slaven as a 'colossus ... unrivalled by any other nation', had been vanquished.

Piers Brendon, in *The Dark Valley*, his masterful account of the interwar years, paints a vivid picture of the worst affected areas:

> The tragedy of unemployment was enacted against a background of sordid streets, foetid alleys, mephitic courts, decaying houses and suffocating rooms. Here were be-shawled women shuffling over the cobbles in clogs, gaunt children in ragged hand-me-downs who even at play on scrubbed pavements looked like 'little old people', and an army of mufflered men in shabby suits and patched boots.

---

* In the 1930s, the breed was hugely popular on both sides of the Atlantic. In America, Franklin D. Roosevelt's Scottish terrier Fala received regular fan mail. Celebrities from Humphrey Bogart to Charles Lindbergh also owned Scottie dogs.

Brendon also quotes the playwright Ted Willis who put things more succinctly. He wrote of an 'atmosphere of fear and foreboding which lay on the district like a frost'.

The early part of the century had seen the introduction of such welfare state staples as unemployment benefit, but this had been reduced in 1931, as part of the government's desperate attempts to 'balance the books'. Furthermore, any individual or family claiming state assistance had to undergo a humiliating ritual known as the 'means test'. Here, the family's possessions would be assessed and any-thing unnecessary to basic survival would be taken away and sold – a heartbreaking procedure for any aspiring family that took pride in its hard-won signifiers of comfort and respectability. A married couple with two children needed four chairs around the dining table. Any more would be taken away to be sold so income could be generated to offset the cost of unemployment benefit. Cherished ornaments and the radio were also fair game for the 'means test man'.

This sheds a bright light on the government's declared insistence that no refugees should become 'a burden to the public purse' – the rather quaint phrase employed to refer to taxation revenue intended for the welfare of British people. For some politicians, this was based on a simple conviction that 'charity begins at home'. For others, it was a fear of stoking resentment and unrest by giving to foreigners what was being denied to the native population. This was a time when tax yields had fallen by a third, and the cost of unemployment benefits had risen from £12 million in 1928 to £125 million in 1931.

And quite apart from the cost, introducing additional contenders to the labour market at a time of high unemployment was obviously going to stir resentment. In the early '30s, one in five working-age men did not have a job.

These legitimate concerns ran hand in hand with other prejudices, most especially regarding the acceptance of Jewish refugees. Antisemitism lurked within the social fabric of the country in a way that was far more open and common than today.

*   *   *

Alongside a resentment and fear of refugees, there was also a general undercurrent of suspicion towards foreigners in general, both of which were kindled by Britain's tabloid press.

Here, for example, is an article in the *Daily Mail* from 2 March 1929, clearly designed to invoke a fear of anyone east of the white cliffs of Dover:

NEW WHITE SLAVE LURE

Rumblings and tremors in the underworld of London have brought fear to the alien criminals who profit by the vices and weaknesses of the great city ... The Home Office is slowly but surely making London too hot for the foreign gangs and their native satellites who since the war have been making tainted fortunes by defying the law.

The white slave traffic, the dope traffic, gambling dens, bogus clubs, smuggling and banknote forging are almost entirely controlled by aliens who hitherto have laughed at passport and registration restrictions.

The piece is a sustained and gratuitous attempt to blame the more insalubrious areas of British crime on the foreigner, implying perhaps that ordinary decent British criminals could not possibly want to engage in such sordid, albeit titillating, endeavours. Such newspaper articles are notable because they offer a lens through which many British people viewed 'the foreigner' in their midst at this time.* It was to this hostile and distrusting environment that refugees from fascism fled.

* * *

The worldwide depression, triggered by the Wall Street Crash of 1929, had a profound impact on Britain. Democracy and capitalism were failing to deliver a reasonable life across the regional and social spectrum. It seemed that the world was coming apart at the seams. Having lost faith in the traditional political and economic models, many people turned to the novel appeal of communism and fascism. Communism was hobbled by the sinister hold Stalin and his fellow Bolsheviks had on the Soviet Union and was more easily dismissed as a barbaric creed by both the Labour leadership and right-wing newspapers.† But Mussolini, and then Hitler, had a more conventional appeal to some sections of the population.

Antisemitism in Britain was nowhere near as open and widespread as it was in the Nazi realm and other parts of Eastern Europe. But, in the words of Labour politician Herbert Morrison, it was 'always lurking under the pavement'.

In its extreme form, antisemitism found its most vocal champion in Oswald Mosley, an aristocratic political chameleon, so memorably dismissed by Conservative politician F. E. Smith as a

---

* The *Boy's Own* parody 'Jack Black and his dog Silver', in the not-as-funny-as-it-used-to-be *Viz*, clearly owes its existence to such reporting and the hostility it aroused.

† George Bernard Shaw was a rare admirer of Stalin, although he admired Mussolini too. H. G. Wells and socialist intellectuals Beatrice and Sidney Webb also spoke positively about Stalin's Soviet Union.

'perfumed popinjay'. Having failed to achieve any political office higher than Chancellor of the Duchy of Lancaster, in either the Conservative or Labour Party, he took his inspiration from Benito Mussolini and launched the British Union of Fascists (BUF). Borrowing shamelessly from *Il Duce's* repertoire of political theatre, his followers wore black shirts, gave the 'Roman' salute and had as their emblem the fascist fasces. By 1934, the BUF had a membership of 50,000 and held mass rallies in venues such as the Albert Hall in London. Lord Rothermere's *Daily Mail* became an enthusiastic supporter. ('Hurrah for the Blackshirts' ran one headline.)

It is tempting to see the exaggerated masculinity of the Mosley 'Biff Boys', as the press sometimes dubbed his thuggish followers, as a backlash against a rising tide of female emancipation, which had swept through the country before the war and into the 1920s and '30s, where women had at last been granted the right to vote and were becoming an increasingly visible presence in the world of work and politics.

But Mosley overplayed his hand. At one mass rally in 1934, widely publicised and attended in the Olympia Exhibition Hall, Kensington, hecklers were savagely beaten and support for the thuggish BUF rapidly dropped away, not least in the *Daily Mail*.

The *Mail* is often pilloried as 'the paper that supported the Blackshirts' and this has been the cause of some indignation among its apologists. They point out, for example, that the *Daily Mirror*, now renowned as a left-of-centre newspaper, also supported this new force in British politics. It's conveniently forgotten, however, that the *Mirror*, at the time, was owned by the same man who wrote the *Mail's* 'Hurrah for the Blackshirts' editorial – proprietor

Rothermere. Although he quickly came to the conclusion that the Blackshirts weren't worthy of his backing, this did not stop his continual support and admiration for Hitler.

Perhaps a clue to the *Mail*'s reporting on the behaviour of the Nazis towards their own Jewish citizens can be gleaned from an extraordinary article in the paper from 25 May 1937 entitled 'An Anglo-German Pact Means Peace', also penned by Rothermere. Accompanied by a photograph of himself and the Führer standing side by side and staring out at the reader in a manner reminiscent of a death metal band trying to look hard, the piece declares that storm clouds are gathering over Europe and thunder and lightning are in prospect. Rothermere pronounces himself a pragmatist and argues that to placate the Nazi desire for its own empire, Germany should be given colonial territory in Africa despite the myth that Germans were 'temperamentally disqualified for the administration of native races'. This, argues Rothermere, can be disproved by the loyalty shown by the devotion to the German cause of troops under General von Lettow-Vorbeck* in the former colony of German East Africa† during the First World War. He then adds, wistfully: 'These native troops maintained a fidelity to their German officers much in excess, I regret to say, of that shown to Great Britain by the people of Egypt, who had enjoyed the benefits of British administration for over thirty years.' The ungrateful wretches.‡

The article goes on to rail against 'Ignorant Left-Wing British journalists [who] bamboozle their readers with the complacent

---

* Rather thrillingly, von Lettow-Vorbeck turned out to be a strident anti-Nazi in his later days, and such was his prestige among the German people that he reportedly told Hitler to 'go fuck himself' and lived to tell the tale, when offered the position of ambassador to Britain in 1935. He died in 1964.

† Now territory comprising or including Rwanda, Burundi, Tanzania and Mozambique.

‡ You sense that Rothermere would have loved the idea of any future criticism of 'the empire' being greeted in his 21st-century paper with the taunt 'YOU HATE BRITAIN'.

assurance that Britain and France united could intimidate Germany and Italy … In my knowledge of the facts I denounce that idea as both foolish and perilous.' Sadly, here he turned out to be partly correct, although I do wonder what sort of sinister world we would now be living in if his Anglo-German alliance had come to pass.

The article goes on to declare: 'Let us rid ourselves of the delusion that Hitler is some sort of ogre in human shape. I have been his guest at Berchtesgaden and had long conversations with him there. *He has assured me of his desire to meet the British Government halfway.*'*

Rothermere goes on to assure his readers that the loss of life during the Nazi takeover was 'nothing like that caused by the Russian Revolution, or the rivers of blood now flowing in Spain … The death toll of the German revolution was almost nil.'

He ends his piece by beseeching the reader to 'remove the causes which may prevent two kindred nations whose [individual] members, when they meet [feel] instinctive mutual sympathy'.

Curiously, there is no mention at all of the Nazis' antisemitism and the brutal treatment of Germany's Jews.

Nonetheless, the *Mail* was as appalled as other British papers by Kristallnacht. Writes Robert Philpot, in a 2018 article in the *Times of Israel*: 'It made no attempt to disguise the horror of Kristallnacht and its editorial column flailed the Nazis' "wholesale oppression" of a "helpless minority" and urged the regime to show "moderation and mercy".'

The *Daily Express*, which outsold the *Mail* in the 1930s, was also sympathetic to the fascist cause, although not quite as fervently as

---

* The italics are the *Daily Mail*'s own.

the *Mail*. As the persecution of Germany's Jews became more acute, and international Jewish organisations tried to organise a boycott of German goods, an *Express* headline in 1933 proclaimed: 'Judea declares war on Germany: Jews of all the world unite in action'. Not only was the piece unsympathetic to Germany's Jews; it also fed into the common antisemitic narrative that 'the Jews' were able to act as a homogenous mass against their opponents. At the end of the decade, on 1 September 1939, the *Express* excelled itself by declaring: 'There will be no war in Europe'.*

Having lost the mainstream support of the tabloid press barons and seeking to revive his fortunes, Mosley embraced full-scale antisemitism and the BUF remained a presence in British politics until the outbreak of the Second World War, where many of its leading lights were interned. Still, throughout the 1930s, and most significantly in upper-class circles, fascism had an almost fashionable appeal.

* * *

Surprisingly, after the carnage of the Great War, many British people had a sneaking affection for Germany and its new Nazi rulers. Some felt Germany had been treated harshly at the Treaty of Versailles, most especially by 'the French'.† (Here lurked an antipathy which still exists, especially among right-wing tabloid newspapers and their readers.) And this affection made many British

---

* This was a prediction only slightly more inopportune than the *Express*'s recent spate in the 2010s and 2020s of headlines on the future of Britain under four Tory Prime Ministers. ('Only Cameron Can Save Britain', 'Vote May or We Face Disaster', 'Why We Must Put Faith in Boris' and best of the lot 'Put Faith in Truss to Deliver for Britain'.)

† In the cold light of day, the French government did behave with extraordinary ruthlessness towards Germany at Versailles. But then again, half of all French men aged between eighteen and thirty-five had been killed or suffered mutilating injuries in the war – a casualty rate twice as high as Britain's.

people resistant to both believing and sympathising with news stories about Jewish persecution, if indeed they ever read any. Such stories rarely, if ever, featured in right-wing tabloids at least until Kristallnacht (see Chapter 5).

Attitudes to Jewish arrivals desperate to flee the Nazi Reich were also shaped by an adoration of Hitler by some British politicians, newspapers and members of the upper class. Lloyd George referred to Hitler as 'Germany's George Washington' and in the early '30s, the Nazi leader was considered in a frankly astonishing light.[*] Edward VIII (king from January to December 1936) was a visibly enthusiastic supporter of Hitler.[†] Another establishment figure who was so pro-Nazi he was actually interned during the war was Admiral Sir Barry Domvile. In 1935, he wrote in relation to the Nazis and their hatred of the Jews:

I am very far from adopting the sloppy sentimental attitude towards the Jewish race which is so popular in this country. Because we ourselves are tolerant of the aliens and Jews in our midst to the point of stupidity, that is no reason for being intolerant with the policy of others: Jewish ways are not our ways.[‡]

Rothermere, owner of the *Daily Mail*, wrote to Hitler in 1939 congratulating him on annexing Czechoslovakia and praised his 'great

---

[*] In America, too, Hitler had many influential admirers. Frank Buchman, the founder of conservative religious group Moral Re-Armament, described him as an agent of the divine. 'Through such a man God could control a nation overnight and solve every last bewildering problem.' Charles Lindbergh, the first man to fly the Atlantic, and a huge celebrity in his day, was awarded the Order of the German Eagle in October 1938 by Hermann Göring on behalf of Adolf Hitler, for his support of the Nazi cause and not least his anti-communism and staunch belief in the supremacy of the white race.

[†] In 1940, shortly before the Blitz began, Edward, now Duke of Windsor, even told a Spanish diplomat that Britain ought to be bombed to bring it to its senses and stop opposing the Nazis.

[‡] Domvile remained an unrepentant fascist his whole life. When he died in 1971, he was a member of the National Front's National Council.

and superhuman work in regenerating your country'.* Socialite tabloid luminaries Unity and Diana Mitford were spellbound, too. 'For me he is the greatest man of all time,' Unity wrote to her father. You could understand the attraction. As James Wolcott wrote in a 2016 *Vanity Fair* article on the Mitford sisters: 'Compared with the maundering walruses running England and Europe downhill, here was a man who had dynamized, industrialized, and mobilized a nation – destiny incarnate.'

Unity's admiration for Hitler went hand in hand with a repellent antisemitism. She gloated approvingly at an ugly incident where Nazi Brownshirts forced German Jews to crop grass with their teeth, and even wrote to the Nazi newspaper *Der Stürmer* to declare: 'We think with joy of the day when we shall be able to say with might and authority: England for the English! Out with the Jews!'

Her infatuation with the Nazis ended in tears. When Britain declared war on Germany, she shot herself with a pearl-handled pistol given to her by Hitler. The suicide attempt left her with brain damage, but she lived until 1948, dying of meningitis caused by the bullet which was still lodged in her head.†

* * *

It was not just the 'smart set' who adored the Nazis in the 1930s. Ordinary people were fascinated too. Right up until the closing years of the decade, Germany remained a popular tourist destination.

---

* One plausible school of thought holds that Rothermere's praise for the Führer was part of his attempt to prevent a war in Europe. In the same letter, he writes: 'The British people, now like Germany strongly rearmed, regard the German people with admiration as valorous adversaries in the past, but I am sure that there is no problem between our two countries which cannot be settled by consultation and negotiation.'

† I can think of no comparable UK celebrity espousing such an extreme cause in the 2020s. It would be like Helena Bonham Carter or Liz Hurley touting for Britain First or the British National Party or telling us that Putin is the saviour of white Western civilisation.

The Nazi regime was barely six months old when Hitler ordered a tourist department to be created within the Ministry of Propaganda. Not only would this be used to counteract negative depictions of the Nazi state; it could even inculcate foreign visitors with National Socialist ideas. Diverting attention away from the brutal suppression of regime critics and the open persecution of Germany's Jews, the Nazis were keen to present an image of normality.

Joseph Goebbels and his Propaganda Ministry were shrewd enough to fund advertising for trips to Germany with British travel agency Thomas Cook between 1934 and 1937. The agency promoted low-cost tours of the 'New Germany' with its 'clean streets' and 'cheerful, happy people'. Student exchange trips were also common at this time.

The Nazis were particularly keen to encourage an entente with racially acceptable potential allies, and here the Anglo-Saxon British were top of the list, along with the Scandinavians. Both were fellow Aryans who were considered so 'racially valuable' they were even permitted to marry into the *Volksgemeinschaft* – the 'national community'.

Americans, too, were entranced with the new Germany. This was ironic as the country was despised by Nazi ideologues as a 'cesspit nation' where racial mixing was commonplace.* By 1937, over half a million Americans were travelling to Germany to see the Nazi state for themselves. How much this contributed to the popularity of America's Nazi Party can only be guessed. But right until the outbreak of war, wealthy American and British families continued to send their sons and daughters to German universities and finishing schools.

---

* This racial mixing meant between Aryan and non-Aryan European nationalities rather than between whites and black or Asian Americans, which was still considered taboo and was in fact illegal in most American states.

As thousands of British people visited the Nazi realm on these package tours in the decade before the war, many returned home with fulsome praise for Hitler's Third Reich. In 1934, for example, John Garstang, of Chorley, Lancashire, is recorded in a Thomas Cook promotional brochure as saying: 'Everybody seemed happy and carefree, far remote from the ideas of Germany our newspapers give us.'

Edward Bourgoin's academic paper 'British tourists and travellers in Nazi Germany, 1933–1936' contains further fascinating glimpses of British impressions of Nazi Germany. It's said that travel broadens the mind, but this seems to have been only partially the case with the following two examples.

Journalist and soon-to-be Liberal MP Robert Bernays noted: 'I really imagined that all Germans were bullet-headed ... and [had] a penchant for bayoneting babies. It was a real surprise to me to find slim, laughing, fair-haired girls* waiting upon us in the Rhineland restaurants.'

Bourgoin also tells us that another journalist and soon-to-be Conservative MP, Beverley Baxter, noted on his own travels that while the Germans of the west and south were warm-hearted and charming, those further east had 'the yellowish skin, the narrow Mongol eyes and the square brutish head which betrays the Slav in every Prussian'. From the twenty-first century, it's curious to see this open and unguarded British racism directed against the most infamously racist regime of the twentieth century.

The Berlin Olympics of 1936 also served its purpose well enough as a positive showcase for Nazi Germany. During the Games,

---

* How many of these girls were natural blondes is open to question. With the Nazi obsession with 'Nordic' looks, sales of blonde hair dye went through the roof, with a record 10 million packets being sold in 1934 alone, according to Julia Boyd in *Travellers in the Third Reich*.

antisemitic posters, graffiti and newspaper articles were all toned down or vanished from the streets as the country tried to present a decent face to the world.

And outside of tourism, diplomats and other foreign dignitaries who expressed concerns were taken on selected tours of Nazi concentration camps. Here they were introduced to healthy, happy and energetic prisoners who were actually camp guards in prison uniforms.

This bonhomie all contributed to the positive feelings many British citizens had towards the 'new Germany'.

*   *   *

So, this was Britain in the 1930s: haunted by the prospect of another great war and staring industrial and imperial decline in the face. It was fertile soil for Nazi propagandists, particularly given many British people's admiration for the 'new Germany', and ripe with the prospect of social unrest. Those in power who were sympathetic to the plight of refugees wanting to escape to the United Kingdom walked a tightrope. Introducing and supporting thousands of new arrivals to the UK job market would antagonise those most affected by the Great Depression and risked pushing them into the arms of political extremists. It was doubly unfortunate that the vast majority wanting to come here were perceived to be a feared and despised racial group. Clearly, the arrival of Jews desperate to flee Hitler's Reich would have to be handled extremely carefully.

Chapter 2

'Scurrying' from Germany: The First Arrivals

'Hundreds of thousands of Jews are now leaving Germany
and scurrying from there to this country.'
EDWARD DORAN, CONSERVATIVE MP, 9 MARCH 1933

Government-sanctioned persecution of Germany's Jews began
as soon as the Nazis came to power in January 1933. Within
weeks, Jewish university lecturers, schoolteachers, civil servants,
lawyers, doctors and dentists faced severe restrictions or were
thrown out of their jobs. Those who sought to leave were immediately penalised by a 'flight tax' designed to fleece them of their
financial resources. Furthermore, many countries which would
welcome immigrants were looking for skilled labourers, technicians
and agricultural workers – skills and abilities that most middle-class
Jewish professionals lacked.

German Jews fled where they could. Anne Frank's family, for example, fled from Frankfurt to Amsterdam within a year of Hitler's
coming to power. Many others turned east or west within Europe

– an ill-fated choice that would provide only a temporary respite from Nazi persecution.

Right from the start, Britain, or British-controlled territory such as Palestine, was a popular choice among those seeking to flee. In late March 1933, Frank Foley, a British passport control officer in Berlin, reported: 'This office is overwhelmed with applications from Jews to proceed to Palestine, to England, to anywhere in the British Empire.'

So, how did Britain view the prospect of playing host to Germany's reviled Jewish population? The opinion makers in British newspapers were often ambiguous and, in some cases, plainly hostile.

The arrival of Hitler as Chancellor of Germany inspired this breathless piece of adulation in the *Daily Mail* on 31 January 1933, although its author remained anonymous (the byline reads 'A Political Columnist'). Beneath a picture of a frowning Führer, with fist clenched mid-oratorical flourish, is the headline 'Hitler's Hour of Triumph'. Only hindsight would give those words an ominous ring, for the article that follows fizzes with fanboy adoration.

For Adolf Hitler, yesterday was 'Der Tag.'

The importance of Hitler's victory is difficult to exaggerate. The German chancellorship is one of the highest political offices in the world and … seemed utterly beyond the reach of the leader of the young generation of German patriots.

The story of Hitler's rise to fame opens in 1921. The sullen and dispirited Germany of those days needed a virile young leader, and one came to them in the beer-gardens and cafes of Munich. Adolf Hitler, a handsome young corporal who, with two wounds and the Iron Cross, had survived the war, and suddenly appeared among the listless idlers and proclaimed his message to them over the foaming steins.

After emphasising how much Hitler and his crew detested Bolshevism and the Jews, the article concluded: 'Good looks and a charming personality have helped him on his way, but most of all, he owes his success to his intensity of purpose and his ability to inspire the masses with his burning oratory.'

That same day, the editorial to the left of the article took an overview of goings-on with the charmingly archaic headline 'Britain and the World Welter'.* As part of an analysis of Europe, the *Mail* declared: 'Germany is on the brink of a great political adventure under a Ministry headed by Herr Hitler ... Let us hope that it will practise moderation and provide a success.'

This was, of course, a forlorn hope. Still, the blatant thuggery of the Nazis, particularly in regard to their political opponents and the 0.75 per cent of the population who were Jewish, seemed not to have overly bothered the *Mail* or its proprietor, who would go on to write an article calling for a close alliance with Germany in 1937 (see Chapter 1).

Early and blatant examples of Nazi brutality also cut little ice with the *Mail*'s reporting. On 27 March 1933, the paper declared:

HITLER AND THE JEWS
Statement to 'Daily Mail'

'NO MISHANDLING'

Dr Hansstaengel,† one of Hitler's closest co-operators, told me today: 'The Chancellor has authorised me to say that all reports of the mishandling of Jews are barefaced lies.'

---

*   I had to look that word up. It means 'to move in a turbulent fashion'.
†   Some sources spell the name 'Hanfstaengl'.

The *Mail* journalist then asked whether it would be safe for eminent exiles Albert Einstein and novelist Lion Feuchtwanger to return home after their criticism of Germany's new rulers. Dr Hansstaengel's ominous reply: 'What would England do to British subjects who abused their country abroad?' passes without further comment.

The following day, the paper carried another story, again framing the persecution of Jews through the prism of 'fake news', under the headline 'Hitler's Warning to Jews: Reprisal for Propaganda'.

The story reports that the Nazis are taking practical defence measures against 'the "atrocity" propaganda let loose by interested Jewish circles in the United States and Great Britain against the new National Government'.

Other papers were more sympathetic to Germany's Jews. Earlier that month, the *Daily Telegraph* had printed an editorial on 11 March 1933:

GERMANY UNDER MOB RULE

What prevails today throughout a great country at the heart of European civilisation is mob law, tolerated and even protected by the regular police.

The *Daily Mirror*, in its pre-left-leaning days, was also more sympathetic to Germany's Jews, albeit in a way many today would find offensively patronising.

In an article from 19 May 1933, entitled 'Here's to the Jews, A Race That is Misjudged, Says Andrew Soutar', accompanied by photographs of Jews being bullied by Brownshirts in German streets, Soutar examines the reasons for antisemitism and reports:

Even the most bitter of his critics and transducers cannot deny that [the Jew] makes an excellent citizen, is phenomenally industrious and is seldom before the courts as a malefactor. There are poor Jews but how often do you find one in the role of a beggar?

Take into consideration the numerical feebleness of the race and you must agree that the Jew has contributed very largely to progress. Every ramification of art bears his impress. In literature, painting and sculpture he stands, a compelling figure.

Following a slightly tortured discourse on usury which is quick to admit that 'not all usurers are Jews', Soutar concludes:

The alpha and omega of the persecution of the Jews all over the world may be summed up in one word – money. They are hated because they are so clever in getting so much of it. If the Christian had the brains and the energy to get it as easily, the bulk of his prejudice against the Jews might disappear.

Even if money were to become obsolete in the future, Soutar reflects, 'even then the Jew will not escape our contumely. He will get so far ahead of us in another direction that we shall have to gather together our scattered forces and hurl more verbal brickbats at his head.'

Such articles provide a good insight into how Jews were perceived in the years just before the Holocaust and how British people felt about potentially hosting them. Undoubtedly, the tabloids and their readers were either ambivalent and sometimes patronising or hostile and discriminatory towards Jews.

* * *

The wealthiest Jewish businessmen were in the best position to leave Germany – especially if they had business concerns and bank accounts in other countries. But most Jews were caught in an ugly catch-22 where countries refused to have them because the 'flight tax' would leave them destitute. And rather than prompt sympathy, this awful situation seemed to provoke scorn and suspicion. Some British politicians were quick to make hay. Alongside Mosley and his Blackshirts were also-rans such as the Conservative MP Edward Doran who announced in the House of Commons in March 1933 that 'hundreds of thousands of Jews are now leaving Germany and scurrying from there to this country'.

Aside from being a bare-faced lie, reminiscent of the UKIP canard that Turkey would be joining the EU and hundreds of thousands of Turks would soon be flooding into the UK, Doran employed the Nazi practice of depicting a reviled ethnic group in animalistic terms. Cockroaches and rats scurry.

Doran, you feel, would have had plenty of admirers in today's right-wing circles. He was an early adapter when it came to stirring up dislike of the BBC – calling for a cut in funding barely ten years after the state broadcaster had come into existence. He also had the shameless knack of saying whatever he thought his listeners would like to hear. After summoning the image of a Jewish invasion, he warned: 'If you are asking for a Von Hitler in this country, we will surely get one.' (Perhaps he assumed that everyone in Germany had the aristocratic appellation 'von' before their name. Or perhaps he knew better but thought that's what his constituents would think?)

You sense that he would have been quite comfortable with 'a

von Hitler'. Soon after this speech, Doran hosted a meeting in the House of Commons where Nazi representatives were invited to explain their anti-Jewish policies.

Doran lasted only a single parliament. His Tottenham constituents rejected him in the 1935 election, much to the displeasure of right-wing magazine *The Patriot*, which blamed the Conservative Party for not being robust enough to accommodate his views.

But more broadly, this desire for a more fascistic Tory Party was a viewpoint that had already been aired in the mainstream *Daily Mail*. On 25 April 1934, for example, Lieutenant Colonel T. C. R. Moore CBE MP had written an article, entitled 'The Blackshirts Have What the Conservatives Need', in a report about a Blackshirt rally. Among other heated observations, he asked his reader: 'What is there in a Blackshirt that gives apparent dignity and intelligence to its wearer?' Perhaps in need of a cold shower, he goes on to write that 'the men were fine examples of a healthy and intelligent mind in a healthy and well-made body. The girls, straight-eyed, vivacious and comely, well-matched their male comrades.' Building to a thunderous climax, Lieut. Col. Moore declared that 'the Blackshirts want Britain to be strong enough, physically and morally, to maintain her great historical position as a leader of civilisation and guardian of world peace. That is a fundamental demand in every truly Conservative heart.'*

*   *   *

A great number of talented and capable people were being hounded from Hitler's Reich, but they met mixed fortunes if they wanted to

---

* Moore, Conservative MP for Ayr Burghs at the time, wrote many newspaper articles in favour of Hitler and the Nazis. He held the seat until 1964 and died in 1971.

come to Britain. The British Medical Association and the British Dental Association were anxious to prevent German doctors and dentists from coming to the UK, seeing them as rivals to their own members. This, of course, was a time before the National Health Service and such medical professionals operated as businesses in their own right, as private health practitioners do today. Those Jewish doctors and dentists who did manage to obtain visas were required to undertake substantial retraining if they wished to practise their profession (this is covered in more detail in Chapter 5).

The universities, on the other hand, were quick to welcome their German colleagues. The Academic Assistance Council (AAC) was established in April 1933 to help Jewish academics and scientists find roles in universities, industry and research institutions. Established by none other than William Beveridge, who went on to become a leading architect of the welfare state, the AAC was given office space by academic science's most prestigious institution, the Royal Society. The AAC's first president was the Nobel Prize-winning scientist Lord Rutherford. With friends like these, the council looked set to achieve marvellous things – and it did.

Among scores of other eminent scientists and academics, the atomic physicists Leo Szilard,* Edward Teller, Rudolf Peierls and Otto Frisch all arrived in the UK in 1933 as Jewish refugees from German universities. All were to make significant contributions to the development of the first atomic bomb. Peierls and Frisch, for example, authored a paper in March 1940 which accurately described the exact calculations necessary to detonate such a weapon. Max Born, another Jewish scientist who fled to Britain, went on

---

* Szilard, who moved to a variety of American universities from 1938, was perfectly placed to escape the Nazis. He kept his savings in Zurich and was able to transfer over £1,500 – worth £120,000 today – to a London bank.

to develop the science of quantum mechanics. Biochemist Ernst Chain arrived in England from Friedrich Wilhelm University, Berlin,* in April 1933. He was virtually penniless but was quickly offered a research post at University College Hospital, London, and then the opportunity to take a PhD at Fitzwilliam College, Cambridge. Chain went on to pioneer the therapeutic use and manufacture of penicillin alongside his colleague Howard Florey. Its use was greatly beneficial to injured soldiers during the war. Although the Germans also made use of penicillin, they lacked the expertise to manufacture it in sufficient quantities.

Lyn Smith, in her book *Heroes of the Holocaust*, writes about the German Jewish biochemist Hans Krebs, who was to be knighted in 1958 for his pioneering work on cell metabolism and molecular biology. He was already a valuable member of the University of Freiburg when the Nazis came to power and as he contemplated the end of his academic career, he was swiftly approached by the British.

I was somewhat surprised when I got a letter from a German colleague who worked in Cambridge, England, telling me that people had heard I was in difficulties. He told me that if I was interested in coming to Cambridge I should write to Hopkins [Sir Frederick Gowland Hopkins, a noted English biochemist] and I would be sure of a sympathetic response. So I wrote to Hopkins and got a reply which I found very touching because it began with the sentence: 'I admire your work so much that I am anxious to help you'.

I decided to emigrate.

---

* Friedrich Wilhelm University is know now as Humboldt. The great Bebelplatz in front of Humboldt's law department was the site of one of the Nazis first book burnings, on 10 May 1933. Here, works by Jewish scientists and academics were burned by Nazi students and other Nazi groups. The site is now marked by a haunting underground sculpture by Micha Ullman called *The Empty Library*, visible from the pavement via a glass window.

Krebs became one of 1,500 refugees to find a home in British universities in the 1930s, thanks to the work of the AAC. Lyn Smith points out that sixteen of the AAC scheme beneficiaries would go on to win Nobel Prizes, eighteen would receive knighthoods and over 100 would be elected as fellows of the Royal Society.

The fact that such extraordinary minds* were rejected by the Third Reich was a poor advert for the swivel-eyed zealotry of the Nazi mindset. Hitler was aware of what his country was losing but blithely waved away such concerns: 'If the dismissal of Jewish scientists means the annihilation of contemporary German science, we shall do without science for a few years.'†

Perhaps the scientists had an easier time of gaining entry to Britain because they were seen as co-creators and valuable additions to university departments. British doctors and dentists merely saw their German and Austrian colleagues as rivals.

Away from the academic community, prospects were bleaker, although Germany's Jews were not without allies in Britain. The Quaker Society of Friends were quick to organise practical help and backing and worked with Jewish charities to help Jews make a new home in Britain. They even set up offices in Germany, and later in the decade in Prague and Paris, to help negotiate visas with the Home Office.

Jewish charities such as the Central British Fund (CBF) for German Jewry (an organisation which still exists today as World Jewish Relief) were established to provide financial aid to fleeing

---

* Albert Einstein, a German Jew and already the most famous scientist of the twentieth century when the Nazis came to power, was in the United States in January 1933. His Berlin home and offices were ransacked by the Nazis and he realised that a return to his post as director at the Kaiser Wilhelm Institute for Physics was out of the question. He remained in America for the rest of his life and became an American citizen.

† Notwithstanding, the Third Reich still went on to pioneer several key developments in military technology, not least the Me 262, the first combat jet aircraft, and the V-1 and V-2 rockets, the first cruise missile and the first ballistic missile, respectively.

Jews. The Jewish Refugees Committee also arranged admissions, training, employment and financial maintenance – particularly for Jews who could persuade the Home Office that they were here en route to another country. Many of the Jews who did arrive here were permitted to do so only on transmigratory visas.

So, between January 1933 and September 1935, a small number of mostly wealthy or well-connected refugees arrived in Britain. But as Nazi persecution increased, particularly after the passing of the Nuremberg Laws on 15 September 1935, which enshrined Nazi racial theory in fiercely antisemitic terms, pressure continued to mount on Jews to leave Germany. And as that pressure increased, so did official resistance to accommodating these refugees. But it was not just simple prejudice that prevented British officialdom from accepting Jews. Politicians feared that by 'encouraging' German and Austrian Jews to flee to Britain and its empire, other countries which considered themselves to have a 'Jewish problem' (most notably Poland and Romania, which were fiercely antisemitic) would also provoke their Jewish populations to flee into the open arms of friendly nations.

As such, the Home Office continued to operate a 'policy of rigid but sympathetic control' of immigration. By 1937, several thousand 'desirable, industrious, intelligent and acceptable persons' had been admitted to Britain. But trouble lay ahead.

In addition to the possibility of emigrating to Britain, European Jews fleeing persecution before the war broke out turned their attention towards the British mandate of Palestine. Here, the wants and rights of Palestinians came up against the recently minted concept of Zionism – a belief that the Jewish people should have their own homeland in this eastern Mediterranean territory.

Following the First World War and the fall of the Ottoman Empire, Britain had been granted a mandate by the League of Nations to rule Palestine. The ill-thought-out Balfour Declaration of 1917 pledged support for a Jewish homeland in Palestine, regardless of the feelings of the existing Arab inhabitants. Over a century later, the turmoil occasioned by this declaration still boils and rages, and the Middle East is still one of the world's most troubled regions. In the 1930s, when Hitler came to power and antisemitism viciously increased throughout Europe, the hope the Balfour Declaration engendered among the persecuted Jews of the Nazi realm led to fatally wrong-headed decisions which cost hundreds of thousands of lives (see Chapter 4). Palestine became a symbol of hope for Jews trying to flee, and by the middle of the decade, some 355,000 Jews resided in Palestine, amounting to 25 per cent of the population. This hope of Palestine as a sanctuary, however, was hindered by several British policies enacted to limit further Jewish emigration to Palestine (it was restricted to 12,000 per year in 1937 and then to 75,000 in total over the next five years in 1939). With a global war looking inevitable and tensions within Palestine rising, the British went through a series of policies, trying to find a workable solution for power sharing between the Arabs and Jews, but none of them gained the support of either faction. Balfour's declaration was clearly not worth the paper it had been written on.

Not only did Britain's disastrous foreign policy here, and the precarious state of Palestine and its Jewish residents, have a direct and calamitous impact on the options open to Jews hoping to flee the Nazi realm; they also directly shaped British attitudes towards Jewish people and influenced the reaction of sympathetic governments hoping to help refugees in the 1930s, when something could have been done to save at least some of the 6 million who died in the Holocaust. This churning tumult and uncertainty over Palestine carried on until war broke out in September 1939. And for the duration of the conflict, the future of Palestine was put on hold.

The years before the war broke out would put even greater pressures on both Germany's Jews and countries which showed an inclination to accept them. And in the middle of the decade, another problem arose. Civil war had broken out in Spain and other refugees were now clamouring for the thin gruel of public sympathy.

Chapter 3

Feeding Red Children:
The Spanish Civil War

The horror and scope of the Holocaust have lent a particular focus to the Jewish arrivals in Britain. But in the middle of the 1930s, all that was still to come. In 1936, another calamity descended on Europe, producing its own share of uprooted people and disrupted lives.

The Spanish Civil War began in July 1936. In essence, it was a struggle between the Republicans – the democratically elected left-wing government – and the Nationalists, Spain's right-wing establishment, essentially the Roman Catholic Church, the aristocracy and much of the military. Support for the Catholic Nationalists was strongest in rural regions.* The big cities were mostly on the side of the Republicans.

The participants were aided and abetted by political bedfellows, most especially two regimes of exceptional barbarity from either end of the political spectrum: Nazi Germany and the Soviet Union.†

---

* This is a common feature in religion-inspired civil conflict. The Taliban have their strongest supporters in the Afghani countryside. Likewise, Iran's Islamic theocracy.

† Such was the scale and horror of both regimes that we tend to forget that most of Europe was ruled by ugly, repressive governments in the 1930s. Sweeping west to east, Portugal, Spain, Italy, Hungary, Poland and Romania all hosted fascistic regimes where political opponents feared for their lives – and Jews were often a common scapegoat for the country's ills.

Hitler sent aircraft and armoured divisions,* as did Fascist Italy. The Nazis' infamous Condor Legion, several squadrons of bombers and fighter aircraft, offered invaluable aid to the Nationalists. They also allowed the German air force to give their pilots and aircraft first-hand military experience. In the words of the United States Holocaust Memorial Museum: 'Spain became a military laboratory to test the latest weaponry under battlefield conditions.' The Republican side received aid from Stalin's Soviet Union, mainly in the form of military equipment, although a small number of Soviet soldiers also fought in Spain. Tellingly, while fascist allies Germany and Italy sent their own soldiers to help the Nationalists, the Republicans were helped by thousands of volunteers from countries all over Europe, most especially the 'International Brigade'.

The Nationalists, although greatly dependent on their fascist allies, were able to present a more united front. The Republicans, as so often the case with left-wing politics, were a fractious, divided crew – comprising a broad spectrum from liberals to communists to anarchists. Independence movements in Catalonia and the Basque region added to their troubles. George Orwell's heartbreaking *Homage to Catalonia* illuminates this farrago in harrowing detail.[†]

The conflict was a merciless one, with massacres on both sides. Of the 500,000 people killed during the civil war, it's thought at least 200,000 were murdered away from the heat of battle. In Britain's right-wing press, attention was particularly paid to the 7,000 or so Catholic priests, monks and nuns murdered by the far-left

---

* Hitler had hoped his support would lead to a military alliance with Fascist Spain, but it was not to be. Francisco Franco was canny enough to keep the country out of the carnage of the Second World War, although around 40,000 Spaniards volunteered to fight against the Soviets on the Eastern Front.

† Describing the factionalism of the left, Orwell writes: 'As time went on, the Communists and the POUM [another Spanish communist party] wrote more bitterly about one another than about the Fascists.'

and anarchist fringes of the Republican forces. For the other side, the Nationalists are thought to have executed 100,000 Republican soldiers during the war, as well as 50,000 after the conflict ended.

The civil war saw particularly bitter fighting in the Basque region and produced a flood of refugees to nearby France – 5,000 women, children and elderly men had fled across the Pyrenees by the end of August 1936. Altogether, around 120,000 Spanish citizens escaped to other countries during the conflict. When it ended in a Nationalist victory in April 1939, a whopping 500,000 Republicans also fled to France. Just as the Jews of Germany and Austria who fled there before the war only postponed their fate, so it was with many of the Republican soldiers. When the Nazis occupied France, Republican Spaniards were rounded up for forced labour, and some were murdered in Nazi concentration camps.

The Spanish Civil War created a great deal of interest in Britain – the conflict seemed to be a microcosm of the great political rivalries of the age. And there was support for both sides along predictable lines. Right-wing newspapers, including the *Catholic Times* which was understandably keen to highlight the killing of Catholic priests, supported the Nationalists. Other papers supported the Republicans, as did a sizable majority of the population.

And it soon became apparent that France alone could not accept the wave of refugees fleeing the fighting. However, there was great reluctance to admit some of these desperate people to Britain.

But just as newspaper front pages featuring the drowned body of two-year-old Syrian refugee Alan Kurdi on a Turkish beach in September 2015 spurred a surge of sympathy towards Middle Eastern refugees in the 2010s, so shocking events in the 1930s triggered a similar desire to help in a reluctant Britain.* In April 1937, German and Italian aircraft bombed the Basque town of Guernica, killing around 1,600 of the town's 5,000 inhabitants.

The issue provoked both predictable support and hostility. Tony Kushner and Katharine Knox in their book *Refugees in an Age of Genocide* point out that while most people sided with the Republicans, the Conservative government and British business organisations favoured General Franco's Nationalists. One particular outspoken 'anti-alienist', the Conservative MP Sir Henry Page Croft, declared with a lack of empathy that would have done justice to Katie Hopkins: 'We are not going to support the feeding of Red children.'

Fortunately, many British people did not share Croft's vengeful sectarianism. The Aid Spain Movement raised £2 million and provided over 2,000 British volunteers for the International Brigade, to aid the Republicans. A group of British MPs set up a cross-party National Joint Committee for Spanish Relief, an umbrella organisation for over 150 local fundraising groups and 850 local and national bodies with an interest in helping the Republican cause. Support and objection to allowing Spanish refugees into Britain came cross-party too. Kushner and Knox write that a proposal by Conservative MP Colonel John Macnamara† to provide temporary shelter for Basque children to the UK was opposed by Labour's Lord Listowel, who felt it was inadvisable to bring these children to 'cold and Protestant' England. Here, Lord Listowel shared the same opinion as Conservative Prime Minister Stanley Baldwin,

---

* Much the same happened after Kristallnacht, as we shall see in Chapter 5.
† Macnamara volunteered for active service when the war broke out and was killed in Italy in December 1944. He has the sad distinction of being the last serving member of Parliament to have been killed in action. A fascinating figure, he was part of a coterie of gay MPs and diplomats with strong links to fellow gay individuals in Nazi Germany.

who also felt Britain was an inappropriate refuge for Spanish children because 'the climate here would not suit them'.

But eventually, on a groundswell of popular opinion, the British government was moved to act in 1937. On the strict understanding that the children would be entirely supported by donations, rather than the public purse, and that the arrivals would be repatriated as soon as possible, 4,000 (negotiated up from 2,000) were allowed to embark on a liner bound for Britain.*

Once Britain had agreed to take children, there was fierce competition in Spain for places on the ships. Reports vary, but between 10,000 and 20,000 children were put forward for the 4,000 places available. All travelled with the expectation that they would stay for a few months until the crisis blew over.

The children who were destined for Britain were selected among the various political factions contesting the Basque region – Basque separatists, Republicans and Nationalists. On 21 May 1937, 3,889 children, together with 219 teachers and fifteen priests, sailed aboard the passenger ship *Habaña*. One child described the first day of the voyage as 'a bad and a sad day for everyone; the sea was very rough and everybody was sea-sick. Everywhere one could hear crying and lamentations. Some asked for water and others asked to return them to their parents.'

The children's arrival in Southampton prompted great interest and was even reported live on the BBC. The *Daily Mail*'s coverage reads exactly like the cheery commentary from a Pathé newsreel and waxes lyrical about the kindness of the British people:

---

* France, by this time, had taken 10,000 Spanish refugees and the government had provided them with a daily allowance of 10 francs apiece.

Colourful, yet forlorn, young Juans, Juanitas, Miguels and Carmens made Southampton ring from dawn onwards today, while they were being 'decanted' from the weather-scared ship. The sight of green meadows, and ordered life of the sort they have almost forgotten, affected the children remarkably. Some of the older ones burst into tears, but the younger ones showed that they regarded England as little short of Paradise ... The cries of delight as they caught chocolates and other tit-bits which Southampton folk threw up to them as they passed through the streets in buses and vans testified to the suffering that had ended.

However, Amador Díaz, writing about his experiences as a refugee fifty years later, remembers his arrival in Southampton in less gushing tones: 'The impression I received passing through the streets of Southampton was not favourable.' He found the buildings small and upon seeing a thatched cottage, 'there were cries of surprise that an advanced country like England should still have cottages with "straw" roofs! In the industrial area of the Basque Country the roofs of even the poorest of farm cottages were covered in tiles or slates!'

Once disembarked, the children's destination was a campsite in Eastleigh, Hampshire. Curiously, the Spanish authorities had permitted the children to leave their country only on the condition that they would be kept together rather than farmed out to private houses. Although this was intended to offer these children companionship and support, the request was a mixed blessing. To honour this arrangement, the children lived under canvas – an unenviable arrangement in Britain, even in the summer. Arriving at the campsite, Amador Díaz recalls: 'I did not feel elated though

I knew not what to expect.' He remembers one girl exclaiming: 'I can't sleep there!'

The Eastleigh campsite was set up by a combination of volunteers from the boy scouts and girl guides, the YMCA and organisations such as Toc H,* rotarians and university students. Despite the disparaging remarks of Sir Henry Page Croft and his ilk, the people of Hampshire donated food, clothes and toys to over twenty depots set up for the children.

The camp itself was well provided with a cinema and concert stage. Celebrities of the day, such as singer Paul Robeson and the heavyweight boxing champion Joe Beckett, and even the new King and Queen of England, came to visit. The camp was also inundated with sightseers come to gawk at the novelty. Amador Díaz remembers them throwing 'sweets, chocolates and even apples' at the children. 'In retrospect,' he reflects, 'I can see the spectacle had a resemblance to the monkeys' enclosure at a zoo!'

But day-to-day life in the camp was sometimes challenging. The lavatories made available were not for the faint-hearted. A lack of proper drainage for such large camps meant that latrine pits had to be dug. They were so heavily doused with bleach that anyone who visited them returned with streaming eyes. Meals were often 'chaotic', as Amador Díaz recounts about the evening distribution of bread and milk:

It became obvious that in order to eat one had to become somewhat aggressive, so we began to help ourselves from the trays to as many slices of bread as we could and to dip the mugs into the billy-cans

---

* Toc H is a largely forgotten Christian charity with origins in the trenches of the First World War. Still going, just about, in 2023, its commendable mission statement reads 'to build the common good in local communities through mutually supportive friendship, neighbourly service and reconciliation, with a commitment to social justice and a sustainable environment'.

[of milk] for as many times as we were able … I learned two [other children] had got apples at supper, but I saw none!

There were also problems that immediately became apparent – not least the lack of a common language. Amador Díaz recalls: 'The young man that saw us off the bus, the men and women in the canteen, the two scouts who showed us how to prepare the bedding, could not communicate with us, they knew no Spanish, we knew no English.' Some English people who spoke Spanish had volunteered as interpreters, but their task was made harder by the fact that many of the children spoke the Basque dialect, which sometimes led to confusion and distrust among the children towards their new carers. Amador recounts: 'The language barrier did not help to reduce the mistrust and smooth over [any] misunderstandings.'

Having left their loved ones behind in a warzone, the children were often in a traumatised state. Volunteers at the camps recalled the younger ones diving under beds and trembling with fear, shouting 'bomba, bomba' whenever an aircraft flew by. Volunteer Freda Sibley recalls: 'We comforted them as best we could, till they calmed down.' Further compounding the children's anxiety, Amador Díaz describes the camp being split in two, one half full of children who had been 'washed and deloused' and 'given new clothes' and the other full of children who had yet to be 'decontaminated'. Amador continues: 'It took a long time for this Second camp to lose the stigma of being contaminated. In some cases brothers and/or sisters had been separated which created a resentment and mistrust of the Camp Authorities that was to last during the whole of our stay at North Stoneham.'

Another issue was the fact that the camp authorities often

underestimated the extent of the children's political awareness. Amador Díaz recalls: 'Even before the beginning of the conflict, politics were very much a part of everyday life in Spain.' As such, the children 'were well aware of the double-talk and unsavoury dealings of the European powers' with regard to the Spanish Civil War, and this fostered some distrust of the authorities, as the children felt like the British had been ambivalent towards the conflict that robbed them of their homes and families.

As the civil war went on, becoming more bloody and vengeful, the temporary arrangement of the camps was abandoned and children were found homes with volunteer families. Many of them ended up in Manchester and surrounding towns and their experiences were recorded in a chapter in Bill Williams's book *Jews and Other Foreigners*, published by Manchester University Press in 2011. Williams writes that the Manchester Mayor Joseph Tool declared his intention to take care of these children, telling a political rally: 'This country was famous for many things, but one great thing was the right of asylum.' Elvira Buckley remembers that they 'were all welcomed with open arms' when they arrived. But as Williams notes, 'there were nonetheless signs of anxiety amongst children moving to yet another unknown destination. On the first night they chose to sleep together ... rather than be separated from their friends and siblings.'

Although some articles in the right-wing press called for the repatriation of these children, households from all around the Manchester area, and as far away as north Wales, offered to take them in.

Unsurprisingly, the charity offered to these children stirred up resentment in an area that had been hit hard by the Great Depression. Williams writes that letters in local papers such as the *Bolton*

Evening News and *Salford City News* complained that 'starving' children in 'grim Welsh Valleys' and the 'stricken areas of the north' had a prior claim on people's kindness and donations. The *Catholic Times*, already predisposed towards supporting the Nationalists, not least following the massacres of Catholic priests, monks and nuns by the Republican communist and anarchist fringe, published a piece characterising the children as 'Red terrorists'.*

As the civil war reached its bloody climax, the Basque region came under the control of the Nationalist forces, creating uncertainty for the children. Amador Díaz recalls:

The news [of the fall of Bilbao] was received in silence but soon some of the young ones began to cry while the older ones marched to the Administration block asking for more news. Camp personnel were everywhere. Afterwards I learned that they had all been alerted to calm the hysteria expected from us, but the feeling was rather of repressed tragedy and anger ... Nobody had received letters from our families since we left Bilbao, four weeks previously. We did not know what was happening to them. Have they left the town? Have they been jailed? After all, most of us had somebody in the ranks of the Basque army.

Unsurprisingly, as Amador Díaz details, the stress of this uncertainty left

us in a state of tension which tended to explode at any small provocation. I remember a visitor, who spoke tolerable Spanish, coming to

---

* It is always distressing to note how easily nuance is lost in the ugliness of war. Former British Conservative politician and now travelogue TV personality Michael Portillo's father Luis Gabriel Portillo fled from Spain as he was a renowned left-wing academic. But he was also a devoted Roman Catholic.

the Camp some days after the fall and saying to a small group of us that now we will soon be going back to Bilbao; this comment produced a sudden angry reaction calling him fascist and worse, while two boys threw on the ground the chocolate he had given us because it was from a fascist.

And once one or two began to misbehave, particularly the older boys, some of whom had actually seen combat, sections of the press scented blood. Stories of 'violent young refugees' and 'bad Basque boys' circulated, causing local youths to pick fights with the refugees. One hostel in Bolton which accommodated these children prompted locals to complain that Manchester 'do-gooders' had foisted these children on them. Overlooking the fact that these traumatised children deserved some leeway, the British press echoed Conservative MP Sir Henry Page Croft's revulsion towards 'Red children'.

Altogether, seventeen boys were returned to France in disgrace and out of seventy camps containing Basque children, only three were affected. But this did not stop their perceived behaviour becoming a national joke. Kushner and Knox write that parents of badly behaved children would quip that their offspring had been 'playing with some Basque children'.

Many of these children returned to Spain when the civil war ended, although around 500, whose families were on the losing side, stayed behind.

The whole episode is something of an anomaly in our refugee history. Unlike the Jews who came here fleeing from the Nazis, who had a significant impact on the political and cultural life of Britain, the Spanish refugees have remained a low-key addition. Support or hostility towards them depended on existing political affiliations and, as ever, was impervious to facts. Franco's fascists murdered far more of their opponents, but that did not stop conservative newspapers and politicians demonising 'Red children' and making the focus of their hostility Republican war crimes.

But looking back from the present, despite the hostility of the press and some sections of the British public, refugees who came and stayed remember the kindness of the British with affection. Venancio Zornoza travelled with his two brothers and ended up in Keighley in Yorkshire. In a BBC News article from 2016, he recalled a family who 'took us out to tea – and we kept in touch with them for about 80 years'. He goes on to say: 'The government didn't want us here ... but really the British people they behaved so well to us, it was just unbelievable, I can never thank the British people enough and, whenever I get the chance, I do so because they were fantastic.'

Chapter 4

A Lost Opportunity:
The Évian Conference

'The world seemed to be divided into two parts – those places where
the Jews could not live and those where they could not enter.'

CHAIM WEIZMANN, 1936

'There is only one thing I hope to see before I die and that is that
my people should not need expressions of sympathy any more.'

GOLDA MEIR, JEWISH DELEGATE AT THE ÉVIAN CONFERENCE
AND ISRAEL'S FUTURE PRIME MINISTER

By early 1938, approximately 150,000 of Germany's 600,000 Jews had managed to escape. The remaining 450,000 were increasingly desperate to follow them. So, in the summer of 1938, President Franklin D. Roosevelt called together a conference with European democracies and other interested countries to try to find a solution to the rapidly escalating refugee crisis. His motives, according to some historians, notably Piers Brendon who described the conference as 'a hypocritical charade', were far from altruistic. Behind the desire to offer assistance to the victims of Hitler's racism was a need to divert criticism away from the American government's desire not to admit more of Europe's Jewish refugees.

To be fair to Roosevelt, he was plagued by problems familiar to any student of recent American history. He was faced with the open racism of the Ku Klux Klan and their bedfellows, who were happy to admit their desire was for America to be home to 'Nordic' inhabitants, rather than the 'lower races' who had arrived in great profusion around the turn of the century, not least Jews fleeing from Russia and Eastern Europe. America was also beset with a vivid fear of Bolshevism, linked inextricably in the public mind with Jewish people. As with today, crackpot conspiracy theories concerning both Jews and Bolsheviks were also flourishing in the economic uncertainty of the Great Depression.

The conference was held in the French town of Évian. Half-hearted ideas were floated, such as allowing a few hundred families to settle in the British Empire territories of Northern Rhodesia or Kenya. Vague intentions were promulgated, such as 'we shall undertake negotiations to improve the present conditions'. The whole affair was a damp squib. British protectorate Palestine, the destination of choice for many fleeing Jews, was now becoming a hotbed of Arab resistance, so further emigration there was discouraged. All participating countries were anxious not to 'provoke' Nazi Germany, and no one wanted to appear too generous in case this prompted other countries which saw themselves as having a 'Jewish problem', such as Poland, Hungary and Romania, to expel their own Jews.

The urge not to 'provoke' the Nazis was everywhere in British foreign policy dealings with their German equivalents, especially regarding the issue of the clearly iniquitous 'flight tax'. Despite declaring their intention to make the Reich *judenrein** ('clean of Jews'), the Nazis made it very difficult for Jews to escape – not least with this 'flight tax' which fleeced anyone who intended to leave. As the British ambassador in Berlin, Sir Nevile Henderson, mentioned to Foreign Minister Joachim von Ribbentrop, the British government were concerned about the 'difficulties which will be created if the present restrictions on the export of Jewish property are maintained', highlighting that countries were unlikely to want to receive destitute refugees. Naturally, the Nazis sniped and sneered at the goings-on at Évian, with von Ribbentrop dismissing the conference as a forum for Jewish propaganda. Henderson replied that the damage caused by such propaganda 'might be mitigated' if the Nazis allowed their Jewish émigrés to take at least some of their property. A. J. Sherman's *Island Refuge* quotes Henderson as saying: 'I would deprecate too dogmatic an attitude by British delegates as regards German policy towards Jews. However uncivilised and deplorable, it is, in the Chancellor's[†] eyes, Germany's own business.'

The illogical conundrum of the flight tax's prohibitive effect on emigration seems characteristic of the Nazi mindset – a hatred of a racial group so deep they must be driven from the country, coupled with vindictive regulations making their leaving extremely difficult. Here, plainly, spite trumped practicality.[‡]

* * *

---

*   This was another heartless variation of the Nazi turn of phrase *judenfrei*, meaning free of Jews.
†   Meaning Hitler.
‡   This illogicality would be a major contributor to the Nazis' defeat. In the final year of the war, for example, the Nazis devoted huge but dwindling resources to the transport and extermination of Jews. Such resources would have been much more effectively employed against the Allied and Soviet armies approaching Berlin from east and west.

The Évian Conference was prompted by alarming events. In March 1938, the plight of central Europe's Jews took a further turn for the worse when German soldiers marched into Austria and an *Anschluss* was proclaimed.*

The *Anschluss* was a clear rejection by Hitler's Germany of the post-war settlement. It also created an additional problem for Jews desperate to escape the Nazi realm. Austria had a higher number of Jews among its population than Germany (nearly 4 per cent, as opposed to 0.75 per cent in Germany). Now an additional 192,000 Jews were faced with the same restrictions and persecution as the Jews in Germany.

In a reaction reminiscent of our modern-day response to climate change, a nebulous anxiety that 'something must be done' hung in the air. Roosevelt, especially, felt under pressure to be seen to be doing something. America, alongside the British mandate of Palestine, was the favoured destination for Europe's Jews. The United States, though, had a strict annual quota on immigration, from country to country, and far more Jews wanted to go there than were permitted to do so.

Roosevelt's America was beset with exactly the same problems that made Britain wary of opening its doors to an influx of refugees. The vast country had been hit hard by the Great Depression, and antisemitism was a powerful sentiment. (Like Britain's Blackshirts, the Americans had their own fascist party – the German American Bund. Like the Blackshirts, it had limited appeal but nonetheless

---

* Not only did the two countries have a common language; they had been linked together historically for many centuries. Initially, they were both part of the Holy Roman Empire and then part of the German Confederation. Modern-day Austria, as an independent nation, had existed only since the post-First World War settlement of Europe at Versailles, a treaty which had explicitly forbidden a union between Germany and Austria.

was able to pack out New York's 20,000-capacity Madison Square Garden for a rally in February 1939.)

Following Roosevelt's call for an international conference to address the problem, in July 1938 delegates from thirty-two countries met in Évian to discuss what could be done for Jewish refugees. The conference was also attended by 200 journalists and reported all around the world. And, of course, its outcome was anxiously awaited by the Jews who remained in Germany and Austria.

Alas, the cards were marked from the start. Before the conference began, the British and Americans agreed that the two most desirable destinations for Jewish refugees, America and Palestine, were not to be discussed. Furthermore, and tellingly, the heads of the delegations from both countries were hardly senior government representatives. The Americans sent a businessman friend of the President, industrialist Myron Taylor, rather than a politician. The British delegation was headed by the Irish aristocrat Edward Turnour,* who held the lowly Cabinet post of Chancellor of the Duchy of Lancaster. Turnour was highly attuned to the resentment likely to be stirred up by the process of sending destitute refugees out into the world, requesting that 'the country of origin, on its side, will equally assist in creating conditions in which the emigrants are able to start life in other countries with some prospect of success'.

Despite the many expressions of sympathy offered to the persecuted Jews of Germany, actual help was in meagre supply, aside from the small Caribbean nation of the Dominican Republic. Their delegation agreed to take 100,000 settlers and put agricultural land aside for them. But only 800 Jews ever managed to reach the

---

* Turnour also appears in accounts of Évian as his aristocratic title Lord Winterton.

Dominican Republic, the first arriving in May 1940, eight months after borders had closed and the war had begun. Why this was so lay in a combination of complications, not least the difficulty in reaching the republic from Nazi territory. Refugees who arrived in the coastal town of Sosúa remember the ramshackle accommodation – there was 'no electric light and the mosquitoes were humming' and 'very often we had no water'. But despite 'all this, we were glad to be alive', reflects Ruth Kohn.

America decided to consider its quota of immigrants from Germany and Austria and agreed that the annual 30,000 limit should be made available specifically for Jews. Britain decided to accept a similar number. Other nations in the British Commonwealth also considered their intake. Australia proposed to take 15,000 Jews over three years, but its chief delegate, Colonel T. W. White, demurred: 'As we have no real racial problem, we are not desirous of importing one."* South Africa conceded to allow Jews with existing family connections to enter and Canada made no commitment at all.

Assistance from outside the Anglosphere was equally unforthcoming. France, for example, declared itself 'saturated' with Jewish refugees. Soviet Russia, which had its own historical tradition of antisemitism, also refused to accept any refugees. In 1939, guards on the Soviet border were ordered to treat any refugee seeking to flee the Nazis as a spy – a death sentence in the sinister Bolshevik state.†

In a further attempt to be seen to be 'doing something', the

---

* Presumably, the Aboriginal population weren't worthy of his consideration. Coincidentally, an Australian Aboriginal leader, William Cooper, led a delegation of the Australian Aboriginal League to the German Consulate in Melbourne at the end of the year and delivered a petition condemning the 'cruel persecution of the Jewish people by the Nazi government of Germany'.

† Russia was unlikely to have been any Jewish refugee's first-choice destination. Pogroms in the late nineteenth century had already driven millions of Jews to other countries. In the upheaval of the aftermath of the Russian revolution, a reported 85,000 Jews in Russia were murdered in 1919 alone. Stalin's own antisemitism reached peak fruition after the war, when he became convinced that Jewish doctors were seeking to murder him. A full-blown purge began to gather momentum, but Stalin's death in 1953 put an immediate end to this completely fabricated conspiracy.

conference agreed to establish a body called the Intergovernmental Committee on Refugees. Its intention would be 'to develop opportunities for further settlement'. But the organisation had no authority or support from member nations and unsurprisingly proved to be wholly ineffective.

One of the tragedies of Évian was that even the Jewish refugee organisations, which had been invited as observers rather than participants, could not agree on a united course of action. The American Jewish Committee, conscious that their fellow Americans would likely think they were trying to flood the United States with Jews and anxious about the increase in antisemitism this would provoke, even advised Roosevelt not to increase America's immigration quota.

The two most prominent Zionist leaders, staunch advocates for a Jewish homeland in Palestine, also wildly overplayed their hand. Chaim Weizmann and David Ben-Gurion, who would become the first President and the first Prime Minister of Israel, respectively, both declared that Palestine should be the only destination for Europe's persecuted Jews. They both firmly opposed proposals to enable more Jews to escape to Western nations. Their strategy was intended to create a crisis where hundreds of thousands of desperate Jewish refugees would simply have nowhere else to go, and Britain would be forced to permit them to flee to Palestine. The leader of the British delegation despaired for this approach, describing it as 'stubbornly unrealistic'.

*   *   *

As we have seen in Chapter 2, the possibility of emigrating to Palestine had indeed become the dream of many of Europe's Jews, even before the arrival of the Nazis. Since 1933, the eastern Mediterranean territory had seen an influx of 60,000 German Jews, encouraged by the Balfour Declaration of 1917. Now at Évian in 1938, it was plain that the declaration had led Jewish organisations up a blind alley. Turnour, as leader of the British delegation, played down the prospect of allowing more refugees to flee to Palestine. Although he did not mention the territory by name, he alluded to overseas territories under British jurisdiction where 'local political conditions hinder or prevent any considerable immigration'.

Weizmann and Ben-Gurion had underestimated the sheer malignancy of their Nazi opponents, and their focus on a Palestine-only solution at Évian backfired disastrously. At exactly the same time such an escape route was most needed, the British were desperately trying to dissuade Jews from reaching this hotly contested territory.

* * *

The Évian Conference had been prompted by the Nazi takeover of Austria. But in the months that followed, Kristallnacht increased the desperate necessity for Jews within the Nazi realm to flee. And eight months after the conference, the Nazis occupied Czechoslovakia and a further 357,000 Jews fell under their control.

The conference was watched closely by the British press. Not only the right-wing tabloids fretted over the potential arrival of thousands of Jews. *The Observer* was concerned that a great influx would provoke a massive outburst of antisemitic anger 'unless every great country takes her proportionate share'. Trade unions were also concerned: 'We appreciate that often the refugees have committed no crime against the country that harries them; but charity begins at home,' wrote one prominent trade unionist in a letter to the *Daily Herald* on 25 August 1938. 'We shall never keep the standards that have been won for us, if the influx of aliens goes on unchecked.'

At the conference, France, Switzerland, the Netherlands and the Scandinavian countries all claimed that they had already admitted what they considered to be large numbers of refugees and were unable to absorb any more. The South American countries claimed likewise.

A. J. Sherman comments that thirty governments made statements that 'seemed to most observers unhelpful, repetitious and designed largely for domestic consumption', all of which further underlines the image of Évian as a 1930s equivalent to the 'greenwashing' of the 2020s. A public relations sleight of hand by a government or corporation designed to encourage a worried population that 'something' was being done.

The Nazi Party were quick to mock the failure of the conference. Hitler sneered:

> I can only hope and expect that the other world, which has such deep sympathy for these criminals [by which he meant Germany's Jews], will at least be generous enough to convert this sympathy into practical aid. We, on our part, are ready to put all these criminals at the disposal of these countries, for all I care, even on luxury ships.

Turnour returned from Évian to report to the Cabinet that the conference had gone well. He also observed, writes A. J. Sherman, that the fact that the American and German governments were on bad terms with each other was 'not unconnected with the fact that the Jewish vote in the United States was a large one'.* He also pointed out that America had wanted to issue a denunciation of Germany but that this had been successfully resisted by the British delegation.

The British Home Secretary, Sir Samuel Hoare, writes Sherman, was 'anxious to do his best, [but] there was a good deal of feeling growing up in this country – a feeling which was reflected in Parliament – against the admission of Jews to British Territory'. Notwithstanding, Cabinet papers reveal, he intended to 'go on quietly considering individual cases on their own merits'. This was an alarming prospect for those tens of thousands of individual cases whose future hung on an urgent positive decision in their favour.

The summer of 1938 saw further resistance across the political spectrum towards help for Europe's desperate Jews, from trade unions to the British Medical Association, which was demanding a further two years' clinical study before any German or Austrian Jewish doctors be allowed to practise. Alfred Feiner, a Jewish GP from Vienna, had to complete these extra qualifications in order to practise when he arrived in the UK. His wife, Herta, worked as a housekeeper and cook to keep the couple and their young son afloat while Alfred was studying. They had to overcome 'a great deal of suspicion and animosity' from the locals, but eventually they 'gained [their] respect and admiration'.

Even Jewish refugee organisations were alarmed by the scale of refugees wanting to come to Britain, not least because they had offered to guarantee that Jewish arrivals would not need assistance from the state and were anxious that their existing funds would no

---

* These days we'd consider this a classic case of 'victim blaming'.

longer be enough to do this. So, at exactly the time when a more open refugee policy would have helped those trying to escape, vetting of incoming cases increased.

Incidentally, around this time, America had its own *Kindertransport* opportunity when the Wagner–Rogers Bill to accept 20,000 Jewish refugee children was put to the Senate. Prompted by Kristallnacht and proposed by Democrat Senator Robert F. Wagner and Republican Senator Edith Rogers, the bill was defeated by a combination of anti-immigrant and antisemitic sentiment.

And adding to the disquiet, British newspapers were always keen to cover stories about 'aliens' who had smuggled themselves into England to face expulsion or imprisonment. One London magistrate, Herbert Metcalfe, was reported in *The Times*, on 20 August 1938, to have said: 'It was becoming an outrage the way in which stateless Jews were pouring in from every port of this country. As far as he was concerned, he intended to enforce the law to the fullest extent.'

Not all newspapers approved, notes A. J. Sherman. The *News Chronicle* wrote that Metcalfe might like to 'hound homeless and helpless refugees [with] less obvious pleasure'.

The failure of the Évian Conference haunted politicians for the rest of the century. Jimmy Carter's Vice-President Walter Mondale remarked in 1979: 'At stake at Évian were both human lives and the decency and self-respect of the civilized world. If each nation at Évian had agreed on that day to take in 17,000 Jews at once, every Jew in the Reich could have been saved.'

Mondale's remarks were prompted by the international response to the Vietnamese 'boat people' fleeing the country following the communists' victory in the long-running civil war. Évian, he implied, had failed the test of civilisation.

Not long after the conference ended, the *Daily Express* ran an editorial on 23 August 1938 entitled 'The Wandering Jew', conjuring images of an 'underground railway', alluding to the escape route of slaves in Civil War-era America. 'Certainly there is no room for the Jews in Britain, where we have 1,800,000 of our own people out of work and biting their nails ... There are plenty of uninhabited parts of the world where, given a touch of the Christian spirit, [the Jews] may yet find happy homes.'

From the title headline onwards,* these words seem cruelly flippant, a thin veneer of nicety to disguise their heartless sentiment. You wonder where they had in mind. The Sahara Desert? Eastern Siberia? The Antarctic? Wags at the time pointed out that Évian spelled backwards was naïve. But I think the spirit behind it was far more cynical.

---

* The Wandering Jew is a mythological figure who cursed Christ on the way to his crucifixion and was thereafter condemned to walk the earth until the end of time.

Chapter 5

Escape: The Lucky 80,000

As the Nazi persecution of Jews increased and the world edged closer to war, the prospect of thousands of German and Austrian Jews arriving in Britain caused uproar in the tabloids – and much of their reporting carried a clear echo of the 'migrant invasion' stories in today's papers.

The *Daily Express* editorial 'In They Come' of 9 July 1938 demands:

NO WORK FOR FOREIGNERS

Foreigners should not be allowed to work in Britain, particularly in the professions. Already we have too many young men trying to crowd into the professions. And our young men are just as clever, just as well educated, and just as able to discharge the duties which will fall upon them as any foreigner … As for the working-classes, the unemployment in that section of the community has already reached immense proportions. We cannot afford to add to the numbers. Such a proceeding would be an act of cruelty for which the responsible Ministers should be severely punished.

But these words are immediately followed by two paragraphs entitled 'Sanctuary':

Do not suppose from this argument that the *Daily Express* wishes to exclude political refugees or to stand in the way of those who are brought here as guests of big-hearted and open-minded British citizens willing to bestow benefactions on their unfortunate friends in those foreign countries where persecution prevails.

On the contrary, the *Daily Express* stands against persecution and for the oppressed. It stands for Britain as a sanctuary, but against those who, given refuge in the sanctuary, attempt to deprive our own people of their living.

A classic example of having your cake and eating it, and the idea that immigration of any type is a zero-sum game.

Five weeks later, the *Express* carried an article by journalist Sydney Smith on its opinion page of 23 August 1938 with the headline 'It's Too Easy to Get into Britain'.

'Britain is the land of the free – for the fugitive foreigner,' it begins, then goes on to warn: 'They see Britain from their persecution-ridden corners of Europe, as a wide-open space, barred to them by nothing much more formidable than the English Channel.'

Given the perturbed tone of the article, the numbers causing such anxiety seem laughable. 'This year already, the police have found twenty-four men and women in London and on the south coast, who had managed to enter this country without passports.'

Backing up his argument, Smith returns to the popular foreigners = criminals prejudice of his readership by reminding them that 'only this month a woman and two men, described by Scotland Yard as "a gang of dangerous international criminals", were found at work in the East End'.

Looking at the various routes into the country, Smith goes on to claim:

> There are 8,000 servant girls of German and Austrian nationality working in Britain now. They enter the country with all facilities because they had work to go to.
>
> They got it at wages far below those that would be accepted by English girls, and therefore the servant employment agencies are able to say there is a shortage of English labour.
>
> Then the German or Austrian servant girl leaves her job and drifts off into the wide-open spaces of free Britain.

The article goes on to claim that the Alien Registration Form required by the government is too easy to forge. 'And even if it is discovered to be a forgery, who cares what he fills in? He'll be gone somewhere else before it's verified.' The article ends abruptly with the puzzling sentence: 'The Englishman is kind to dogs, horses, children and foreigners.'

Yet only a month previously, the *Express* had been carrying articles on 'the servant problem' – such as 'The difficulty in getting a well-trained "daily"'. There clearly was an issue with middle-class families finding a 'suitable' servant, not least because after the First World War the number of British people wanting to 'go into service' declined considerably.

On the same page as the 'It's Too Easy to Get into Britain' article, the opinion pieces are in full anti-refugee flow. 'Keep Them Out!' demands one paragraph, railing at the arrival of 'aliens smuggled into the country. ... For every one caught many escape recognition.'

The following opinion piece, with a total lack of irony or recognition that these two subjects may be linked, asks 'Who Makes the Fuss?' and complains about demonstrations against a German football team currently touring the UK.

> This wicked business of being offensive to foreign visitors is not an English characteristic at all' ... Too often it is found that the attacks are made and engineered by people who are foreigners themselves ... If they are not prepared to conform to our ways let us send them to their homes again. They must not introduce here the controversies of their own lands.

Curiously, this 'send them back if they don't like it' argument is frequently repeated today in the reader comments section of the *Daily Mail*. No doubt if the term were *en vogue* in the 1930s, the *Express* and *Mail* would have described such demonstrators as 'woke'.

Following on from this blinkered comment is another about the *Express* reporter William Hickey, currently 'motoring' through Germany. Just in case any reader had the temerity to think: 'Hang on, aren't these foreigners here because they are being brutally and murderously persecuted in their own land? No wonder they're demonstrating against the German football team,' Hickey puts them right. He discovers 'no air of tension, no difficulties at frontiers, and nothing to support the alarmist warnings given out by

---

* Perhaps they should have added 'unless they're Jews'.

panic-makers in this country. Coblenz, great Rhineland town, is peaceful he says, even gay.'

Throughout this time, there were many other stories of this nature in the *Express* about people arriving 'illegally', including 'Crews are Bribed to Help' and 'Aliens Land with Forged Passports'.

But ten months before the war broke out, closing borders between combatant nations, a particular savage event provoked a change of heart towards refugees wanting to come to Britain, within both government and much of the population. Two months after Chamberlain's dramatic 'peace for our time' Munich settlement, the Nazi Party bared its teeth in a shameless Jewish pogrom.* On 7 November 1938, Herschel Grynszpan, an aggrieved Jewish refugee, shot a diplomat named Ernst vom Rath at Germany's Paris Embassy.† After lingering a day, vom Rath died, and this became an excuse for the Nazis to unleash wholesale reprisals on their own Jewish population. During the night of 9–10 November, synagogues, Jewish businesses and homes were attacked and burned throughout Germany and Austria – now under Nazi control following the *Anschluss* eight months earlier. The Sudetenland, seized from Czechoslovakia barely a month before, also saw violence against its Jewish inhabitants. Altogether, nearly 100 Jews were murdered and between 20,000 and 30,000 Jews were arrested and sent to concentration camps. Many never returned. These events became known as Kristallnacht – after the wholesale smashing of glass windows during the disturbances. The Nazis declared their actions to be a spontaneous and righteous display of German, Austrian and Sudeten anger. But they were

---

* This Russian word, meaning 'to wreak havoc', was first used in the early nineteenth century to describe Russian attacks on Jews in Odesa. It has now come to mean any murderous attack on Jews.
† This event is cloaked in irony. Vom Rath was under Gestapo investigation at the time as an anti-Nazi and Jewish sympathiser, so his assassin, a young Pole called Herschel Grynszpan, certainly picked a poor victim. Incidentally, if any keen-eyed readers are wondering if 'vom' is a typo, I understand it's a German variation of the aristocratic appellation 'von'.

carefully orchestrated by the Gestapo and the SA (the paramilitary wing of the Nazi Party). The message was clear enough: Jews who remained in Hitler's Reich were risking their very lives.

With the sort of warped, sadistic 'humour' that would see the gates of concentration camps adorned with the message *Arbeit macht frei* ('Work sets you free'), the Nazis then fined their Jewish population a billion Reichsmarks for the cost of cleaning up the destruction – estimated to be 20 per cent of the wealth of the 300,000 Jews who still remained in their territory. Kristallnacht marked a point of no return for the Third Reich's Jews. Any hope that Hitler's behaviour towards them would mellow was plainly a lost cause. Now, in the closing months of peace, most Jews made plans to leave. Depending partly on family links, some only postponed their fate by going east or west to neighbouring countries. The lucky ones fled to America or Britain.

In Britain, the harrowing events of Kristallnacht generated greater, albeit sometimes grudging, sympathy, and these final months before the war broke out saw a substantial influx of mainly Jewish refugees. Prime Minister Chamberlain privately noted in a letter to a friend: 'I believe the persecution arose out of two motives: a desire to rob the Jews of their money and a jealousy of their superior cleverness.' Chamberlain added: 'No doubt the Jews aren't a lovable people; I don't care about them myself; but that is not sufficient to explain the Pogrom.'* Not all leading Tories were so ambivalent. Former Prime Minister Stanley Baldwin† launched a public

---

* Chamberlain was a man with many of the prejudices of his era. Piers Brendon reports he thought America 'a nation of cads' and that the French 'couldn't keep a secret for more than half an hour'. He famously dismissed the Czechs and their tribulations with Hitler in 1938 as 'a quarrel in a faraway country between people of whom we know nothing'.

† Baldwin had form here. As early as 1933, he spoke out in a radio appeal asking for financial assistance to help Jews wanting to flee from Nazi Germany. 'I ask you to come to the aid of victims not of any catastrophe in the natural world, nor of flood, nor of famine but of an explosion of man's inhumanity of man.'

appeal on behalf of Jewish refugees: 'Thousands of men, women and children, despoiled of their goods, driven from their homes, are seeking asylum and sanctuary on our doorsteps, a hiding place from the wind and a covert from the tempest."* Rules of entry were changed. A system of visas was introduced for German and Austrian Jews so the government could select who they were prepared to admit. Wealthy businessmen, who could employ British people in their enterprises, were welcome, as were those prepared to work in domestic service. But anyone who came here had to have a guarantor who would support them. The 'public purse' was not available to these new arrivals.

Kristallnacht prompted a series of evacuations known as the *Kindertransport*, undoubtedly the achievement most readily recalled to demonstrate our 'proud tradition' of helping refugees. Perhaps because compassion for children rarely rankles and the young can hardly be accused of stealing jobs and fomenting crime or revolution. Up to 10,000 Jewish children under the age of seventeen were placed on trains from Berlin, Vienna, Prague and other cities and transported to Harwich and then on to further UK destinations. Many of them bade a tearful farewell to parents they would never see again. Significantly, this was not a government initiative but one funded and organised by members of the British public, most especially the Central British Fund (CBF) for German Jewry, the Jewish Refugees Committee and the Quakers, who set up an office in Vienna to process the paperwork needed to obtain a visa and find an organisation or private individual who would act as a guarantor that any refugee would not need assistance from the British state.

---

* On a curious tangent, Margaret Thatcher's family, staunch Grantham working-class conservatives, helped her sister's Austrian Jewish pen friend to escape Vienna after the *Anschluss*. The girl, Edith Mühlbauer, came to live with the Roberts family for a while. Future Prime Ministers Clement Attlee and Jim Callaghan also took in refugees at this time.

At first, selection was based on need. Children whose parents were in concentration camps, or who were homeless or orphaned, were given priority. But in order to encourage more private individuals to come forward in Britain, the focus shifted to middle-class 'attractive' children, who were more likely to assimilate and not exhibit awkward behaviour. Thus were the cards stacked against the poor and less educated. Lacking connections with overseas relatives and friends, and less able to cope with the mountain of bureaucratic forms required to obtain a visa, working-class Jews were ill-adapted to survive this Darwinian struggle for survival. The search for visas was, of course, not just limited to children under seventeen. By late 1938, British broadsheet newspapers were flooded with adverts from desperate German and Austrian Jews seeking employment opportunities in Britain for both their older children and themselves. There were strict rules regarding the kind of work available to them, prompted by the fear that they would take jobs away from British workers. This concern was felt across the British class spectrum, from shop workers to doctors and dentists. But since the First World War, there had been a dearth of domestic servants for middle-class households, so this became the most prudent occupation to apply for. Well-to-do Jews in professional occupations had to advertise themselves, and their children, as willing and able to do such work – maid or cook for the women, chauffeur or manservant for the men.

The Guardian was widely considered the best place to advertise for work or foster families, not least because it, more than any other British newspaper, was most likely to carry stories about the Nazi persecution of the Jews. It was also based in Manchester, which had a large Jewish population, and it was a popular paper among

Quakers, who were at the forefront in the rescue and care of Jewish refugees, both in sponsoring individuals and setting up institutions to care for groups of children.

One refugee to arrive via these *Guardian* small ads was fourteen-year-old Gertrude Batscha, described thus by her desperate parents: 'Well mannered, able to help in any household work, speaks German, French, and a little English and plays the piano.' Taken in by a family in Somerset, she had said goodbye to her parents at Vienna's main railway station in February 1939. Like many other *Kindertransport* children, she never saw them again. 'I hope never to know such desperation as prompted them to decide to part with me and send me away alone,' she wrote in her memoir. Her parents prepared to leave for England, hoping for work as a butler and housekeeper, but were just two of the hundreds of thousands who never obtained a visa or sponsor. Gertrude discovered their fate after the war, when the Red Cross informed her that they had been killed by the Nazis in the Maly Trostenets death camp in Belarus, probably in late 1942. Gertrude herself emigrated to Israel after the war ended.

Eighteen-year-old Liese Feiks, who had advertised herself as a multilingual 'shorthand writer and typist', was offered work as a servant and remembers her time in England as 'the most miserable years of my life'. Walter Laqueur offers such refugees sympathy in his book *Generation Exodus*. These girls 'were not accustomed to being treated as social inferiors ... Very often they had been of a higher social standing and better educated than those they were working for in Britain ... They forgot they had been hired to wash the dishes, not to play the piano.'

As well as pleas for work, the adverts often asked for families to foster children – a far more agreeable fate for bright, well-educated young refugees. But how they fared after they arrived was, of course, a matter of luck. Some have entirely happy memories of coming to Britain, others not so much. Charities sometimes offered to pay carers to take in children, and these instances were often among the most unhappy placements. Those who were too young to work fared far better when they were placed with volunteers.

But matching refugees with hosts could be difficult for a variety of reasons, not least because of social awkwardness. Martha Immerdauer left her middle-class Viennese parents in the summer of 1939. Then nine years old, she was very close to them and would never see them again. A bright child who had all but taught herself to read, she was fostered by a Jewish couple in Bow, east London, who had arrived in the 1900s, refugees themselves from the pogroms of Tsarist Poland.

Annie and Will Greensztein had no children of their own, following a string of miscarriages and stillbirths, and showered Martha with love. When their refugee arrived, Annie thoughtfully explained that she should call her 'Auntie' as she already had a mother. Will would be known as 'Uncle'. Alas, Martha immediately felt uncomfortable with them. Annie, who could not read or write, spoke with a pronounced accent peppered with Yiddish expressions. She was also given to wild gesticulation and passionate outbursts. Martha cringed with embarrassment at Auntie's exchanges with her more reserved, undemonstrative British neighbours. Looking back, she had wished she had been sent to live with a family more like Greer Garson's cut-glass Mrs Miniver (from the 1942 MGM film of the same name). Martha recalled that Annie had no great interest in her own love of classical music, referring to it as 'sympathy music' (rather than symphony) and believing a concerto to be a musical instrument.

Martha frequently quarrelled with Annie, but her taxi-driving 'uncle' was more palatable to her. He was a quiet, steady man who had his own little foibles and quips. (When asked if he'd like another cup of tea, Martha relates, he would invariably respond: 'No, but I'd like some more tea in the same cup.') She writes that he was 'a simple but loving man. He spoke English, Polish, Yiddish and some German, yet he had few words.' When she learned at the end of the war that her parents had both been murdered by the Nazis, she did not want to be formally adopted by the Greenszteins but remained in their foster care. She writes: 'I had the feeling that, kind as they were, I was not of their kind.'

But the story has a happy ending, and as she grew older, Martha began to show a greater appreciation of her auntie and uncle. Her memoir, *A Child Alone*, first published by Vallentine Mitchell & Co. Ltd in 1995 under the name Martha Blend, is dedicated equally to her biological parents and the auntie and uncle who fostered her.

Will and Annie ensured she went to academically ambitious schools, and she quickly learned to speak English without an accent, taking pride in her ability to 'pass' as an ordinary middle-class schoolgirl. 'On the surface,' Martha writes, 'it was though I had shed my Austrian language and personality as a snake sheds its skin and had grown a protective English covering.' She went on to Queen Mary College, University of London, to read English and married a medical student.

Will died soon after Martha married, but Annie remained a frequent visitor. 'She did enjoy being with my children and came regularly to see me with supplies of home-baked biscuits and other offerings. We kept up a thorny but affectionate relationship until she too died suddenly whilst staying with friends,' writes Martha.

A Child Alone is a telling reflection of the awful upheaval many *Kindertransport* children experienced. Martha's intolerance of her 'auntie' should be seen in the light of her experience of coming to 'a strange house in a strange country with a strange language and worst of all, utterly separated from the parents I loved deeply and might never see again'. Martha was lucky to have such understanding fosterers. Many other carers would have resented a rather aloof and rebellious child, who kept them at arm's length. But the three of them reached an understanding. Martha's regard and loyalty for her foster parents comes through in her decision to marry young rather than 'live in sin', which she had contemplated with her fiancé. This, she writes, 'would have given my Auntie a heart-attack'.

The ultimate success of the relationship with her 'auntie', Martha reflected, lay in their complementary needs. 'Fortunately for us both, her strong need to express her maternal feelings dovetailed with my need for comfort and security.'

Martha carried an 'otherness' with her throughout her life, haunted by the parents she had left behind and her twin Viennese and British identities. She also had an almost subconscious feeling that there was something wrong and shaming about being Jewish – the pernicious effect of intense Nazi propaganda. 'What had happened to me was so painful that it was quite beyond my powers to talk about it,' she writes. Only thirty years later, having purposely shut out contact with other survivors and any other information about the Holocaust, could she bear to return to Vienna to find out what had happened to her parents and fellow Jews.

Many Jewish refugees who came here in similar circumstances learned not to talk about their experiences of Nazi persecution. They found that people did not want to know. Others found the British to be comically insular. The publisher George Weidenfeld, who came to Britain from Austria after the *Anschluss*, recalled being asked by a society hostess: 'I hear you come from Germany. Did you know the Goerings?'

In London in the 1980s, I came to know two people who had arrived on the *Kindertransport* programme. One was a woman called 'Ella'* who worked part-time as a receptionist in an archive where I worked. As a tiny child, she had left her famous parents (both well-known film actors) who were then interned in the 'model' concentration camp of Theresienstadt in Czechoslovakia. Here, conditions were more tolerable than in other camps, and it was used in Nazi propaganda films to fool the world about how well they treated interned Jews. Sometime later, both her parents were sent to death camps and did not survive the war. Ella could have been no more than fifty when I met her, an elegant, poised individual whose English was good, although she still spoke with a marked Austrian accent.

My other friend was a lively, sharply intelligent woman named Ilse Gray, who ran the copy-editing department of a publisher. As required by the demands of her job, her English was faultless and, incidentally, entirely without an accent. Ilse too had come over as a small child, arriving from Vienna in one of the first *Kindertransport* consignments in December 1938.

---

* I have lost touch with this person and was unable to ask her permission to use her story, so I have changed her name.

Six and a half at the time, she had travelled with her nine-year-old sister Eva. Ilse's family were entirely secular – she didn't even know she was Jewish until the *Anschluss* of 1938.

At first her parents had been unable to obtain a visa for their two daughters, as these were mostly available via Jewish religious groups. But fortunately, the Quakers had set up an office in Vienna and were happy to help anyone Jewish – religious or secular.

At the time of writing, Ilse is ninety and lives in Primrose Hill in London. She wrote:

We arrived in England round about 14th December. Eva and I were being sent to Norfolk to live with a single lady and her niece in a village called Cringleford, but, as it was late in the day, Miss Hope, one of the Quaker ladies who had looked after us on the journey, took us to her home in Park Village East, just south of Camden Town. Eva remembered the taxi journey in the dark from Victoria round Hyde Park Corner and up brightly lit Park Lane and later described how she marvelled at the people in evening dress outside the Dorchester hotel. All I remember was the humiliation of being sick in the taxi as we arrived at Miss Hope's house! Cringleford, a village with a history going back to Saxon times, lies on the outskirts of Norwich. In 1938 it was still fairly small. We lived with a lady and her niece (or possibly, we thought later, her daughter) and went to the local school – a building divided in half, like so many village schools then, juniors on one side, seniors on the other. I don't remember any of the teachers or what we learnt, just as I don't remember the transition from not speaking English to speaking English fluently, but it seemed to be a happy, friendly place. I even had a 'boyfriend'; a small, ginger-haired lad who walked me to school every day, for which we were much teased by the other children. Out of school, we were allowed to wander the countryside without adult supervision. Many of our friends were farmers' children and we played in the fields and woods. I remember finding hens' eggs in the hedges; presumably the chickens were completely free range. Then suddenly around Easter we were transferred to a family in Birmingham. I have never been sure why, but think it had something to do with my mother trying to find a sponsor and suitable home for her parents whom she had persuaded to leave Vienna before it was too late. We now found ourselves in the midst of a large Jewish family in Edgbaston under the watchful eye of a formidable mother. I suppose father was mostly out at work because I hardly remember him at all except that he seemed nice and friendly. The oldest two boys were mostly away at college, the others went to school locally, where we soon joined them. An eleven-year-old boy frequently wet his bed and sadly got into much trouble from the adults and teasing from the children.

However, Eva, now nine years old, and the family did not get on so well and, without consulting anyone, they moved her to another home. This was to a woman who lived on her own and with whom Eva got on very well. The lady was a film addict and Eva had a lovely time going to the cinema almost every day during the Easter holidays.

Ilse was also looked after by two Quaker women called Lilibet and Isobel. As well as sheltering child refugees, they were also active in rescuing adults from Nazi territory. Ilse remembers they were particularly helpful in getting her mother and baby sister out of Austria. She told me that her and her elder sister came to realise the two were a couple and that the Quakers were 'quite relaxed about this', even in the 1930s.

Eva's own memories of this time are darker – not least because she was older and more aware of what was happening. Here is an excerpt from her account of the journey from Vienna to England:

On December 13th 1938 a silent unhappy group of relatives were as-sembled at the Westbahnhof to bid us good-bye. Most of them were fully aware that this might be the last time they would ever set eyes on us, and some were right ... It was a grim occasion, and although I was terribly excited to be going on such a long journey, I did know, deep down in my heart, what it was all about. By this time I had experienced Gestapo brutality and the fear with which we lived day in day out. As the last tearful farewells had been said and the train drew out of the station, my mother broke loose from the little group and ran along beside the train in desperation. It was terrible to see her anguish and this, more than anything else, made me fully realise the possibility of losing her for ever.

Eva also gives us another glimpse of Miss Hope, evidentially a woman of formidable courage:

At Aachen the Germans searched the train and examined visas. A boy and a girl in our group were ordered out and Miss Hope was told to leave them behind. (I understood later that the reason was that they were only half-Jewish, whatever reason that was!) Miss Hope refused to leave without them. She threatened to make an international incident out of the whole business. At this point the Nazi regime still had some respect for the British, and they let the children go. Because of all the confusion, the train was held up, and the rest of us sat, silent and trembling, watching the German soldiers with their machine guns over their shoulders, parade up and down the platform outside our carriage window. All of us knew what the fate of those two children would be if Miss Hope were not to succeed.

After what seemed like years, Miss Hope and the children returned and we proceeded on our way through the frontier, into Belgium. How we cheered, once we knew we found ourselves in the free world!

Meanwhile, Ilse's mother and stepfather had also been able to escape. Her mother had obtained a visa in the spring of 1939. Her stepfather had been refused a visa in Vienna, so he travelled to Helsinki and was granted one there. He immediately took a boat to England and was rapidly reunited with his wife. Ilse's father (her parents had divorced when she was three but remained on good terms) also failed to get a visa in Vienna. So, he crossed the Alps to Italy by bus and took a boat from Genoa to Uruguay. Here he settled in Montevideo and continued to work as an ear, nose and throat consultant. His parents were not so lucky. They stayed and were looked after by an aunt in the family, but they died in a Jewish ghetto and the aunt later died in a concentration camp.

Ilse writes about the reunion with her parents:

They came to see us in Birmingham but were unable to take us back to London because they were living in only one room in Belsize Square while Heinrich [her stepfather] was preparing to take dental exams – a condition for working in the UK, despite that everyone knew that at that time dentists from Austria, Germany and some other European countries were much better trained and qualified than those in Britain – and so had no money to move to somewhere with enough room for all of us.

Ilse told me her mother also succeeded in getting her own parents out of Austria. They arrived three days before war broke out. They got to England thanks to a stroke of great good fortune. As she was travelling to meet up with her children, Ilse's mother met a friendly man on the bus who was a publican. They got talking and she told him about her parents being stuck in Vienna. Though a complete stranger, he immediately offered to sponsor them.

Ilse's maternal grandfather, incidentally, had led an extraordinary life. In the First World War, he had been fighting with the Austro-Hungarian Army and had spent much of the conflict as a prisoner of the Russians in Siberia. Before the war, he had owned a well-known patisserie in Vienna and in captivity he was immediately employed in the kitchens by the Russian officers who ran the camp. He eventually escaped and made his way across Russia, arriving back in Vienna just as the war ended. Following the *Anschluss* of 1938, like many veterans, he mistakenly assumed that fighting for his country would protect him from Nazi persecution. Only a chance random act of kindness, hundreds of miles away, by a stranger on a bus, saved him and his wife from a death camp gas chamber or the execution squads of the *Einsatzgruppen*.[*]

Ilse also told me of another extraordinary episode in her family history, which happened in the early 1960s. While she was trying to get out of Austria in 1939, her mother remembered, she had met a Nazi official at the Viennese visa office who was most kind and

---

[*] Best translated as 'task force', these specialist squads were created to execute Jews in conquered territory. The death camp gas chambers were introduced because this method of killing Jews by mass shooting was inefficient and 'dispiriting' for the soldiers involved.

helpful to her. In 1962, with the Adolf Eichmann* trial in Israel making headlines around the world, she saw his photograph and exclaimed: 'That's the man who helped me! He was the only person in the office who was nice to me.'

The majority of *Kindertransport* children came from Germany or Austria, but, thanks again to the dedicated work of individuals and charities, some 3,500 Jews and other enemies of Nazism were also rescued from Czechoslovakia between December 1938 and March 1939, when the German Army occupied the entire country. Most famous of these individuals was the British stockbroker Nicholas Winton, who arranged safe passage to Britain for 669 Jewish children while working with the British Committee for Refugees from Czechoslovakia.†

Käthe Fischel, a sixteen-year-old art student, was one of the Prague children Winton helped. She recalled her journey in Lyn Smith's *Heroes of the Holocaust*. 'My brother was seven years younger and my mother couldn't bring herself to add him to the Winton list … It was a terrible wrench, but I remember that I very much wanted to go.' The train journey itself was chaotic. 'I was the oldest by far in this compartment. There were four or five very little ones which I was supposed to look after. I wasn't very good at it because they were sick, and they cried and dirtied themselves and I had no idea how to handle this.'

In his book *Generation Exodus*, Walter Laqueur suggests that the youngest *Kindertransport* refugees adopted to their new circumstances most easily. Just as Ilse Gray cannot now even remember

---

* For readers not au fait with the gallery of Nazi villains, Eichmann was one of the leading architects of the Holocaust. He is played, rather magnificently, by Stanley Tucci in the 2001 BBC/HBO film *Conspiracy*.

† Many people will be familiar with Winton because he was featured on the 1988 British television programme *That's Life*, where the studio audience was entirely comprised of either the now adult children he had rescued or their descendants.

learning English as a six- or seven-year-old, so other tiny children quickly adapted to their carers, especially if they were lucky enough to be taken in by loving foster parents who treated them as their own. This, of course, could sometimes lead to heartbreaking scenes when biological parents occasionally turned up to claim them and discovered their children barely recognised them. Language here was another barrier. Even if the biological parents spoke English, almost all of them did so with a heavy accent, which the children struggled to understand.

Nonetheless, many refugees adapted to the culture of the country that had offered them refuge. Laqueur recalls one child saying: 'The whole lifestyle opened up entirely new vistas for us. The quiet courtesy, the freedom to express any opinion, the sincerity and honesty of the people, the ability to live undisturbed in whatever eccentric manner one preferred. We, as many others, became Anglophiles.'

But others were not so lucky. Laqueur also writes of Marion Harston, who arrived in London aged thirteen and who was placed with a wealthy Jewish family in Wandsworth. She felt like Cinderella, she recalled, and the family soon dropped her. Another teenage refugee, Bertha Leverton, had to hand over her entire wage packet to her foster parents, even though they received an allowance for looking after her. Six-year-old Renate Beigel found herself in a very cold foster home: 'It was a horror … All of a sudden I'm with an elderly couple who don't know a single word of German. I don't know a single word of English … I just could not stop crying.'

Other refugees recall freezing houses and terrible food, not to mention bullying in school. One headmaster even insisted on trying to convert his newly arrived Jewish children to Christianity by making church attendance compulsory. A few unlucky children complained of sexual harassment only to be dismissed as troublemakers.

Sadly, even fellow Jews could be standoffish to young refugees. Laqueur writes about Sylvia Rodgers, who was sent to the exclusive Henrietta Barnett School in north London. She found that the Jewish girls there 'entirely ignored her', never speaking to her or inviting her to social events. Sylvia thought the Jewish girls might have feared that their tenuous acceptance by their British peers might be endangered by the arrival of this refugee girl speaking broken English.

*　　*　　*

Six-year-old Ilse seems to have been especially lucky in her experience of coming to England. But once safely arrived at Harwich or Victoria, what happened to older arrivals who had found work in domestic service? Most were likely to be their new employers' social and educational equals, and many had had their own servants before they were forced to flee. Even before the Nazis came to power, Germans and Austrians had come to Britain to escape the economic hardships of the 1920s. Lucy Lethbridge, in her book *Servants*, observes that Germans and Austrians had a reputation for *tüchtigkeit* – a German word that best translates as 'proficient' or 'methodical'. The British might mock their starched Teutonic mien, but these hardworking, thorough qualities were so appreciated a UK recruitment agency even set up an office in Vienna, intending to hire exactly these kind of people for British households.

Servants is an empathetic study of twentieth-century domestic service and contains a fascinating chapter on the German and

Austrian Jews who came to Britain in the late 1930s. Lethbridge writes at some length about the Groszmann family – he a wealthy Viennese accountant, she an accomplished pianist who had studied at the Vienna Academy. After the *Anschluss*, the family apartment and contents were commandeered by the SS and the Groszmanns took shelter with relatives. Their ten-year-old daughter Lore got a place on a *Kindertransport* and was sent to live with a Jewish family in Liverpool. She later wrote a book about her experiences, entitled *Other People's Houses: A Refugee in England 1938–48*, written under her married name Lore Segal.

In Liverpool, Lore was in constant contact with a domestic bureau in London and persuaded them to grant her parents work permits – an extraordinary responsibility and achievement for one so young. She succeeded in facilitating their escape and the Groszmanns took jobs in a household in Kent, as a butler and cook for the pitiful combined sum of £1 a week. Before the war, the average annual wage of an agricultural worker had been £80, considerably more than the Groszmanns' £52 a year. Their accommodation was a small attic room above the kitchen with a single lumpy mattress.

The elderly Herr Groszmann struggled with his butler duties, finding the heavy trays he was required to carry, and other manual work, a strain. Within three days, he was demoted to the rank of gardener. Frau Groszmann was permitted to play the drawing room piano, but only when no one else was in the house. She attempted to make friends with the chef next door by baking her an apple strudel but was rebuffed. Having been used to modern apartments with central heating and continental quilts, the new arrivals found that their washing cloths froze on the side of the basin and that thin blankets were no substitute for a cosy duvet. Lore writes that the

Kent family displayed to her mother 'an exquisitely judged combination of surface kindness and patronising condescension – making sure to impress her inferior status on her and refusing to believe that members of the servant class, especially foreigners, can be as educated, cultured and in every way as middle-class as members of the British middle-class'.

Poor Herr Groszmann, who could hardly be imagined as a threat to anyone, was later interned on the Isle of Man in 1940. Here, he suffered a series of strokes and then died a few days before the end of the war.

*   *   *

There were other avenues, too, to enter Britain aside from the *Kindertransports* and visas for domestic service. Narrow though they may be, compared with the number of Jews who wanted to escape, these further routes away from the Nazis did save thousands of lives. Although the British Medical Association was keen to exclude Jewish doctors, there was work available for German or Austrian nurses. Students and schoolchildren were permitted to come to study, but on the strict understanding that they returned home as soon as their course was completed.

Another scheme, set up by the YMCA, enabled young men to come to Britain for agricultural training. This too was on the understanding that the UK would be only a temporary haven. Successful applicants were issued with transmigration visas and were expected to seek work in South America, South Africa, Australia or Canada when they were done. By the end of 1938, 30,000 refugees had arrived on these visas.

A further scheme was sponsored by the Central British Fund (CBF) for German Jewry. They too provided transmigration visas for young men to come to Britain to train in agricultural work. Here, refugees arrived at a former army base known as the 'Kitchener Camp', on the outskirts of Sandwich, Kent. Many had been arrested on Kristallnacht and held in Nazi concentration camps. To obtain visas for them, the CBF had to guarantee that they would support them financially and that the arrivals would not make Britain their permanent home. Some 4,000 male refugees were saved in this way and a handful also managed to arrange for their wives and children to follow. Helmuth Rosettenstein recounts his experience of being in the Kitchener Camp:

> I don't know who put me forward for the camp to this day. All I know is that they saved my life ... They needed 200 tradesmen and I was a signwriter, so I was asked to come over ... When I arrived I was given overalls and rubber boots and we all worked day and night to put up huts, level roads and install such things as showers. Each hut could take forty-eight refugees and in the end we provided shelter for 3,600 Jews.

Although restrictions were eased and more Jews were allowed into the country, entry was still strictly controlled and those without the exact paperwork could be barred from entering Britain. One infamous incident occurred on 29 March 1939, after Germany had taken over Czechoslovakia, adding considerably to the numbers of Jews desperate to escape. On this day, thirteen refugees arrived by chartered plane from Nazi-occupied Bohemia and Moravia via Copenhagen. It had been a busy day at Croydon Airport, with between

240 and 400 Jewish refugees (reports vary) already arriving and being admitted as they had either the correct visas or sponsors waiting and vouching for them to ensure they would not be 'a burden to the state'.

One of these thirteen passengers on the chartered flight was admitted to the UK as they had family already in the country who guaranteed they would offer financial support. But the other twelve were detained and refused entry. Some were 'stateless', having fled from other hostile countries to Czechoslovakia with no identity papers during the First World War.

And on that day, none of them had the correct visa or sponsor. The British Committee for Refugees from Czechoslovakia also refused to guarantee them when they arrived.

So, the twelve passengers were returned to the plane they had arrived on with the intention of flying them back to Europe. Convinced they were returning to their deaths, they began to scream and protest and throw themselves to the floor. When manhandled back on the plane, they continued to protest and the pilot refused to fly them. The cover of this book depicts two of the passengers during this incident. They were then handcuffed and taken to Croydon Police Station, with the intention of deporting them by boat to Copenhagen and then back to Eastern Europe.

Another of the passengers was Oskar Goldberg, a stateless Jew from Galicia. He was inspired to stage his protest by the presence of press photographers at Croydon, there to cover the other arrivals throughout the day, and his picture appears in the plates in this book. His dramatic behaviour did indeed draw considerable attention and photographs were printed in the following day's newspapers. The newspaper publicity (some sceptical, some more sympathetic) led the British Committee for Refugees from Czechoslovakia to change their minds and guarantee these twelve refugees after all, so they were allowed to stay. (Oskar's brothers also managed to escape, but his parents and sisters and their families were all killed in the Holocaust.)

*   *   *

How did Britain compare with other countries in the assistance offered to Jewish refugees? The issue of who came to Britain is especially important because it was the most accessible country for Jews who would actually be able to survive the war. But, of course, no one knew that at the time. Only hindsight tells us that the unimaginable actually happened.

When Hitler came to power in 1933, there were 523,000 Jews in Germany – approximately 0.75 per cent of the population. By the time the Nazis forbade any further emigration to neutral countries in October 1941, there were 163,000 Jews left – most of them elderly and unable to face the upheaval of leaving. Where the others had gone in the eight previous years of Nazi rule took on grave importance. With characteristic playground spite, in 1938, the Nazi Foreign Minister von Ribbentrop remarked to Hitler that he had told one eminent French politician that 'we all wanted to get rid of our Jews but that the difficulties lay in the fact that no country wished to receive them'. This was not true. By September 1939, when the war began, 282,000 Jews had left Germany, plus another 117,000 from Austria. (These figures, and those immediately below, come from the United States Holocaust Memorial Museum and do not tally with other given figures.*)

---

* It is difficult to settle on exact figures for numbers of refugees. The number of *Kindertransport* refugees arriving in Britain varies from 10,000 (United States Holocaust Memorial Museum) to 7,700 (*Jewish Chronicle*, among other sources), for example.

Of that number, 95,000 had managed to reach the United States* and 75,000 had settled in Central and South America. A further 60,000 went to Palestine and 18,000 managed to get to Shanghai in Japanese-occupied China. During the war, Japan's German allies tried to persuade them to allow the deportation of these Jews, but this request was never granted.

Shanghai was both a last resort and the easiest option for a refugee. To go there you did not need a visa. But the Chinese city was controlled by Japanese troops in their ongoing war with their huge but militarily weak neighbour. Despite its globally renowned cruelty, the militaristic regime that controlled Japan in the 1930s and '40s had a benign view of Jewish people. This was partly connected, writes Steve Hochstadt in the book *Refugees from Nazi Germany*, to the fact that the Jewish banker Jacob Schiff had helped bankroll Japan's triumphant 1904–05 war with Russia. Many in the Japanese government also believed the classic antisemitic canard that 'international Jewry' were able to influence world affairs and that it would be unwise for the Japanese Empire to antagonise 'the Jews'. At the time, Japan also hoped it could maintain a peaceful relationship with the United States – not least because its ambitions for empire centred on the colonial possessions of the dwindling European powers of the Netherlands, France and Britain. This was why there were no barriers to immigration to Shanghai. This was also why Japan resisted all demands within the territory under their control for a hostile attitude towards Jews from Axis ally Nazi Germany. Bizarrely, having allowed Jews to leave for Shanghai in the 1930s, in the 1940s, with the war raging around them, the Nazis started to

---

* Antisemitism was rife in the United States, too. In 1943, a poll suggested that 25 per cent of US citizens agreed that Jews 'were a menace to America'.

pressurise their allies to send the Jews back to them so they could exterminate them. Such requests were ignored.

Others, in smaller numbers, reached safety in Spain, Switzerland and Portugal. Britain, in comparison, took between 70,000 and 80,000 refugees – although some of these came on transmigration visas and did indeed migrate to other countries rather than settle.

At the time, of course, many of these refugees did not understand how lucky they had been. Only hindsight tells us how fortunate they were to have escaped. And this was sometimes something that those helping refugees did not appreciate either. In his book *Generation Exodus*, Walter Laqueur relates how Britain's chief rabbi during the war, Dr Joseph Hertz, complained that *Kindertransport* children had not been given kosher food and had desecrated the Jewish Sabbath by travelling between sunset on Friday evening and after dark on Saturday evening.

As the threat of war with Germany grew more intense, Britain's new arrivals faced increasing public hostility. Blind to the logic that these persecuted refugees had escaped with their life, the *Daily Mail* informed its readership in April 1939 that 'we are nicely honeycombed with little cells of potential betrayal' and that 'even the paltriest kitchen maid ... is a menace to the safety of the country'. When war did break out and fear of invasion hit its heights, Britain's refugees would face even greater indignities.

Chapter 6

The Enemy Within:
The War Begins

The Second World War began on 1 September 1939, following a series of false-flag operations by German special forces along the Polish border. The most notorious of these was a bogus attack on a German radio station close to the border at Gleiwitz, where SS troops murdered several prisoners from the Dachau concentration camp along with a local farmer said to be a Polish sympathiser. These doomed souls were dressed in Polish Army uniforms and left as 'evidence' of a Polish attack.* American journalists were called to witness the scene and the German people were provided with a *casus belli*.† The attack, and other stories, many about supposed violence towards ethnic Germans in Poland, were enough for the Nazis to convince their people that they had to attack the Poles. Soldiers and tanks crossed the border in the middle of the night and a German battleship bombarded the city of Danzig (present-day Gdańsk) at 4.45 a.m.

---

* Oskar Schindler, made famous by the book *Schindler's Ark* and film *Schindler's List*, is alleged to have provided the operation with Polish uniforms. The story seems plausible, given his reputation as a black marketeer and all-round ducker and diver.
† Hitler reportedly told his generals: 'I will provide a *casus belli*. Its credibility doesn't matter. The victor will not be asked whether he told the truth.'

After a fierce campaign, Poland fell in little more than a month. Nazi forces behaved with predictable brutality. Civilians were executed in mass killings and German aircraft strafed women and children fleeing from the front lines.

But there was worse to come. On 17 September, the eastern border of Poland was invaded by the Soviet Union – all pre-arranged with the Nazis in the August 1939 German–Soviet Pact. But despite it all, the Polish government, much of the country's gold reserves and thousands of soldiers still managed to make their way to the West.

Britain and France had made the invasion of Poland their red line to Hitler, and they honoured their promise by declaring war on 3 September, although they did not send their own forces to help defend the country. In Britain, war began with Chamberlain's famous broadcast from Downing Street at 11.15 a.m. on Sunday 3 September.

This morning the British ambassador in Berlin handed the German government a final note stating that unless we heard from them by 11 o'clock that they were prepared at once to withdraw their troops from Poland, a state of war would exist between us. I have to tell you now that no such undertaking has been received, and that consequently this country is at war with Germany.

Lacking the melancholy sound bite of Sir Edward Grey's 'The lamps are going out all over Europe...', often quoted by historians to mark the beginning of the Great War in August 1914, Chamberlain declared rather clumsily: 'For it is evil things that we shall be fighting against – brute force, bad faith, injustice, oppression and persecution – and against them I am certain that the right will prevail.'

Was Chamberlain's certainty shared by the population as a whole?

For sure, the prospect of war had been long dreaded by the British people,* not least the likelihood of aerial bombardment.† Guernica had offered a graphic example of the dreadful destruction and slaughter that would ensue when a town or city was bombed. Prime Minister Stanley Baldwin had used the phrase 'the bomber will always get through' in a speech to Parliament in 1932 contemplating the future of warfare, and his words had brought many a sleepless night to the citizens of Britain. 'I think it is well also for the man in the street to realise that there is no power on earth that can protect him from being bombed,' he said with a frankness that would shame a modern politician.‡ What was particularly harrowing for people was the thought that civilians hundreds of miles away from 'the front line' could be victims and that a country at war faced the prospect of losing the wealth, history and culture of its cities.

To protect British skies, the Royal Air Force had the magnificent new technology of radar – a device which sent out and then intercepted returning radio waves which enabled operators to spot an incoming attack much further away than the previous method of detection using just eyesight and hearing. They also had the Spitfire, regarded as one of the most elegant and effective fighter planes of the war. But the principal fighter in 1939 was the Hurricane, its slower and considerably less glamorous sibling.

---

* In island Britain, new technology features highly in projected fears of invasion. A brilliant piece on the British Library website by Mike Ashley details a fear of fleets of massive hot air balloons carrying 3,000 soldiers and horses apiece during the Napoleonic Wars. The prospect of vast troop-carrying German airships haunted the Edwardians in the years before the First World War. Another alarmist and highly unlikely prediction featured a tunnel being dug beneath the English Channel.

† Britain had been bombed by Zeppelins in the First World War, but these aerial behemoths carried only a small payload and damage was minimal.

‡ Baldwin was only partly right on the bombers. The German Luftwaffe and British and American airpower did indeed wreak terrible destruction on civilian targets, but bombing alone was never going to win a war. In fact, it stiffened enemy resistance rather than caused it to collapse. Although the bomber did indeed almost 'always get through', the bombs regularly missed their target and casualty rates among bomber crews were often extremely high.

Other aircraft were even less promising. When I was young, I enjoyed perusing my father's childhood books on Britain's military capabilities from the 1930s and early '40s. Harborough Publishing's *Aircraft of the Fighting Powers*, with glossy adverts for model aeroplanes and Parnall power-operated gun turrets ('More power to your elbow!'), offered little to inspire confidence. Readers looking at the beautifully executed line drawings, designed to help model builders produce an accurate scaled-down facsimile of the aircraft of their choice, could not fail to notice the difference between the RAF's feeble-looking Bristol Blenheim and Handley Page Hampden bombers and the Germans' sinister, angular Heinkels and Dorniers, the aircraft that had already brought destruction to cities in the Spanish Civil War. In September 1939, the Lancaster, one of the greatest bombers of the war, was still a design concept and sixteen months away from its first test flight. It would not come into service until February 1942.

Aside from the fear of aerial bombardment, there was also a very real prospect of a boots-on-the-ground invasion. What would happen when German troops arrived via landing craft and parachute? Most realistic assessments assumed that a successful landing would lead to the fall of London in a matter of days. In September 1939, the British Army, never the most prestigious fighting force, numbered some 900,000 men, both full-time soldiers and members of the part-time Territorial Army. The army was modernising and expanding as war broke out, but no one could seriously claim that it was a match for Germany's *Wehrmacht*.

But away from the army and air force, there were indeed grounds for optimism. Readers of publications such as *Jane's Fighting Ships* and Ward, Lock and Co.'s *Wonder Book of the Navy* had much to reassure them. Britain, still in command of 'an empire upon which the sun never sets', had a navy to match. Mighty battleships such as the extraordinary HMS *Rodney* could still conceivably be said to rule the waves.

HM Stationery Office, publisher of a fascinating cutaway diagram of the battleship, informed awed readers that *Rodney* had nine sixteen-inch guns,* 'each with a range of 35,090 yards' (twenty miles) which was approximately the distance between Trafalgar Square and Windsor Castle. A full salvo, said the Stationery Office, 'cost £700', which was then only slightly less than the average price of a London house.

For refugees, once the war began, the wisdom of fleeing to the variety of countries open to them became apparent.† For those newly arrived in territories east or west of Germany, the chances of survival were slim, although those in Western countries especially, such as France and the Netherlands, did at least have a more sympathetic local population, many of whom were prepared to risk their lives to harbour them. Those who had managed to reach America or other overseas territories away from Europe were safe. But now Jews who had fled Hitler's Reich for Britain faced the prospect of a Nazi occupation.

Adding to this appalling possibility for refugees who had already endured years of persecution and deprivation was the British government's decision to treat them as enemies. As soon as war broke out, all German and Austrian refugees in Britain were labelled 'enemy aliens'. And by 1940, as the Nazis swept through Europe,

---

* For anyone not steeped in the jargon of military technology, the sixteen inches here refers to the width of the shell a gun fired. A shell like this would be the height of a man.

† The outbreak of war did not entirely cut off the arrival of refugees. On 10 May 1940, a shipload of 200 German Jewish refugees, including eighty children, left the Dutch port of IJmuiden for England at 7 p.m. German soldiers arrived in the town two hours later.

they were even suspected to be part of a much-feared 'fifth column' – an enemy within, likely to help the Germans when they arrived.

This alarming designation was to be calibrated into three categories labelled A, B and C, which also included perceived home-grown threats from British nationals on either end of the political spectrum. Some 120 tribunals were set up all over the country, tasked with the job of interviewing and classifying potential enemies of the people.

Category A were people considered a threat to national security – either refugees or Britain's very own political extremists. They were to be interned immediately. Up to 300 people were arrested within days of the war breaking out, followed by a further 600 who were known to be Nazi sympathisers. But it was not just fascists who became Category A prisoners. German and Austrian communists and British trade unionists who were thought to be opponents of the British war effort were also arrested.

Like God, the tribunals moved in mysterious ways. Oswald Mosley, astonishingly, was not arrested until May 1940 and was then allowed to live in a house within the grounds of Holloway Prison with his wife Diana.* The Duke of Windsor (previously Edward VIII)† was allowed to join the general staff in France as a major-general. Scandal followed in his wake as the German ambassador to The Hague claimed that the duke had sent him plans for the defence of Belgium. (This treasonable offence was rapidly denied.) The duke remained a thorn in the side of the British government and following a series of embarrassments, he and his wife

---

* They were close enough to the Nazis to have married at Joseph Goebbels's Berlin home in a ceremony that was attended by Hitler.

† The Nazis had big plans for Edward, who had been chummy with Hitler before the war. If the Germans occupied Britain, Edward was to be reinstated as monarch in return for his support. Historical records are hazy about whether or not he would have been prepared to do this, and luckily for him, and us, the opportunity never arose.

were sent to the Bahamas for the rest of the war, where he served as governor of Britain's many colonial possessions in the region.

After this initial round-up of fewer than a thousand people, most recently arrived 'enemy aliens' remained free to go about their lives, although they were forbidden to live in particular areas such as the coast.

Category B contained suspects of considerably less concern than Category A. Among this group were 6,700 recently arrived refugees. The overwhelming majority of 'enemy aliens', some 66,000, were designated Category C – those considered to be genuine victims of Nazi persecution. As previously mentioned, the tribunals, consisting of magistrates and other local worthies, were notoriously unpredictable. Just as they had been over-lenient with members of the British 'upper crust' like Mosley and his wife, they were also inclined to be overcautious with their 'aliens' and some obviously Category C refugees were placed in Category B.

So, what was to be done with these Category B and Category C 'enemy aliens'? At the start of the war, the British Cabinet, not least the Home Secretary Sir John Anderson, were determined not to repeat the internment policy of their predecessors in the First World War. Here, from barely two and a half decades previously, was a clear indication of how not to proceed. But Peter and Leni Gillman, in their 1980 book *Collar the Lot!* which outlines the failures of the Great War internments, make a strong case that lessons were not learned in 1940.

When the war began on 4 August 1914 and was welcomed by cheering crowds in city squares all over Europe, the British Home Office and the War Office both decided that interning their 'enemy aliens' was the prudent thing to do. In the face of a tsunami of racist rhetoric in the British press, enhanced considerably by the German invasion of Belgium, which occasioned grotesque exaggerations of the sometimes brutal behaviour of German soldiers against Belgian civilians,* the pressure to 'do something' about the German students currently studying in the UK, and sundry other German nationals living in Britain, was intense.

Here, for example, is a piece by editor J. L. Garvin in *The Observer*[†] from 21 September 1914:

> The cup of German culture is not yet full. With cruelty, lust, and ruin poured into it in full measure, with every refinement of savagery borrowed from the shame of humanity's past, the cry of 'the blonde beast' is still for more rapine and horror, for continued destruction for destruction's sake.

One particular disaster upped the hysteria considerably. On 22 September 1914, British cruisers *Aboukir*, *Hogue* and *Cressy* were caught out in the North Sea by a German U-boat, which made swift work of all three of them. In truth, they were carelessly deployed and had made themselves vulnerable to such an attack. But the British press, egged on by Admiral Lord Charles Beresford, keen to divert criticism away from the ineptitude of the Senior Service, had a ready-made excuse. Beresford wrote to newspapers that 'numbers of men have been caught red-handed signalling'. For good measure, he added that these were clearly 'assassins in the shape of spies. All enemy aliens should be locked up.'

---

* During the invasion, German soldiers had sometimes executed Belgian civilians in towns and villages where they were fired upon. But they did not make a habit of bayoneting babies and raping nuns, which was widely reported in the British press.

† Throughout its existence, *The Observer* has had a varying history of political allegiances and was not the centre-left newspaper it is today.

Admirably, the Department of Public Prosecutions wrote to the admiral enquiring: 'Would you kindly tell us what are the particular cases to which you refer?' Further useful information was not forthcoming.

But advocates of British 'fair play' were fighting against a rising tide of tragic events, which served only to wind up the hysteria the press were carelessly generating. After the Belgian atrocity stories came the indisputably real casualty figures for British and French troops fighting to stop the German Army reaching Paris, an early indication that this was a war like no other, and loss of life was going to be on a monumental scale.*

The pressure to round up Germans 'at large' in Britain was now too great to resist. By early November 1914, 1,500 miscellaneous German citizens – from students to butchers and bakers – had been incarcerated in the drafty cavern of Olympia Exhibition Hall in London.† They slept on straw palisades and were fed from great dixie cans with stew and soup. The Gillmans relate that the lavatory facilities were sufficient, unlike many internment camps, but that the doors had been removed from the water closets to discourage escape via windows.

By the end of November, the total number of detained German nationals in Britain had reached 10,000. They were housed in locations around the country, from skating rinks to jute mills and even passenger ships moored on the Thames Estuary. A camp was set up on the Isle of Man, but this was a disaster as too few huts were

---

* The Great War was fought at a time when the tactics and weapons for defence – barbed wire, machine guns, trenches – were infinitely superior to those for attack: essentially an infantry man with a rifle and a bayonet. The result was unprecedented slaughter. ·
† The hall, in west Kensington, has been the venue to everything from rock concerts by Jimi Hendrix, Pink Floyd and the Rolling Stones to TV roadshows like the *BBC Good Food Show* and the *Dr Who* Experience. It is still used as a concert and exhibition venue.

provided for the incoming flood of internees. A riot ensued and soldiers opened fire, killing five.

As the country settled into what was clearly a war that would not be over by Christmas, the government decided to release 2,700 of the more innocuous German internees. Rather quaintly, they were asked to sign a pledge which ran: 'I hereby promise and undertake that I will neither directly nor indirectly take any action in any way prejudicial to the safety of the British Empire, or to the safety of her Allies, during the present war.'

But the following year, a further outrage swept across the country when a German submarine sank the passenger ship *Lusitania* off the south coast of Ireland on 7 May 1915, with 1,201 passengers dying.

Shops with owners of German heritage were ransacked. It was said that dachshunds were stoned in the street, presumably by the great-grandparents of the people who attacked Sikhs after 9/11. Within a week, the British Prime Minister H. H. Asquith had announced an intention to intern all 'enemy aliens' of fighting age. Subsequently, an extraordinary collection of nationalities connected to or allied with Germany – Turks, Boers, Bulgars and even Duala tribesmen from German Cameroon* – had been herded into a camp at Knockaloe on the Isle of Man. In all 20,000 were imprisoned there in appalling conditions. Aside from imposing much upset and discomfort upon thousands of people, Peter and Leni Gill-man write that 'the need to house and guard a large number of innocuous civilians had diverted precious resources'. It is difficult to disagree with this assessment, but the events that followed in 1940

---

* Captured as prisoners of war.

clearly show that the British government was not prepared to learn from the First World War's disastrous internment policies.

*   *   *

During the Second World War, the fortunes of refugees could be entirely random. Some met the fate of Anne Frank – whose German Jewish family fled from Frankfurt to Amsterdam in 1934. Anne's family's story is too well known to bear repeating, but it is still a wrench to know that, having endured so much, she died in Bergen-Belsen only a month or two before the British and Canadians arrived to liberate the camp.

And while the German and Austrian Jews who made it to Britain certainly had no expectations of losing their life, some still faced the most extraordinary hostility from British people.[*]

This was not necessarily antisemitism; it resulted from a plain hatred of Germany. Extraordinarily, many British people did not make a distinction between Germans and German Jews – perhaps because many British newspapers did not make a point of featuring stories about Nazi persecution of the Jews. Perhaps they felt their readers would not be sympathetic or indeed even be interested.[†] To give just one example of this, Walter Laqueur in his book *Generation Exodus* relates the story of refugee Naftali Wertheim, a secondary school pupil in Bethnal Green whose Welsh geography teacher hauled him out in front of the class to tell him: 'Come out here, you Prussian swine. You think this is Nazi Germany, with a lot

---

[*]   Mosley and the BUF sometimes referred to Jewish refugees as 'refujews', a tellingly childish insult that neatly encapsulated the playground spite of their racism.

[†]   I am reminded of an article in *The Sun* during the Thatcher era instructing its readers 'how to spot a commie' in the workplace. Among several other indicators of a dangerously subversive political leaning was an interest in foreign affairs, such as the then hot topic of Nicaragua. Presumably, they thought ordinary working people should be interested in only sex and football.

of Jerries doing what they bloody well like? Well, let me tell you this is a democracy and you do as you're bloody well told.'

And even the governor of the Isle of Man felt able to declare: 'The only good Hun is a dead Hun.' When refugees were sent to the island (see Chapter 7), they were met by jeering locals who shouted 'bloody Nazis' at them.

A world away from the suffering of the Frank family, and those hapless Jews who were despatched with such ruthlessness in Treblinka and other death camps, we have the refugees who made their escape via the *Kindertransports*. Some of them found themselves living out the war years in the idyllic surroundings of Yealand Manor School, on the fringes of the Lake District. Set up by Manchester Quakers in 1939 as a refuge for children evacuated from the northern cities, the ivy-clad manor also became home to several Jewish refugee children between 1939 and 1944, the year it closed. The school was run on the most benevolent of principles, with great emphasis on those human activities that nourish the soul – music, drama, art and nature studies.

There were fifteen refugees at Yealand in all, from six different European countries. Three arrived with their mothers, who had managed to escape to England soon after their children and who were incorporated into the volunteer staff. Accounts from the school offer insight into the torments that these children had endured before their arrival and the difficulties that they carried with them throughout their childhood. As kind as their treatment often was, it would be a mistake to believe that everything worked out fine once they had arrived in England. Headmistress Elfrida Vipont Foulds* reports:

---

* Foulds was an extraordinary multifaceted character who was also a children's author. Her novel *The Lark on the Wing* won the prestigious Carnegie Medal for Writing in 1950. She also wrote *The Elephant and the Bad Baby* with the magnificent Raymond Briggs.

The dark haired little Czech girl who was quite clearly going to be brilliant (she won a scholarship to secondary school when she was only nine) had very loving kindly foster parents who cared for her very tenderly. But in class she needed much reassurance, feeling conscious of the language difficulty, and of the many subtle little ways in which she was different from these English children – she, for example, didn't know their weights and measures, and used a different style of writing. And out on walks she always wanted to hold the grownup's hand.

Foulds's daughter Robin Greaves – at the time of writing, a lively ninety-six – remembers this child as Renata Polger, who left both parents behind to come over on a *Kindertransport*. Robin, slightly older than most of the children at Yealand, worked as a volunteer at the school while on holiday from her own boarding school and has vivid memories of the place. Robin recalls Renata forgetting how to speak Czech and having to relearn the language by visiting the local RAF squadron of Czech pilots, who were happy to help her with her native tongue. Through extraordinary good luck, both Renata's Jewish parents survived the Nazi occupation and were reunited with her after the war. Foulds's assessment of the child as someone 'who was quite clearly going to be brilliant' was spot on. Renata became professor of paediatrics and medical genetics at the University of Wisconsin.

Not all the refugees had such a successful adult life. Foulds also writes about another girl, Marianne Lask, who came to Yealand after some time in an internment camp with her mother on the Isle of Man. Prior to this, they had walked across France in their deter-mination to escape from the Nazis. Foulds described the damage that the refugee experience had done to the child's character:

[Initially] she was subject to dramatic outbursts of fury which at first did not fail to attract the attention of which the poor child subconsciously felt that she had been deprived. She was a brilliant, handsome, delicate little girl, with an outstanding dramatic talent which found full vent in her temperamental tantrums, as she raged and screamed and spat.

In the book *The Story of Yealand Manor School*, written by Foulds's niece Susan Vipont Hartshorne, we're told Marianne never really recovered from her traumatic early life. She settled well into the school, but after the war 'she had difficulties ... in adjusting to life away from Yealand, [and] suffered severe bouts of depression and tragically died young'. Robin Greaves remembers hearing that Marianne had 'starved herself to death', possibly suffering from anorexia. Some children, notes Hartshorne, 'had unfortunately been so damaged by their difficult experiences that they had to move [from Yealand] to more specialist education elsewhere'.

Also of note in Hartshorne's account is the way Nazi propaganda ate into the children's thinking. Just as some Jewish children (as we have seen in Chapter 5) could not escape a sense of shame about being Jewish, so some refugees, influenced by Nazi propaganda, even carried a dislike of each other based on their nationalities. In a letter to a friend, one Yealand refugee wrote:

There was Lorelinde from Germany who hated me because I was Czech ... She was hostile to me because, as she maintained, the Czechs were enemies of the Germans, so there was no way that she could treat me as a friend, even as a fellow refugee in a similar situation to her own. She forgot that we were both Jewish ... Akim (from Poland) too hated the Czechs. If the Czechs hadn't surrendered to Hitler and given up their land, then Hitler would never have invaded Poland.

Robin Greaves also remembers this sense of grievance quite clearly. 'There was quite a lot of argument between the children who came from Vienna … the children who came from Czechoslovakia,' she told me. 'They all said if it wasn't for YOU we wouldn't have to be refugees. It's your fault … What they didn't realise was that they were all Jewish.'

Some of the children resented the British too – feeling that they could have done more to prevent the Nazi occupation of their respective countries. Nazi propaganda minister Dr Goebbels would be rubbing his hands with glee had he been party to these exchanges.

*   *   *

A year into the war, fear of invasion was palpable. And as this fear grew, Walter Laqueur writes of the likes of Viscount Elibank in the House of Lords pointing out in relation to the many refugees now working as domestic servants that thousands of female spies were out and about in England, and did the government not have a national duty to get rid of these Mata Haris as quickly as possible?

It was entirely plausible that the Germans who had been resident in Britain at the start of the First World War were likely to be sympathetic to the war aims of their country. But in 1939–40, to regard the refugees who had fled years of persecution in a similar vein was at best lazy and at worst simply bizarre. John Anderson had resisted the calls to intern these refugees, but pressure was building to an insufferable degree.

The opening months of the war had got off to a slow start. After the invasion of Poland by Germany and Russia, and a few shocking incidents such as the sinking of the British battleship *Royal Oak* by a German submarine in October 1939, not a great deal happened and this period of the conflict was known as the 'Phoney War'.

But this changed with the German spring offensive in Western Europe. In April and May, the German Army swept through Denmark and Norway, and then the Netherlands, Belgium and Luxemburg. France, which had fought the Germans with extraordinary tenacity for over four years in the Great War, fell in just six weeks in May and June.

Now, as Nazi troops swept through Western Europe, the prospect of an invasion of Britain became all too real. And newspapers turned the anxiety of their readers against refugees and other foreigners in their midst. While the use of 'fifth column' participants in Nazi offensives was a widely held fear, evidence of this happening in the spring conquests is thin on the ground. But this did not stop the British government and the right-wing press from assuming that the thousands of Jews who had fled with their lives from Nazi territory to Britain would automatically join up with the Germans if they did invade.

Stories began to appear stoking this fear.

On 17 April 1940, the *Daily Mail* printed an article entitled 'I Would Lock Up Doubtful Aliens'.

Written by Ferdinand Tuohy, it is intended 'for the particular attention of his brother-in-law, who is chairman of one of the new regional committees dealing with aliens'.*

---

* I can imagine subsequent family gatherings were rather awkward following this exchange by newspaper article.

'How do they do these things in France?' thunders Tuohy.

Well, all male enemy aliens in France aged 17 to 50 have been interned without any tribunal stuff … We could do with a spot more
of French suspicion instead of carelessly vouching for Germans and
Austrians because they are 'such nice, inoffensive people', and in
some cases are useful … Seemingly, all a Nazi agent has to do is to
be attractive and well behaved, build up a façade of respectability and
curse Hitler, in order to bring out a perverse strain in many English
by which they think it smart to stick up for the enemy and shield
him.

  Intellectual snobs are good at it, though how Oxford, with 800
enemy aliens in the district, imagines it would fare under Nazi success I can't think.

Having vented his spleen against the valuable Jewish scientists and
intellectuals absorbed into the British universities, Tuohy now turns
his attention to 'servant girls':

[The Home Secretary] declined to interfere with respect to the
presence of hundreds of German and Austrian women in domestic
service round Aldershot, a large number in the homes of serving
officers. I'd shift the lot. This is a potentially terrible show we are in,
and if one of those girls is not noting the growth, training, equipment, movement, morale, chat of the army, I'll chew my beret!

I searched in vain for any acknowledgement that these people had
fled with their lives from a regime that was ruthlessly persecuting
them.

On the same page is an editorial entitled 'The Enemy Within'. The author declaims: 'We have a miscellaneous assortment of doubtful enemy aliens, Communists, peace cranks, and Fascists whose activities are a menace. Some of this collection may be spies. Others are openly doing their utmost to sabotage our war effort.'

And German and Austrian Jews weren't the only target of Britain's newspapers. As Italy's fascist dictator Benito Mussolini prevaricated about committing himself to Hitler's war, the *Daily Mirror* printed this extraordinary piece by John Boswell about Mussolini and the Italian residents of Britain on 27 April 1940. Excerpts from the article are reproduced below, formatted as it appears in the paper:

In his own time and in his own way [Mussolini] lines up against us.

The tommy-gun is greased. The sawn-off shotgun is loaded.

There is a stinking wind from the Mediterranean which bodes no good.

Yet we still tolerate Mussolini's henchmen in this country!

There are more than twenty thousand Italians in Great Britain.

London alone shelters more than eleven thousand of them.

The London Italian is an indigestible unit of population.

His first object is to start a business; frequently a café.

He often avoids employing British labour.

It is much cheaper to bring a few relations into England from the old home town.

And so the boats unload all kinds of brown-eyed Francescas and Marias, beetle-browed Ginos, Titos and Marios...

So now, every Italian colony in Great Britain and America is a seething cauldron of smoking Italian politics.

Black Fascism. Hot as Hell.

Even the peaceful, law-abiding proprietor of the back-street cof-fee-shop bounces into a fine patriotic frenzy at the sound of Mus-solini's name.

We are nicely honeycombed* with little cells of potential betrayal.

We ought to smoke out our fascist wasp-nests.

At least we ought to watch them.

Mussolini would never for a moment tolerate twenty thousand such nests of divided loyalty, or worse.

But we always were the mugs of the world... AND WE ARE ALWAYS SORRY AFTERWARDS.

As has been so often the case in the stories related in this book, events and their interpretation by Britain's newspapers would now drive the government's actions towards refugees.

---

* The *Mail* used exactly the same term in an article about German and Austrian refugees in April 1939. Perhaps Boswell borrowed it?

Chapter 7

Satellites of the Monster: Internment

'Regrettable and deplorable things have happened.'

JOHN ANDERSON, HOME SECRETARY,
HOUSE OF COMMONS, 22 AUGUST 1940

Now, every child with a glimmer of interest in history knows that the Germans did not invade Britain in 1940. The great tide of Nazi victories in Western Europe stopped at Calais and the fjords of Norway. Although Hitler's armies would go on to succeed in the East,* their victories in the West had come to an end.

Hitler, like Napoleon 140 years before him, was prevented from deploying the greatest army in Europe on British soil by the likelihood of his landing craft being blown to pieces by British warships and aeroplanes. The Battle of Britain was fought to allow the Luftwaffe control of the skies, which in turn would allow them to attack British warships with greater ease. The failure of this campaign showed that the British Navy and the Royal Air Force presented

---

* General Charles de Gaulle, when observing the ruins of Stalingrad after the war, famously offended his Soviet hosts by declaring his admiration for the German Army for coming so far into Russia.

too great a threat to any invasion fleet – exactly as the Battle of Tr-afalgar ensured that Napoleon's troops would never be able to cross the Channel in the teeth of Britain's formidable men-o'-war. But in 1940, no one knew that the invasion would fail, and it is difficult for us to imagine the level of fear and apprehension among the population of the British Isles in that far-off summer. And an awful anxiety, too, must have gnawed at the guts of every refugee who had reached this safe haven, knowing that the only thing that separated them from the Gestapo and further murderous persecution was a twenty-mile stretch of water across the Channel. They, more than anyone, knew first-hand how cruel the Nazis could be.

As Rotterdam fell to German troops in May 1940, the *Daily Express* declared: 'He is only 180 miles away – remember carry your gas mask with you always.'

And following the surrender of France, the *Daily Mirror* advised its readers on 14 June 1940:

DON'T RUN FROM HOME IN INVASION

Stay where you are in the event of an invasion. That was the advice given in the House of Commons yesterday. [Civilians] should not attempt to evacuate on the roads and embarrass the operations of our forces.

As is their wont, the British tabloids also fed the fear of invasion with a procession of far-fetched stories, stoking the suspicion and resentment many of their readers already felt towards newly arrived refugees. The foreigners in our midst, they told them, were the enemy within and Hitler's spies. You would have thought that someone must have noticed that most of these arrivals spoke English with a very thick middle-European accent, if they spoke it at all – surely something that would have ruled them out as inconspicuous spies able to pass themselves off as locals.

Author and journalist Simon Parkin writes movingly about this climate of fear in his book *The Island of Extraordinary Captives*, published in 2022. He tells us that the British police and intelligence services were 'deluged with tip-offs about suspicious refugees and foreigners'. The real-life examples he gives would have been a gift to a 1970s TV writer seeking inspiration for a sitcom like *'Allo 'Allo!* or *Dad's Army*. One busybody reported their art historian neighbour because she kept hearing suspicious knocking, which she took to be coded messages. Further investigations revealed the source of the noise was a bed that creaked when the neighbour had sex with his fiancée.* Even more ludicrously, another refugee, who had taken up beekeeping, was questioned when investigators discovered a diary entry noting 'Exchange British Queen for Italian Queen'.

Some newspaper stories from the time seemed to be straining to create fear and resentment on the flimsiest pretext. On 16 April 1940, the *Daily Mirror* ran the headline 'Spy Watch on South Coast', reporting: 'Worthing Information Committee announced it was stated that women aliens had taken furnished flats on the front of Worthing. Some were on the telephone and used glasses for screening the sea.'

In a classic *Daily Mail* tactic, where obscure events are magnified beyond their actual importance, the *Mail*† reported on 20 April 1940 'Council Say Intern All Enemy Aliens', referring to a meeting in Lytham St Annes. 'There was not a shadow of doubt, said

---

* Actually, this one sounds more like an unholy wartime version of *On the Buses*. (Mercy!)

† This technique is still used by the *Mail* and *Express* today, often in relation to the BBC, where a handful of complaints on websites are magnified into a headline that reads 'Viewer Fury At…', which then starts a 'pile on'.

Alderman W. Hope, that members of the "Nazi Advance Guard" were among the 64,000 Aliens at liberty.'

The *Daily Express* ran this inconsequential story on 9 May 1940, highlighting the prejudices foreigners faced in Britain:

WAITRESS SEES ALIEN MAKING NOTES – TELLS

Pretty Miss Theresa Donald went to serve a man customer in a café in Hamble (Hants) – a protected area adjoining Southampton Water – and was asked in a foreign accent for a glass of milk and the loan of a pencil.

When she took him the pencil the man began to write busily in a book. Miss Donald became suspicious and told the police.

Yesterday, the man – Gerhard Esser, aged thirty-nine, an enemy alien who teaches German and Music – was fined £2 at Eastleigh (Hants) for entering Hamble without written permission from the chief registration officer.

And other stories that made the tabloids were sometimes even more bizarre. On 13 May 1940, the *Daily Express* strayed into Monty Python territory by telling their readers that the German occupation of Rotterdam began with an airborne assault by machine-gun-wielding German parachutists dressed in skirts and blouses. (Assuming they weren't wearing high heels, their army boots would have lent quite a modern touch to these fiction-al outfits.) More insidiously, the *Express* told its readers that the cross-dressing paratroops were greeted by men and women emerg-ing from 'basements and backdoors' dressed in German uniforms. These people had come to the Netherlands claiming to be refugees fleeing Nazi oppression and had worked as cleaners and servants while awaiting the invasion.

Again, part of the fear that stories like this generated came from earlier reports from the notion that there was a fifth column of traitors or spies who would support an enemy attack. It was not only the tabloid readership that were stirred by this largely fictional 'menace'. A high-ranking British civil servant, Sir Nevile Bland, who had witnessed the invasion of the Netherlands, was convinced that the fifth column had played a decisive role in the German success. Echoing the *Daily Mail*'s pre-war concern that every refugee kitchen maid was 'a menace to the safety of the country', he drafted a report for his fellow Whitehall colleagues maintaining that every German and Austrian refugee in Britain was 'a real and grave menace'. He was certain that when the invasion came, 'there will be satellites of the monster all over the country who will at once embark on widespread sabotage and attacks on civilians'.[*]

The widely circulated report even reached King George VI, who immediately summoned the Home Secretary, Sir John Anderson, and told him: 'You must take immediate action against political fifth columnists ... Men and women.' The report was also broadcast by the BBC and attitudes towards refugees turned distinctly hostile.

Parkin writes that this was particularly sad because a Mass Observation[†] poll had suggested in May 1940 that not a single person they interviewed had thought that refugees were likely to be spies or saboteurs. Before the end of the month, the *Daily Mail* was demanding the rounding up of all 'enemy' refugees. 'Act! Act! Act! Do

---

[*]   In case this sounds familiar, the *Sunday Express* of 20 March 2022 carried a story declaring that female Russian spies may pose as Ukrainians to launch Salisbury-style attacks.

[†]   The Mass Observation social research organisation was established in 1937 and aimed to record everyday behaviours and attitudes via volunteer observers. It existed until the mid-1960s and was revived again in 1981. It is now based at the University of Sussex.

It Now!' ran one story on 24 May. 'All refugees ... should be drafted without delay to a remote part of the country and kept under strict supervision.' The author, G. Ward Price, wagged his finger at his readers with the hysterical statement: 'You fail to realise that every German is an agent.'*

But there was also a 'damned if you do, damned if you don't' element to this sort of hostility. In fact, for some British people, there was a suspicion of treason in the Jews who had left the Nazi realm. You would have thought that even the most zealous 'my country right or wrong' patriot would understand the logic of rejecting a nation whose government had decided to wipe you off the face of the earth because of your biological inheritance. But this wasn't necessarily so. Peter and Leni Gillman quote one Lieutenant Colonel Slatter, stationed at the Huyton refugee camp in Liverpool, who declared: 'I can respect no man who has no loyalty to his country, especially the country of his birth.'

Pressure continued to mount on the government to intern 'aliens' with further stories in the *Mail* with headlines such as 'Fifth Column Foreign Influence: There is More to Be Done'.

So, with newspaper stories howling in their ears, this was the climate in which the government decided to intern many of its refugees. Initially, the target was all German and Austrian males between sixteen and sixty, living in the coastal regions of the UK. The round-up began in the early hours of Sunday 12 May 1940.

John Anderson was opposed to this mass internment but was outnumbered by his Cabinet colleagues. Parkin writes that Anderson

---

* Price was a well-established foreign correspondent for the *Daily Mail* and was close to the paper's proprietor Lord Rothermere. In the '30s, he had been both a supporter of Oswald Mosley and an admirer of Hitler. He wrote many articles hostile to refugees and in favour of those supporting internment of Jewish refugees. He seemed to suggest that the Jews were so lacking in moral fibre they would spy for Hitler if there was money to be made.

had written to his father earlier in the year about the danger posed to justice by national paranoia occasioned by hot-under-the-collar tabloid news stories. Peter and Leni Gillman also write about this in their book *Collar the Lot!* They note a government report which states:

> We found that the majority of people hardly realised what the phrase [internment] meant. We also found that the level of ordinary people's feelings was much less intense than that expressed in some papers. Detailed interviewing in several areas in London and Western Scotland produced less than one person in a hundred who spontaneously suggested that the refugees ought to be interned *en masse*.

Collar the Lot! goes on to reveal some of Anderson's personal feelings in letters to his father.

On 2 March he wrote: 'The newspapers are working up feeling about aliens. I shall have to do something about it or we may be stampeded into an unnecessarily oppressive policy. It is very easy in wartime to start a scare.' On 26 March: 'There has been a lot of fuss in the papers about aliens, but I have seen no sign of real trouble in Parliament as yet.'

The Gillmans note: 'Within a month the "trouble in Parliament" had started. Anderson met the organisers of the Tory meeting on 19 April ... *The Times* said that he satisfied MPs, but the *Mail* judged him "complacent".'

Winston Churchill tried to justify the internment policy by claiming that it was in the best interests of those who had been arrested. Citing the tabloid hysteria, he declared that 'public temper in this country would be such that such persons would be in great danger if left at liberty'.

Bizarrely, this almost exactly echoed the reasoning of Nazi *Reichs-führer* Heinrich Himmler in his justification for arresting public opponents of the Nazi regime. They were being taken into 'protective custody' for their own safety. Parkin notes that on hearing of the British internments, Hitler gloated: 'The enemies of Germany are now the enemies of Britain, too. Where are those much-vaunted democratic liberties of which the English boast?' Perhaps this incident fed into the Nazi fantasy that the fellow 'Aryan' Britain would one day become an ally to the Nazis.*

Churchill did acknowledge that this policy would affect 'a great many people who are the passionate enemies of Nazi Germany'. But he said that there was nothing that could be done. 'I am very sorry for them, but we cannot draw all the distinctions which we should like to do.'

Here is food for thought for anyone interested in the influence of a 'free press' on democracy and the behaviour of the British people. In this instance, the tabloid newspapers had stoked the paranoia and xenophobia of their readers and cast a malignant spell which was to have deeply unpleasant consequences for many of Britain's recently arrived refugees.

The *Daily Mirror* sometimes took a more emollient approach, describing the round-up measures as 'drastic steps' and even carried this story on 17 May 1940:

'REASONABLE' SAY INTERNED ALIENS

Despite the inevitable hardship that internment involves most of them frankly accept its necessity in present circumstances. 'We all

---

* The Nazis nursed such delusions throughout the war. Even as the Red Army closed in on Berlin, they still hoped the British and Americans would realise that their true enemies were the Soviet Union and switch sides.

hate Hitler and if the round-up prevents one spy out of a thousand refugees from doing harm, we shall consider it a reasonable precaution and not object' was a typical comment.

Perhaps this unlikely story was intended to deflect hostility away from refugees, which cannot be said for this story in the *Mail* published on 22 May 1940:

HOUSING ESTATE IS ALIENS CAMP

The neat homes of a newly built housing estate in the north west of England have been turned into an internment camp for 800 enemy alien boys and men. The estate is in pretty countryside on the outskirts of a large seaport and less than eight miles from an important aircraft factory.* If war had not come it would have provided homes for scores of working men and their families ... When I visited the camp yesterday I saw the aliens ... strolling about or sitting in the sun, reading newspapers and discussing arrangements ... All were well dressed. Some smiled and waved.

This is particularly reprehensible given the *Mail*'s leading role in calling for internment in the first place. There's something queasily reminiscent of the Nazi posters that preceded the T4 extermination of the 'useless eaters' before the war, where the German people were shown photographs of physically and mentally disabled children and instructed that the cost of looking after them would have provided homes for thousands of healthy German people. Obviously, the subject matter is not comparable, but the technique is the same.

---

* It wouldn't take an Einstein among members of German intelligence monitoring the British press to guess this is Liverpool.

Perhaps the piece was inspired by a letter to the *Mail* from A. H. Spicer, London EC, a couple of days earlier which said: 'Intern the lot, including the refugees who are being pressed to spy on us by means of threats to injure their relations in Germany. There are plenty of racecourses, sports grounds etc. which could be used.'

By 28 May, the 'mail bag' was bulging with further outrage. 'Many hundreds of readers continue to write to the *Daily Mail* demanding much more stringent treatment of Aliens,' said the paper:

Here are some of the points made in recent letters:

All foreigners should be made to wear on their clothes a disc of cloth in their national colours says Brigadier CR Terror, Eastbourne.

AT Hill, Edgware, asks whether the homes of enemy aliens are being searched for British or other uniforms that parachutists or 5th columnists might use.

JRW, Torquay, says that aliens should not be allowed to have a telephone on their premises.

On the same day, the paper reported on the internment of 'aliens' on the Isle of Man with the headline: 'Women Aliens "Invade" Resort. It's Theirs – For the Duration', adding: 'Many take their children too.'

So, did the Germans set up 'spy rings' as Britain became the latest target for their all-conquering army? The reality of the spy scare was almost comical. Once the Nazis had decided an invasion was necessary, Germany did attempt to send spies to gather intelligence and carry out sabotage when the attack began, in an operation code-named 'Lena'. Landing via boat or parachute, nearly all these agents were captured almost as soon as they arrived. The History Guild, in a piece entitled 'Deceptive Ineptitude: German Spies in WW2

Britain', reports that the incompetence of these agents was extraordinary. They betrayed themselves by ordering beer in pubs outside opening hours, by showing almost no understanding of British currency when ordering railway tickets, by carrying German weapons and other items and, in the case of agent Karl Theodor Drücke, by not even being able to speak English. Some historians think these efforts to land spies in Britain were deliberate attempts to undermine the planned Nazi invasion by members of the *Abwehr* – the German intelligence service – some of whom were opponents of the Nazis.

It is illuminating to compare perceptions in wartime Britain with perceptions today. Many British people in the early twenty-first century had a completely inflated view of the number of refugees in the world who had fled to Britain, thanks undoubtedly to the prominence of this topic in their newspapers of choice. According to a 2002 poll, when this hot topic was just as hot as it is today, many people estimated 25 per cent rather than the real figure of 2 per cent. Likewise, a poll conducted in wartime Britain showed that people thought there were anywhere between 2 and 4 million refugees from Germany in Britain. The actual number, according to Parkin, was 73,000.

*   *   *

So, from mid-May to early July 1940, 29,000 refugees were arrested, of whom 24,000 were German and Austrian. Most of the rest were Italians who had become 'enemy aliens' when Mussolini declared war on Britain in June 1940.[*]

---

[*] In the USA, according to fabled American historian Paul Fussell, Roosevelt decided not to intern Italian American 'aliens' as they were 'a bunch of Opera singers'.

The intention was to release the refugees once their loyalty was assured. This was not a vote of confidence in the original tribunals which had decided on the A, B and C categories.

While some of the Category A refugees were sent to prisons, they were also housed in holiday camps in Seaton, Clacton and Paignton. (The holiday camp phenomenon had bloomed in the interwar years and there were over 200 in the UK by the end of the 1930s.) Bizarrely, fascists and communists and other left-wing refugees were housed in the same places – which led to occasional violence. It was months before fascists were removed from these camps and housed in a separate camp at Swanwick in Derbyshire.

The process, of course, caused huge dismay among the refugees who had already endured nearly a decade of persecution in the hands of the Nazis. With so many 'enemy aliens' to round up, the quality of accommodation was bound to be problematic and not all these internees could be housed in prisons or camps. Empty hospitals, barracks and even disused cotton mills were requisitioned as temporary and no doubt drafty, uncomfortable accommodation.

No place was more forbidding than the abandoned Warth Mills in Lancashire, where internees from the north-west were initially housed. Parkin describes it with Dickensian relish:

The floor, a mixture of cobbles and wood, was viscid and slippery with old machine oil, the smell of which mixed with the acrid stench of the canal that ran alongside the building, and stuck in the throat. Transmission belts hung like nooses from rafters. Crankshafts, partly dismounted, dangled at Damoclean angles. Clumps of rotting, mouldy cotton decorated the floor. Spiders ruled the shadows ... Corinthian capitals, high up in the vaulted murk, supported a glass roof, the sole source of light inside the building, which was pocked with broken panes that let the drizzle in.

Arrivals were marched four miles from Bury Station, under the baleful glare of the local population, 'like a bloody prisoner of war', remarked one refugee, Pastor Peter Katz. 'I felt degraded.'

Worse was to come. The arrivals were greeted by an overwhelming stench of disinfectant and rows of British soldiers ready to examine their belongings. The contents of their bags were tipped on to tables and anything of value was looted right before their eyes – from money, chocolate and cigarettes to typewriters, watches and medicines. One man, a diabetic, had his insulin taken. Doctors had their stethoscopes stolen. Clearly, these soldiers saw the refugees before them as their enemies. And evidently, the tabloids were not just 'tomorrow's chip paper'. Here, in graphic detail, were the consequences of newspaper hate-mongering.

Parkin quotes Claus Moser, who later became chair of the Royal Opera House: 'I remember very clearly … the feeling of insult. The whole operation was panicky and cruel.'

More than 2,000 internees were packed into Warth Mills with a single bath and eighteen taps between them. There were no lavatories and the inhabitants had to make do with sixty buckets inside an oblong tent. Many of these men had had direct experience of Nazi concentration camps and could say with certainty that Warth Mills was no better. William Ravenscroft Hughes, a Quaker aid worker who had visited camps in Germany, relates what happened when he ran into one particular refugee at Warth Mills:

An interesting incident occurred when a man stopped me and said,

'I saw you at Sachsenburg Camp.' This was true ... Many of these interned men have been in German camps. Several had said to me that the physical conditions in Dachau were better than in Bury. Having seen both, I agreed.

Fortunately, the men rarely stayed at Warth Mills for more than a week, but the experience had a deep-seated effect on their impression of the country that had offered them refuge. Simon Parkin notes one internee observing that 'many [have] ceased to believe in the British spirit of humanity before which they had acclaimed'. Gotfried Huelsmann recalled that 'to be interned by the country of their salvation ... was hurtful'.

Parkin notes that in the modern world this story has received much less attention than the American decision to intern its Japanese American citizens,* perhaps because it 'upsets the prevailing historical narrative of Britain's role in the Second World War: a united, courageous nation, fighting a just war to defend the persecuted'.†

Despite the transparent injustice of this false imprisonment of vulnerable people, this particular cloud had one silver lining. When internment came, many refugees who had been unhappily trapped in the purgatory of domestic service were dismissed. 'This was a blessing on both sides,' writes Walter Laqueur. 'They could not prepare toast or kippers or haddock or Yorkshire pudding the right (English or Scottish) way, they had difficulty making a fire or preparing high tea or cooking venison or pork, which were not kosher.'

---

* In one of the more infamous chapters of American history in the Second World War, 120,000 Japanese American citizens were interned after Pearl Harbor. Britain, too, had Japanese citizens and a hundred of them, out of an estimated 500 resident in the country, were rounded up and sent to the Isle of Man in early 1942. But numbers like this were easy to deal with. These internees were repatriated by the summer.

† The Japanese Americans were interned for most if not all of the war. The 'aliens' here faced only temporary internment.

Following release from internment, many of them found work in factories or hospitals, which was far better than domestic service.

*   *   *

Clearly, these temporary places of detention would not do for the long term. So, the British government turned its attention to the Isle of Man – an island a third of the size of London (in square kilometres/miles) and equidistant from the English and Irish coast. The island was a popular holiday destination so already had plentiful hotels and boarding houses.

The refugees were divided by gender and men were placed in particular streets in the main towns of Ramsey and Douglas, which were then surrounded by barbed wire and guard posts. A further 4,000 women and children were sent to the towns of Port Erin and Port St Mary, where they lived alongside local people in similar barbed-wire enclosed areas. Locals were given passes to allow them to enter and exit these enclaves, suggesting that security was not a great concern to the authorities. The following year, a 'married camp' was established at Port St Mary, allowing couples and their children to live together. Historian and Labour MP Baroness Ruth Henig has spoken about her parents' experiences of internment on the Isle of Man. Initially, they were segregated and her mother 'found the separation very difficult'. But on the opening of the married camp, they were finally 'brought together again at a boarding house on the beachfront. It was a great relief to both of them.'

As internment went, the Isle of Man was certainly far more benign than the idea of enforced confinement would suggest. Internees were allowed to create their own entertainment with concerts and plays and a 'university' was created, with classes given on a wide variety of topics. Walter Brunner recalls: 'If we wouldn't have been parted from our family, it was almost like a holiday camp. I learnt tailoring to make ladies coats and costumes.' Another internee, Edith Whyatt, reflects: 'We had meals provided for us; we hardly noticed we were being interned. My mother was delighted with the situation – she loved the view from the window of the sheep in the green pastures.' She continues: 'On the whole, our experience felt very much as if we were guests not internees ... We had given up our home, I had to cut my studies short, but we were away from the Nazis and that was the main thing.'

This idyllic reflection shouldn't undermine the idea that internment was still a cause of great anxiety. Even if they were comfortable, many Jewish refugees felt that being concentrated together in camps would be a catastrophe in the event of a successful Nazi invasion of Britain. The Jews would then be all too easily rounded up. Other German and Austrian refugees recall being in a perpetual state of fear that they would be repatriated or included as part of a prisoner-of-war exchange and sent back to their deaths.

Simon Parkin's book contains, as a central theme, the story of an eighteen-year-old German boy called Peter Fleischmann who was interned in the Isle of Man. His case illustrates the level of distrust faced by refugees. Peter's anti-Nazi parents had been murdered by the Gestapo, he had arrived as a destitute *Kindertransport* child and he had been interviewed by a senior judge who had declared that he posed no security risk to his British hosts. That did not stop him from being arrested and sent to the Hutchinson internment camp on the Isle of Man. But here events took an unusual twist.

Peter was an artistic child and when he arrived in England, he had managed to find work with a couple in Manchester who ran a business colouring black and white portrait photographs of dead soldiers from the First World War. The Hutchinson camp contained the most exceptional concentration of artistic talent. And its residents had organised themselves, under the benign eye of the camp commander, Captain Hubert Daniel,* into an extraordinary college of further education. Peter benefited no end from the tutelage of some of Germany and Austria's most distinguished modern artists, and showing great ingenuity, was able to manufacture paint brushes from bushy eyebrow hair donated by fellow inmates and paint made from minerals such as brick dust mixed with sardine tin oil. After the war, Peter was able to go to Beckenham School of Art and became a successful artist under the name Peter Midgley.† He was forever grateful for the training he received at Hutchinson camp. 'Everything thereafter was just a recap,' he said.

Yet stories such as this can give a sugar-coating to the refugee experience. Like many of his fellow internees, Peter was also left deeply traumatised. For years afterwards, he would have recurring dreams where he was once again back in the camp. The National Archives, in an article entitled 'Policing migration: researching the lives of foreign nationals in a government archive', discusses Lajos Lederer, a Hungarian national who came to Britain in 1926 to study law and who was interned on the Isle of Man. While Lajos did have Jewish heritage, the National Archives states he was likely interned 'due to his Hungarian nationality – Hungary was a member of the Axis powers – and his profession as a journalist'. In March

---

* Daniel, with classic British eccentricity, used the camp radio network to broadcast the latest cricket scores to bemused inmates. Aware that Hutchinson camp held a high number of artists, musicians and academics, he ensured they had a grand piano at their disposal and art materials.

† He died in 1991. Do have a look at his work on Google images. It's really beautiful.

1942, Lajos wrote about his experiences of the camp and his mental health: 'The loss of liberty – for no earthly reason – is apt to create in you most poisonous visions. I even were wondering at times if my friends who knew me well will continue to stand by me.'

Parkin also tells us that many residents were so wracked with anxiety, occasioned both by their internment and by the prospect of a Nazi invasion, that the Hutchinson camp had a 'suicide consultancy' set up by a clinical pathologist and a retired funeral director. They offered 'lessons to any interested parties on the best and most painless way of killing oneself in the event of invasion. The pair offered demonstrations ... on how to make a reliable hanging noose from either a washing line or a pair of twisted trousers.' Some took their advice. At least fifty-six refugees died during internment, many by suicide.

From the present, it is difficult to imagine how a policy as ugly and blinkered as this seemed acceptable – as mentioned earlier, even Winston Churchill admitted as much when he approved its enactment. The indiscriminate imprisonment of vulnerable people who had already endured years of Nazi persecution was definitely not part of Britain's finest hour.

As Simon Parkin eloquently puts it:

Every government must balance its humanitarian obligations with the need to uphold national security. To categorise refugees from Nazi oppression as 'enemy aliens', however, was to invite populist scorn and hatred upon those in most need of compassion in wartime, and represented a moral failing on a national scale.

But for some interned Jews, there was worse to come. As the hotels and boarding houses of the Isle of Man filled to overflowing, the government realised they were running out of space. Commonwealth countries were approached to see if they would be prepared to take these potentially dangerous German and Austrian refugees. Canada and Australia accepted and ships were duly despatched. Canada had three, Australia just the one. Altogether, 7,500 internees would be sent abroad and some of their stories are tragic and harrowing.

Chapter 8

Punches, Kicks and Painful Prods: Internment Overseas

As the cost and trouble of interning thousands of refugees was becoming apparent, the British government decided that the way forward was to export the problem. It would send them off to the colonies. So, in 1940, passenger ships were sent to Canada and Australia, containing around 7,500 refugees among other prisoners. Priority on the first voyage was given to prisoners of war, but the second and third voyages contained B and C category refugees along with prisoners of war and ordinary Italian citizens who had been living in Britain.

Not all the passengers transported went to these destinations unwillingly. For some, the journey offered an opportunity to emigrate to a new country and Canada and Australia were certainly attractive destinations. For others, a trip away from Britain would end the nagging fear they had that the country would be successfully invaded by the Nazis and once again they would have to live in fear of the Gestapo. Nonetheless, these journeys would prove to be both highly unpleasant and, for some of the passengers, fatal.

The internment policy played out in the worst possible way with the deportation of 1,564 internees aboard the liner *Arandora Star*, which sailed from Liverpool on 1 July 1940. This voyage, written about in some detail by Peter and Leni Gillman in *Collar the Lot!* and in recent newspaper articles from *The Scotsman* to *The Guardian*, makes for a haunting read.

Launched at the end of the 1920s, *Arandora Star* began life as a cargo ship before conversion to a first-class passenger liner. It was such a prestigious vessel that the shipping company the Blue Star Line had its image front and centre in their Regent Street office window. On the outbreak of war, the *Arandora Star* was requisitioned by the British government, and for a while it led a charmed life. Initially, it took part in trials for an anti-torpedo system, which consisted of wire mesh nets being fitted at the side of the ship, an effective protection which only marginally slowed a vessel's speed. Unfortunately, following the trial, the nets were removed from the *Arandora Star* and never refitted.

As part of a convoy returning from the evacuation of Allied troops in Norway in 1940, the liner avoided almost certain destruction by the powerful German battlecruiser *Scharnhorst*, when a destroyer escort *Acasta* sacrificed itself by attacking and damaging the enemy warship with a torpedo. This action resulted in the loss of all but one of the *Acaster*'s 145-strong crew.

Arandora Star went on to take part in the rescue of soldiers stranded in France following the Dunkirk evacuation and picked up British troops from Quiberon and Polish Army soldiers from Bayonne and Saint-Jean-de-Luz.

Its next voyage, taking a consignment of interned Anglo-German and Anglo-Italian civilians, prisoners of war and German Jewish refugees to Canada, seemed to offer less prospect of misadventure.

The voyage started well, with one Jewish refugee, Gerhard Miedzwinski, remembering: 'The soldiers [who were guards aboard the ship] were nice chaps, just returned from Dunkirk. We soon made friends.' The food was good and the deportees were even allowed to drink at the ship's bar, where they listened to gramophone records.

But as the *Arandora Star* sailed away from the north-west coast of Ireland and into the great waters of the Atlantic, its luck ran out. The German submarine *U-47* spotted it at 6.30 a.m. on 2 July. Its commander was Günther Prien,* already a legend to the German people having sunk the British battleship *Royal Oak* barely six weeks into the war. On this voyage, his U-boat had been at sea for three weeks and in that time had already sunk eight British cargo ships. He had one torpedo left and just before 7 a.m. he sent it speeding towards the *Arandora Star*. It struck the rear of the ship, flooding the engine room and generator, plunging the inside of the vessel into darkness.

The ship sank in twenty minutes, taking many of those on board with it. Alerted by a radio distress signal from the *Arandora Star*, rescue arrived six hours later in the shape of Canadian destroyer *St Laurent*. Two and a half hours after that, all the survivors had been hauled from their lifeboats and life rafts and the *St Laurent* headed for Glasgow. Of 700 Italians, perhaps 460 died, many of whom had previously been interned in Warth Mills. Of 500 Germans, perhaps 130. The 174-strong crew lost forty-two, including the ship's captain, Edgar Moulton. The ship's guards lost thirty-seven of 200.

The British press made much of the sinking but framed the story entirely around the behaviour of the 'aliens' aboard. The *Daily*

---

* Prien survived his extraordinarily dangerous job for another eight months, dying at thirty-three when *U-47* was sunk by a British depth charge.

Herald of 4 July 1940 headlined the story 'Aliens Fight Each Other in Wild Panic'. The *Daily Express* was no more sympathetic:

> Soldiers and sailors ... told of the panic among the aliens when they realised the ship was sinking. All condemned the cowardice of the Germans, who fought madly to get to the boats. 'The Germans, fighting with Italians to escape, were great hulking brutes,' said one soldier. 'They punched and kicked their way past the Italians. We had to restrain them forcibly.' The Italians did not stand a chance against the Germans, according to the seaman. 'The Germans made it clear that nobody was going to stand in their way of being rescued. But the Italians were just as bad. The whole mob of them thought of their own skin first. The scramble for the boats was sickening.'

But as these reports poking fun at national stereotypes did the rounds in the newspapers, the Admiralty shipping casualties section were quickly and quietly interviewing survivors. The chief officer of the *Arandora Star* reported: 'There is absolutely no truth in the statement that German prisoners were pushing the Italians out of the way, nor did I notice any fighting between the Germans and the Italians.'

A further official report revealed that 'all the aliens had appeared on the upper deck and greatly hampered the crew on launching. There was, however, little or no panic among the internees.'

Quite aside from discovering that these stories of selfishness and cowardice among the Italians and Germans were false, a group of survivors were so distressed by the reports that they released their own memorandum refuting this representation of events. As quoted by Peter and Leni Gillman, it read:

We wish to put on record that all reports about unpleasant incidents of fighting between the shipwrecked during the period of rescue are untrue and lack basis or foundation. The ship's crew and the internees assisted each other in a most friendly and helpful spirit; and when taking people into the boats from rafts, wreckage or those who were swimming, no differentiation whatsoever was made.

There were more distressing reasons for such a death toll, not least among the Italians. Many of them were older men who had led comfortable lives and were not used to physical exertion. They had also been allocated the lowest decks on the liner and escape from the ship's pitch-black interior had been more difficult. By the time they arrived on the upper deck, the lifeboats had been filled. The German and Austrian prisoners of war had had a much better chance of survival as most of them were active serving seamen who were younger and healthier.

Another indisputable cause for the high death rate was the simple reason that there were enough lifeboats only for 1,000 people. Quite aside from the fact that the *U-47*'s torpedo had destroyed one of them and damaged the launch apparatus of another, there were 1,564 aboard the ship. There were smaller life rafts as well as the boats, but these were far less effective in saving men from the chilly sea. There was also a great deal of confusion aboard the ship as it was sinking. There had been no boat drill and people simply did not know what to do.

British newspaper reports naturally failed to mention the behaviour of one of the highest-ranking German prisoners, Captain Burfeind of the German ocean liner *Adolph Woermann.** He had

* The *Adolph Woermann*'s crew had been in British custody since 1939.

assisted Captain Moulton as they struggled to help men evacuate the ship and both of them went down together in the water. It was far easier to mock the foreigners than admit that a ship on a highly dangerous voyage did not have enough lifeboats and had not bothered to stage a lifeboat drill.

Further cover-ups followed. In the House of Commons, Anthony Eden, Secretary of State for War, told fellow MPs that all on board had been Italian Fascists or Category A Germans. None of them, Eden assured the House, were refugees. When questioned about the veracity of these statements, Eden told his fellow MPs that he was passing on assurances from his own officials. It was proving increasingly difficult to discover who had made the selection of prisoners and ordered the voyage.

Among the older Italians to die were chefs from London's most exclusive and famous hotels and restaurants, such as the Ritz, the Normandie and Café Anglais. Some of them had been in this country for decades and were naturalised British citizens with English wives and children. Some of the Germans who went down with the ship also had no business at all being aboard the *Arandora Star* as they were prominent anti-Nazi politicians or trade unionists. But perhaps it was their left-wing credentials that had alarmed officialdom.

A report was commissioned into the selection of the *Arandora Star*'s passengers and it was completed and delivered to the Cabinet at the end of November 1940. In essence, it blamed the unsuitable selection of internees on 'the need for speedy action' with regard to interning 'enemy aliens', but it also acknowledged, especially with the Italians aboard, that 'among those deported were a number of men whose sympathies were wholly with this country'.

Fortunately for the government, the Cabinet had given no assurance that it would publish the report and it was decided that, as interest had died down in the *Arandora Star* story, there was no point reviving it. The report was squirrelled away and forgotten about.

For the immediate future, the disaster of the *Arandora Star* did not prevent further sailings with ships packed with internees from taking place over the summer of 1940. Luckily, there were no further sinkings, but the British authorities did decide they needed to pick their passengers more carefully. The invalid and infirm were excused, as were boys under eighteen still at school or living with a British family. Refugees 'performing work of national importance' were also let off the hook, as well as those who ran businesses employing twelve or more British people. Some degree of compassion and common sense was seeping in. Removing a family member if this would cause 'gross hardship' was now also a good reason not to snatch an 'alien' away from his family.

As fear of invasion receded, the press outrage and subsequent panic among the population that had driven the government to intern their refugees also abated. It was quietly decided to suspend overseas transportation, but this only happened after the next two planned voyages to Canada and Australia respectively had gone ahead.

The Canadian ship contained an ill-assorted combination of prisoners of war and pro-Nazi and anti-fascist Category A internees. When they arrived in Canada, the Jews were treated exactly like the prisoners of war and interned alongside German soldiers. Eventually, realising these Jewish refugees were in danger from their fellow prisoners, the Canadian authorities set up separate camps. Edgar Lion, who was imprisoned in Quebec and New Brunswick remembers: 'We were on the same side as the Allies. We kept telling them, we're with you, we're against the Nazis. It didn't hold any water.' In a short film made by the *Montreal Gazette*, Edgar spoke of his complete bewilderment in finding himself in Canada. 'We did not know what would happen to us. We were there in a new country with no money, with no connections, with nothing.'

The unfortunate transportees on the trip to Australia had mixed fortunes too. HMT *Dunera* took over 2,500 passengers on an overcrowded and insanitary voyage over seven weeks. Food was poor and fresh water was only given to the men two or three times a week. There were only ten toilets available for the passengers, which resulted in waste overflowing across the deck. The consignment included 450 German and Italian prisoners of war and a number of fascist sympathisers, but at least two-thirds of the passengers were Jewish refugees – some of whom had been rescued from the *Arandora Star*. One Jewish passenger named Peter Eden recalls: '[We] slept on floors and benches, and if you wanted to go to the toilet at night you were walking on bodies. The troops that were guarding us were the worst in the British Army. I remember seeing someone walking off wearing my raincoat and I lost my watch.'

Nobody likes to imagine their own soldiers behaving badly, and even to this day stories criticising the behaviour of British troops are likely to be greeted with swivel-eyed fury by right-wing tabloids. But most people, especially students who stray into the wrong pub on a Saturday night in a garrison town like Colchester, know how ill-behaved a group of young men trained in the art of killing can be.

So, I turn with some trepidation to the behaviour of British soldiers sent to guard the passengers of the *Dunera*. Fortunately, the story involves no rape or murder, although one passenger was goaded into suicide. There was, however, blatant and gratuitous bullying and widespread looting of passengers' belongings.

Perhaps this was a consequence of a mob mentality in soldiers ill-commanded by senior officers who probably sympathised with the prejudices of some of their charges. How much this behaviour was prompted by tabloid demonisation, and how much of it was simply inherited antisemitism, is a PhD study in waiting.

The circumstances of the voyage made it almost inevitable that something ugly would develop. It certainly makes for uncomfortable reading and has now been the subject of several books, including *The Dunera Affair* edited by Paul R. Bartrop and Gabrielle Eisen and *The Dunera Internees* by Benzion Patkin, and is also covered by Peter and Leni Gillman's *Collar the Lot!* Figures vary, but there were approximately 2,700 internees aboard the *Dunera* and 2,288 of them were political or racial refugees, described by one indignant involuntary passenger thus: 'All of them are the bitterest enemies of Nazidom.'

The remaining 444 deportees consisted of 200 Italian and 251 German prisoners of war. The Italians, many of whom had also survived the sinking of the *Arandora Star*, were mainly civilians who had been living in Britain for decades, often working in the restaurant trade. One recalled their treatment by soldiers as they arrived at the harbour side. 'They assisted our boarding with punches, kicks and painful prods with their rifle butts, along with an assault of disgusting language.'

Only the German prisoners of war could in any way be described as a threat to Britain and their fellow passengers. The more fervent Nazis among them did indeed cause trouble for the guards – but this was no reason to treat the rest of the internees in such an appalling fashion.

The voyage began with the looting by soldiers of the internees' luggage. This was regrettable in itself, but especially so as it was carried out in such a blatant manner in full view of the sergeants and officers supervising these men.

'Our trunks are being broken open on deck,' reported one refugee in a diary of the voyage he secretly kept. 'They are being broken open and pilfered. An officer is looking on. Soldiers are filling their pockets openly.'

Another refugee recalled reporting this theft to a sergeant. 'I said to him in English, "You know your man is stealing" … He turned around and said, "Fuck off, you filthy pig" or something like that.'

Suitcases with a change of clothes and washbags were stolen or simply thrown overboard.* Watches, rings and money were taken. Other instances of gratuitous bullying included throwing medicine such as insulin, and false teeth, into the sea. Jewish religious items, such as prayer books and vestments, were also thrown overboard, a clear indication of the soldiers' contempt for their refugee prisoners.

Further recollections of the soldiers' behaviour are even more disturbing. 'One of our fellow internees, Mr P. Fliess, who one night was suffering from diarrhoea and endeavouring to reach the lavatory by means of a gangway … was stabbed through the barbed wire with a bayonet into his stomach.'

Other passengers recall soldiers throwing glass bottles in front of them which would shatter and cut their feet as they attempted to keep fit in their moments of exercise on the upper deck.

---

* However, some of the facts surrounding the *Dunera* are murky, with passengers and researchers writing contradictory claims. For example, Peter and Leni Gillman write that there was plenty of evidence to back up reports of looting but none of items being thrown overboard.

Surprisingly, only two refugees died on the voyage. One, Hans Pfeffen, was already seriously ill when he boarded the vessel and died en route to Australia. Another, Jacob Weiss, died by suicide. Weiss had obtained immigration documents for himself and his family at considerable effort and when these documents were torn up in front of him, he became so distraught he threw himself overboard and drowned.

Yet despite the ill-treatment, the looting and the appalling state of the ship, the *Dunera* did have one stroke of luck. In a bid to avoid U-boat attack, the captain had taken a route past the far north of Scotland and was following a standard manoeuvre of zigzagging along his course. This the ship was doing as it sailed through the Irish Sea and the German submarine *U-56* fired two torpedoes towards it. Both torpedoes missed and exploded on timed fuses further beyond the *Dunera*.* The explosions naturally caused considerable consternation aboard the ship. Indeed, prisoners in the depth of the vessel immediately tried to get to the top deck, only to be blocked by soldiers threatening to kill them.†

So, who were these soldiers? Benzion Patkin's account tells us they were mainly recruited from the Auxiliary Military Pioneer Corps, a branch of the army somewhat notorious for the poor quality of its recruits (see Chapter 9 for further information here). 'They had all been at Dunkirk, and most of them had something to remember that – a glass eye, shell-shock symptoms, fingers missing

---

* Again this is disputed. The Gillmans point out that the *U-56*'s captain, Oberleutnant Harms, recorded in the logbook that he fired two torpedoes and that one missed and the other failed to explode.

† Another contradictory story, reported in the *Jerusalem Post* on 12 December 2015, says the U-boat followed the *Dunera* to establish whether it was a legitimate target. Goods and documents, written in German and thrown overboard by the guards, were recovered by divers from the U-boat, and the captain decided the ship was carrying German prisoners of war so did not attack it. This version of events was convincingly dismissed by the Gillmans in a letter to *The Guardian* on 22 February 2022. There is no mention in the ship's logbook of divers recovering jettisoned luggage or the captain deciding to give HMT *Dunera* safe passage.

… Altogether a forbidding looking crowd. The officers were not much better. Most of them didn't care tuppence what the men did, but were drinking all day.' One officer was particularly remembered by the internees: '[Some soldiers] led by Lieutenant O'Neill were inciting [other] soldiers to fresh deeds. O'Neill had come up from the ranks, he had been in the last war and wore a V.C.'

O'Neill, a hard-faced Scot who stares from his army portrait with the air of a man facing down prisoners in a particularly unpleasant branch of HM prison service,* had indeed won this most prestigious of medals while serving as a sergeant in the Second Battalion, Prince of Wales's Leinster Regiment, where he had performed acts of extraordinary battlefield bravery in the final month of the First World War. He re-enlisted when war broke out again in 1939 and was commissioned as a lieutenant. He gave evidence at the court martial of officers and other soldiers following the *Dunera* disaster but was not charged himself. He died, aged forty-five, of a heart attack in 1942.

But not everyone aboard the *Dunera* behaved in such a deplorable manner. Paul R. Bartrop and Gabrielle Eisen's *The Dunera Affair* contains a fascinating glimpse of the voyage as seen by an ordinary sailor, who wrote about his experience in the *Sydney Sunday Telegraph* in October 1940 under the alias 'Semaphore'. His diary accounts make it hard to excuse the soldiers on the grounds that they must have thought the refugees were loyal German soldiers and hardcore Nazis. The German soldiers had in fact been segregated from the rest of the passengers in the aft of the *Dunera* and

---

* Some accounts claim a number of the *Dunera* soldiers had volunteered for armed service so they could be released early from prison sentences.

appeared to be 'aloof and arrogant'. No doubt fuelling the unease on the voyage, Semaphore writes:

> Several of the Nazis have been boasting that they will see to it that the ship will arrive at no other destination than Germany. Most of the Nazis are the desperate fanatical type and are quite capable of running the ship … There is a feeling of tension in the air.

Sure enough, reported another one of the ship's crew in his diary, the German prisoners did try to stage a rebellion, occasioned by rumours of a German warship in close proximity. A fire was started in the German quarters on the ship and prisoners tried to break out. But the rebellion was swiftly brought to an end with warning shots and the sight of fixed bayonets.

But despite the appalling food and unhygienic conditions, the refugees were not denied some of the decencies of life. Semaphore writes that 'lectures have been arranged. The better educated among the refugees are going to talk about subjects such as "A walk through Paris" and "How to drive a car".'

He also noted that 'a number of small choirs have sprung up among the prisoners … They give really first class shows to an audience of about 1,500.' This he contrasts with the behaviour of the German prisoners of war. 'The p.o.w.s play cards but their main indulgence seems to be fighting among themselves.'

He also noticed a serious antipathy between the Italian and German soldiers:

> Between them is an intense hatred. I must say, however, that to us the Italians seem much more pleasant people. They are agreeable

and have a sense of humour. But whatever individual personalities the Germans might have seems to have been crushed out of them by the imposition of a fanatical Nazi arrogance. You have to see these people, the militaristic Nazis, to realise how this Hitler stuff has got hold of them.

These comments are notable for two reasons. In Chapter 10, this book looks at Britain's treatment of prisoners of war and this positive view of Italian prisoners seems to be a common one. The behaviour of the German prisoners, too, gives us an insight into how deeply the Hitler Youth and Dr Goebbels's Ministry of Public Enlightenment and Propaganda inculcated the Nazis' hateful views into their young people.

Semaphore gradually came to realise exactly what sort of people the British government had deemed worthy of deportation. 'There are some extraordinary people among the refugees ... altogether 14 lawyers, a reporter from the *Berliner Tageblatt*, "Zeppie" a famous acrobat ... There are a number of men whom the others address as "Doctor".'

Semaphore also noted that the Jewish refugees 'appeared indifferent to their fate, whereas the Italian civilians [whom he describes as "unnaturalised English"] were frightened and nervous'.

The thuggish behaviour of many of the guards made a sorry contrast with the conduct of the refugees, and their decency and pragmatism. Their resilience was commendable. In a rather haphazard article about the voyage, reported in the *Jerusalem Post* in 2015, they were said to have appropriated the Scottish folk song 'My Bonnie Lies over the Ocean' and rewritten the lyric thus:

My luggage lies over the ocean
My luggage lies over the sea.
My luggage lies over the ocean
Oh bring back my luggage to me.

Refugees' accounts of ill-treatment were made public only three months after the end of the voyage. 'We have refrained up to now from commenting on treatment on board HMT *Dunera* as we were afraid that those facts might be used for enemy propaganda,' wrote one refugee. The report from the internees ends with 'an appreciation of helpful officers and men ... it would be unjust not to mention ... and we know that those officers and men who maltreated us did not act in accordance with the British Tradition.'

At first, the story of the voyage was given a positive spin by Britain's right-wing press. Seeking to deflect criticism of the British Army guards, the *Daily Telegraph* reported that 'among the internees were parachutists, other prisoners of war, and hundreds who had been carrying out subversive work in England'.

It was a flimsy defence. When the ship arrived in Australia, it became obvious that something appalling had been going on. Medical army officer Alan Frost raised the alarm as soon as he boarded the ship and his report led to the court martial of the officer in charge of the vessel, Lieutenant Colonel William Scott.

Even then, the story was reported with extreme caution. 'Allegations that suitcases belonging to interned German and Italians showed signs of having been broken open while their owners were being taken to Australia in the transport *Dunera* were made at a field general Court-martial,' reported *The Times* on 21 May 1941, under the headline 'Alleged Theft from Interned Aliens'. Couched in such a manner, it seems almost unimaginable that refugees would recall the same incidents in considerably more brutal terms.

In time, an apology came from Winston Churchill himself and a fund of £35,000 was established to compensate the *Dunera*'s passengers for their stolen and disposed of belongings.

In early 1941, the British Home Office sent an army major to Australia to investigate the *Dunera* arrivals and consider repatriation. He concluded that the passengers who weren't prisoners of war should be reclassified as 'refugee aliens'. While some returned to Britain, 900 of the *Dunera* passengers remained in Australia for the duration of the war, many of them joining the Australian Army's Eighth Employment Company, where they contributed to the war effort by building infrastructure such as railways lines, bases and supply dumps.

As 'Semaphore' had noticed, these '*Dunera* boys', as they became known, were an unusually talented group. Many were writers or scientists, and others were musicians or artists. Looking back, on 19 May 2006 the *Sydney Morning Herald* wrote: 'Their arrival ... was seen as the greatest injection of talent to enter Australia on a single vessel.' Fortunately for Australia, many of these refugees decided to stay after the war, where a notable number of them achieved national recognition in fields as diverse as sports coaching and philosophy, photography and furniture design.

* * *

Unease about internment, and voyages such as these, was already apparent in Britain even as the policy was being enacted. On 6 July 1940, *The Guardian* ran a leader entitled '"Enemy" Aliens':

For seven years ... we have offered, under many safeguards and after much jealous enquiry, asylum to men and women fugitives from Nazidom.

Once again we were admitting and absorbing elements of technical and intellectual ability that would strengthen Britain.

When war came, the value of refugees seemed even greater for they, of all people, could be trusted to work and fight to the end, since, if Hitler should win, their only alternative was slavery or execution.

The paper goes on to marvel at the logic that suggests Jewish exiles would support the Nazis:

Hitler and the Gestapo may want his blood, but all the same, so strong will be his desire to help the Nazi invaders that he in innumerable ways will assist to put himself into their clutches again.

This may seem ridiculous but only on such a supposition can one find any credible basis for the decisions of the last few weeks ...

Putting aside the human considerations ... does it not seem unintelligent and wasteful to deprive ourselves of the aid of these thousands of men and women in our terrific struggle? Are we really so stupid that we cannot distinguish good men from bad men?

By the end of 1940, the British government was reconsidering its internment policy. The stupidity of interning so many people so indiscriminately was becoming obvious. The oldest and the youngest had their cases reviewed and those who were working in positions of national importance were given priority.

The Isle of Man internees were gradually assimilated back into the mainland, and by the summer of 1942, less than 5,000 still remained. But this decision to release them was contentious. Western Command, the Chester-based HQ of the Home Defence Force, considered it 'highly dangerous in every way'. Fortunately, the Home Office chose to ignore what was a preposterous claim. And the treatment of those who remained interned also improved. Married couples and families were no longer kept apart.

From 1941, a more sensible approach was adopted. The British government increasingly came to realise that their 'enemy aliens' were actually a highly valuable resource and in the following years they were to make much better use of them. Many went on to serve in the British armed forces and many of those then settled here, becoming naturalised British citizens.

As the war receded into history, former refugees played down the hardship and emotional turmoil they suffered. It seemed like an indulgence, when the full horror emerged of what had happened to their friends and relatives who had not managed to escape the Nazis.

Chapter 9

Valuable Work: Refugees and the War Effort

A s the fear of invasion abated by the autumn of 1940, so the government began to make constructive use of the often highly educated German and Austrian Jews who had escaped the Nazis and who they had interned as 'enemy aliens'. By the end of 1940, 10,000 internees had been released and those who were classified as C after a tribunal hearing, or reclassified after a second hearing, were invited to a variety of roles after they were deemed fit to be freed. They could pursue civilian roles, such as engineering, medicine or farm work, or join the army in the Auxiliary Military Pioneer Corps, like their fellow refugees in Australia.

By late 1940 and early 1941, perhaps 1,000 internees were being released a month. Some had found their experiences so demoralising it had put them off doing anything at all. 'Many [of us have] ceased to believe in the British spirit of humanity which before they had acclaimed,' said refugee Simon Isaac.

But many of them were still keen to help the British, and two accounts of such men appear later in this chapter.

Sir John Anderson shouldered the blame for this sorry episode, although he had been against internment all along. But the press had scented blood and he was the scapegoat they needed to divert attention away from their own responsibility in the hounding of 'enemy aliens'. Calls for his resignation also increased when his decision not to allow Londoners to shelter from German bombing raids in the deep tunnels of the underground led to an open rebellion. People took to the Tube at night and refused to leave. Anderson was replaced by the Labour MP Herbert Morrison, who would remain Home Secretary until the end of the war.

Throughout the war, at least 10,000 Jewish refugees served in the British Army, at first in the Pioneer Corps. Only in 1943 were they allowed to join fighting units. The Royal Navy and RAF were effectively closed to them. Reasons for this are complicated, as many British-born Jews served with distinction in both the navy and the air force. The Royal Navy, for example, had a regulation stating that people of foreign parentage were ineligible for entry, writes Geoffrey Green in 'England expects...: British Jews under the white ensign from HMS *Victory* to the loss of HMS *Hood* in 1941', a piece for the periodical *Jewish Historical Studies*. This was the case even if both parents were naturalised British subjects.* The rule was tweaked on the outbreak of war to accommodate British-born sons of foreign-born parents, providing they were naturalised at the time of the son's birth. But as the war progressed, the navy became more flexible. German Jewish refugees were allowed to volunteer for what Green refers to as 'headache ratings' – radio operators who listened to and translated enemy signals at sea. Established during the First World War, this branch of armed forces communications

---

* There is an irony here. Nelson's ship HMS *Victory* at Trafalgar, arguably the Royal Navy's finest hour, had a crew made up of twenty-two nationalities, from German to Jamaican, Brazilian to Norwegian.

Although the story of angel bowmen protecting British soldiers at Mons in 1914 was originally presented as fiction, many British people were all too willing to believe it was true. By the time of the Second World War, there was much greater cynicism about anti-German propaganda, which contributed to the fact that many British people initially did not believe stories about Nazi Jewish persecution and the death camps.

Source: Wikimedia Commons

Arthur Balfour, the former British Prime Minister and Foreign Secretary, was the architect of the disastrous 1917 Balfour Declaration, which pledged support for a Jewish homeland in Palestine. In the 1930s, this declaration fostered hope among Jews wishing to flee the Nazis, but this was then hindered by a series of British policies enacted to limit Jewish emigration to Palestine.

Source: Wikimedia Commons

Antisemitism in Britain found its most vocal champion in Oswald Mosley, photographed here looking every inch the 'perfumed popinjay' described by Conservative politician F. E. Smith. Mosley founded the British Union of Fascists in 1932. Unsurprisingly, Jewish refugees were a particular focus for its hostility.

Source: Wikimedia Commons

"BRITAIN PROTESTS"

ABOVE During the Spanish Civil War, the British provided temporary shelter to Basque children. Here, the young refugees give press photographers the Republican salute. Many of them were a considerably tougher bunch than the middle-class Jewish children who arrived from Germany and Austria, with some even having seen combat in Spain.
Source: Wikimedia Commons

MIDDLE LEFT This bizarre cartoon, from the October 1937 British fascist magazine *Action*, shows grotesque Jewish stereotypes cheering on Mosley's Blackshirts. The 'humour' here seems to be based on the common belief that Jews were obsequious to anyone who disliked them. Jewish refugees fleeing the Nazis found that Britain too had its antisemites.
Author's collection

BELOW LEFT American representative Myron Taylor addresses the Évian Conference in 1938, convened to discuss the rapidly escalating refugee crisis following the *Anschluss*. The photograph is reminiscent of those from the Paris Peace Conference nearly twenty years before, which is fitting, as both meetings were miserable failures.
Source: Wikimedia Commons

Teenagers en route to England aboard a *Kindertransport* train in 1939. They left parents and other family members behind whom they might never see again. While many appear in good spirits, treating the journey as an adventure, the strain of the ordeal is apparent on some of their faces.

A strangely contemporary photograph of an exhausted *Kindertransport* girl during her journey to England. She looks like she's wearing iPod earbuds, but the white lead around her neck is almost certainly attached to a cardboard label giving her personal details.

LEFT Ilse Gray (*left*) and her sister Eva, snapped in England in 1939. Ilse came to the UK from Vienna as one of the *Kindertransport* children. Her family were entirely secular, and Ilse realised she was Jewish only after the *Anschluss*.
Courtesy of Ilse Gray

BELOW In a photo taken on the same day as this book's cover image, British police forcibly remove a stateless Jew, Oskar Goldberg, from Croydon Airport. He is one of several refugees who chartered a plane to flee from the Nazis only to be denied entry to Britain. The publicity these images generated resulted in the refugees being allowed to stay.
© Wiener Holocaust Library

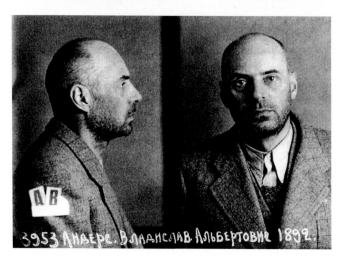

LEFT In a style instantly recognisable to students of Stalin's purges, General Władysław Anders is photographed by the NKVD in 1940. Many recipients of mug shots like this were executed shortly thereafter, so Anders was lucky. He survived to lead a unit of the Polish Army in exile, made up of thousands of former prisoners of war. He died in England in 1970.
Source: Wikimedia Commons

Polish pilots with the Spitfire's less-glamorous contemporary, the Hurricane, in the Kościuszko Squadron. During the Battle of Britain, they shot down more German aircraft than any other RAF squadron.
Source: Wikimedia Commons

HMT *Dunera* transported 2,500 interned 'enemy aliens' to Australia in 1940. Unlike another vessel used to ship refugees off to the colonies, the *Dunera* evaded U-boat torpedoes. When it reached Australia, a national scandal broke over the treatment of its passengers by the ship's British Army guards.
Source: Wikimedia Commons

German prisoners of war are marched off a landing ship at Southampton, shortly after the D-Day landings in 1944. Although the British sailor on the left appears all set to barrack them, they look remarkably relaxed. The British treated their prisoners of war well and only 0.03 per cent died in captivity.
Source: Wikimedia Commons

Auschwitz I, photographed by an American reconnaissance plane in April 1944. The existence of the death camps had been known since 1942, but what happened in them was so unimaginably evil that most British people could not believe it was true.

Source: Wikimedia Commons

Images such as this, from Belsen, brought home the true nature of the Nazi regime and offered a clear explanation as to why so many Jews had been desperate to flee. Alas, the experiences of those who survived the camps and then came to settle in Britain became a taboo subject, and survivors often had to keep their harrowing tales to themselves.

Source: Wikimedia Commons

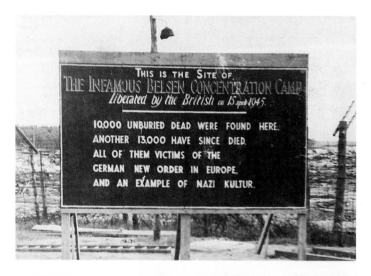

A post-war sign outside the Nazi concentration camp of Belsen. The first camp to be liberated by British soldiers, Belsen set the image of Nazi camps in the public mind. Despite the atrocities visited on Jews in camps like this, many British MPs wanted to send Jewish refugees back to Germany after the war.

© Wiener Holocaust Library

The trial of the Belsen guards. Here, Irma Grese (*right*) leads fellow Belsen accomplices through a gauntlet of Allied soldiers outside a Lüneburg courtroom in September 1945. Tabloid newspaper reports trivialised her trial and the murders she committed, and some even referred to her as the 'beautiful beast of Belsen'.

© Wiener Holocaust Library

Jewish refugees served in many roles in the British armed forces, but none more extraordinary than the X Troop of Jewish commandos, who fought from D-Day to Berlin and then, after the German surrender, hunted down Nazi war criminals. Manfred Gans was one such brave commando.

Courtesy of the Gans family

After hearing a rumour that his parents might still be alive in Theresienstadt concentration camp, Jewish commando Manfred Gans sped off from the Netherlands in a jeep at the end of the war, as the Reich collapsed around him. His rescue mission was successful. Here, he is pictured in late 1945 with his mother, grandmother and father.

Courtesy of the Gans family

Packed to the gunnels with 1,300 Jewish refugees, the *Josiah Wedgwood* seeks to avoid the Royal Navy in the post-war exodus to Palestine. Many of the refugees had survived Nazi concentration camps, but on their arrival in Haifa, they were interned by the British.

was known as the 'Y Service' and German-born refugees proved to be invaluable from D-Day until the end of the war, especially in intercepting radio communications which helped to locate and destroy many vessels in the German E-boat fleet in northern Europe.[*]

In all military organisations, there are varying degrees of prestige and status. In Britain, the commandos, the SAS, the Special Boat Service and the fighter pilots of the RAF were always going to grab the newspaper headlines. At the other end of the scale were those in the catering corps and, most of all, the Auxiliary Military Pioneer Corps – the road builders, the mine clearers, the suppliers of provisions and other essential requirements. There were other even less glamorous aspects to this work – such as lavatory cleaning, digging ditches and humping coal. Despite its obvious essential nature, this branch of the military, say Peter and Leni Gillman, was a dumping ground for 'all human dross'. This was home for the illiterate and those with criminal records. (There was a high correlation between the two.)[†] This was a cause of some frustration among the younger end of the internees who were anxious to join fighting regiments. But this was what was on offer and many refugees took it. Some were hesitant and the authorities were impatient for them to decide, announcing that 'in their own interest, internees should be informed that delays in making up their minds whether or not to join the AMPC may result in their internment for the duration of the war'.

Egged on by this less-than-subtle threat, 4,000 refugees had joined by the end of the year.

Other refugees, who in a former life had been accountants and

---

[*]   These exceptionally fast little boats were armed with torpedoes and flak guns and also laid mines. Operating in the Baltic and English Channel, they were highly effective against both merchant and navy shipping.

[†]   Even today, an estimated 60 per cent of the prison population lack basic literacy skills.

businesspeople, found work in administrative rolls such as the Railway Board, and others were employed as fire watchers atop London's tallest buildings with the Air Raid Precaution organisations.

So, what did happen once Jewish refugees were allowed to enter the British armed forces? Their stories are legion, but here are two – both extraordinary in their way but one so unreal it could be the script of a Hollywood film. (In fact, I'm rather left wondering why it hasn't been…)

Karl Robert Würzburger wrote of his experiences in the book *And Then the Music Stopped Playing*, published by Braiswick. He was one of the last *Kindertransport* children, arriving in Britain from Frankfurt a week before the war broke out. He was seventeen at the time and classed as a 'friendly enemy alien'. Thanks to his youth, and also the vagaries of the local internment panels, he avoided the round-up of 'enemy aliens', although he was required to stay indoors between midnight and 6 a.m. He also needed a permit if he wanted to own a bicycle.

Würzburger was an industrious lad and found work as a houseboy at a hotel in Swiss Cottage, London, where in exchange for seven shillings and sixpence, an attic room and all his meals, he worked a 87-hour week doing everything someone in the hotel trade might be required to do.

While working there, he discovered from an aunt in America that his parents and brother had been murdered at Chełmno extermination camp near Łódź. In one of the book's more poignant passages, sure to strike at the heart of anyone who recalls their childhood home with an aching nostalgia, Würzburger writes:

I had always hoped that when the war was over I would be able to go back to Frankfurt, run up the stairs two at a time to our second floor flat … shouting: 'I am home, I am home!' … I decided I had to get my own back. I was now 19 and I volunteered for the army.

Like almost every other 'alien' who wanted to fight the Nazis, he was permitted to join only the Pioneer Corps and his first experiences were not promising. The duty sergeant at his barracks greeted him with the words: 'I didn't know things were so bad that we have to recruit babies now.' He was shown into a barrack hut with four empty bunks belonging to four boys who had just been killed on a landmine training course. But Würzburger pressed on with the duties required of him – building roads, loading and unloading goods wagons, smashing stones in a quarry. 'I was very proud to wear the British uniform,' he writes, '[but] I wanted to do much more. I wanted to be in the fighting … I felt frustrated and ashamed that I was still in England, while millions of British soldiers fought in the battlefields.'

By the summer of 1943, suspicion of 'enemy aliens' had diminished to such an extent that the British government decided to allow volunteers to join the combat units of the army. Würzburger opted for the Royal Tank Regiment and was enlisted in January 1944.

Now with the prospect of being captured by the Germans, it was suggested that he change his obviously Jewish name. Würzburger decided to retain his initials at least and opted for the *nom de guerre* of Kenneth Robert Ward. He also chose not to have a J for Jew on his dog tag. He was sure he would be shot if he was captured. Würzburger, whom we shall now call Ward, writes: 'The training sergeants and staff wondered why we as Germans were willing … to fight our own countrymen.'

Curiously, according to information provided by the Sydney Jewish Museum, Jewish soldiers fighting on the Western European Front were not treated as badly as expected if they were captured by the Germans. Western governments let the Nazis know that any ill-treatment of any of their captured soldiers would have direct consequences for the way German soldiers would be treated in captivity. So, generally, the *Wehrmacht* would treat Allied Jewish soldiers according to the rules of war – despite pressure from the SS to make them wear a yellow star and hand them over to be murdered.*
Nonetheless, there are still plenty of instances where Jewish soldiers in the Allied armies were subjected to ill-treatment.

Ward trained as a radio operator in a Sherman tank and tried hard to perfect his English pronunciation. He had been warned that the enemy would be able to hear communications between tank crews and his distinctive German pronunciation would enable them to identify the movements of his tank squadron.

The Normandy landings were just around the corner.

Ward arrived in France the day after the first landings on 6 June 1944. He writes: 'Now I had reached my objective I was a fighting soldier. I had at last a chance to avenge my parents and my brother. I would not take any German prisoners.' But his basic humanity took over when he did finally encounter his first enemy soldier:

Two days after we had landed, we were parked in a lane near a hedge
… Suddenly there was some movement on the side and a German
soldier crawled out from under the hedge. He looked very old, di-
shevelled and dirty. He stood there with his hands up, trembling and

---

* This was in sharp contrast to the treatment of Russian Jewish soldiers by German forces, who would be shot as soon as their identity was established. The Nazis treated their Russian prisoners with appalling cruelty anyway, so the odds of surviving capture, even if a Russian soldier wasn't Jewish, were still slim.

very frightened … All my resolutions were immediately forgotten. I felt compassion for this frightened human being and gave him a mug of our compo tea.

For a year, Ward fought on the front line, pushing towards Germany. He was extraordinarily lucky not to be killed and indeed had several narrow escapes, unlike many of the friends he made in the Royal Tank Regiment who were killed in the fighting.*

Following the occupation of Berlin by all the Allied victors, Ward became a valued interpreter with the British military police, dealing mainly with crimes committed by civilians against British military property. He also took part in an investigation into forged currency. While there, he met and married a German woman named Hildegard. At the wedding, the registrar told him: 'You ought to be castrated for wanting to marry a Christian German. What about your family, how do they feel about it?'

But Ken Ward was a big-hearted man. And his basic decency overrode his detestation of the Nazis who had killed his family. He was even moved by the notes and photographs he saw about German soldiers that could be found attached to walls in all major railway stations. 'Do you know Hans Schmitt … last heard of at Stalingrad?'

'It was so pitiful,' he writes, 'that two and a half years after the war finished, hundreds of thousands of German soldiers were still missing.'

On a troop ship back to England, he muses: 'I was now coming

---

* Tank crews make quite a Faustian pact with their calling. Their tank offers them shelter and protection in battle, not to mention a mechanical means of getting from A to B denied to the ordinary foot soldier. But tanks are difficult vehicles to get in and out of. And when a tank is hit, if its crew are not immediately killed, they face the hideous prospect of being burned alive as their vehicle 'brews up'.

again to the country of my choice, which had saved my life, had made me so welcome many years ago.'

But Jewish refugees did not serve only within ordinary British Army combat forces. In what sounds like an implausible action movie fantasy, Winston Churchill and the Chief of Combined Operations authorised the creation of a secret commando unit of Jewish refugees officially designated as No. 10 (Inter-Allied) Commando, 3 Troop – but better known as X Troop.

American academic Leah Garrett has written about these soldiers in her book *X Troop: The Secret Jewish Commandos of World War Two* and tells us that eighty-seven refugees passed through the ranks of this combat group, with over half of them killed, wounded or missing in the later stages of the war.

They fought from D-Day to Berlin, and then, after the German surrender, were active in hunting down Nazi war criminals.[*] All of them were given British identities and dog tags declaring their religion to be Church of England.

The recruits included Lanyi György aka George Lane, Hans Ludwig Hajos aka Ian Harris and Peter Arany aka Peter Masters. All names so ordinary and British they could be Melchester teammates for Roy of the Rovers. These three soldiers all fought with extraordinary bravery in the war in Western Europe. Before they joined up, their experiences were similar to many other Jewish refugees – they were met with fear, suspicion and internment. Peter Masters remembers a British corporal in an internment camp

---

[*]   Quentin Tarantino's *Inglourious Basterds* was allegedly inspired by this group of Jewish soldiers. Manfred Gans's children were anxious for X Troop not to be compared to the soldiers in *Inglourious Basterds*. His daughter Aviva told me: 'Our father made it clear that when he agreed to join the British Army, he knew he would be confronting men like his former German classmates. He also said that his goal was not to kill. He prided himself for taking thousands of prisoners instead.'

screaming at him 'I have the right to shoot you. You have no rights at all!'

But most extraordinary of all is Manfred Gans aka Fred Gray, whose war took him from the Normandy beachhead on D-Day to the Netherlands, via Germany and Belgium. As the war ended, he was in the Netherlands, as a lieutenant in the British Commandos. Here he heard that, in the chaos of the collapse of the Nazi regime, the SS were slaughtering thousands of surviving Jews. Having been informed that his parents might still be alive in Theresien-stadt concentration camp, in Terezín, Czechoslovakia, he asked his commanding officer if he could take a jeep to try to rescue them. Commendably, and not unconnected to the remarkable bravery Gans had shown since D-Day, he was allowed to do this.

Here the story slips the bounds of believability and takes on a *Boy's Own* unreality. Gans sets off with a jeep, a quantity of fuel, a machine gun and a young cockney driver called Bob.

The two of them head through the chaos of bombed-out towns and cities, and thousands of people pushing handcarts and prams, all trying to get home. Passing through territory held by the Amer-ican Army, they refuel when they can from American fuel trucks until they reach Chemnitz, south of Leipzig, and close to the Czech border. This is now Russian Army territory and they are swiftly surrounded by Red Army soldiers. Two Soviet officers ride over on horseback. 'Are you Jewish?' asks Gans. One officer is and he tells them they have to enter Czechoslovakia through American lines as he cannot give them permission to carry on further into Red Army territory.

Gans and Bob find the Americans and a senior officer gives them a letter of safe passage. Here they hear that Germany has officially surrendered. The next day, they set off again from American lines towards Czechoslovakia via the town of Aue, which is still under Nazi control. German soldiers and civilians surround them and they fear they might be lynched. But they press on and the crowd backs away. They drive through spectacular mountain scenery to Schwarzenberg and cross the border into Sudetenland. Here they encounter thousands of German soldiers desperate to surrender to the British rather than the Soviets. The roads are also packed with thousands of Soviet and British prisoners of war and they also run into Red Army soldiers who are ecstatic to see them – the first British soldiers they have encountered. As dusk falls, and three days after leaving the Netherlands, they reach Terezín, and Czech resistance fighters show them the route to Theresienstadt concentration camp.

Soviet guards now control the camp. Gans tells them who he is and announces: 'I have come to find my parents.' The guards let the jeep into the camp and Gans and Bob pass hundreds of starving, ragged Jews. Dead bodies are everywhere. Gans asks how he should find his parents and is pointed in the direction of a registration office. Here he finds a young Jewish woman who goes through the records and tells him his parents are still in the camp. They had been arrested in the Netherlands and were being kept in a part of Theresienstadt known as the 'Dutch Camp'. Here he finds his father – half-starved and almost unrecognisable. His mother is there, too, in an equally fragile state. 'I suddenly find myself in their arms. They are both crying wildly,' he recalls. His mother had survived because she managed to find a job in the SS kitchen and was able to surreptitiously pilfer food. His father had been kept alive as a 'high-value' prisoner, having been a 'councilman' in Borken, a German town close to the Dutch border. He also had a highly distinguished record in the First World War and this may have saved him too. Manfred Gans's children say they cannot say with certainty why their grandparents were spared.

The Soviet commander of the camp tells them typhus is rife and officially he should not have admitted them, and now he should not let them go. But aware of the extraordinary nature of what has just happened, he tells them he will turn a blind eye, but they must leave by 8 a.m. the following day.

Gans and Bob head back to the American lines, picking up as many prisoners of war as their jeep can carry. Two days later, they are back at the headquarters of their unit – No. 41 Royal Marine Commando in the Netherlands.

Here Gans meets representatives of the Dutch government and arrangements are made for him to meet Princess Juliana – an influential member of the Dutch royal family. She arranges for a plane to evacuate Gans's parents and other Dutch residents from Theresienstadt and they are safely returned and cared for.

Having survived the war and this extraordinary adventure, Gans is deployed back in his home town of Borken to assist in the process of denazifying the citizens there.

But not all the Jews who volunteered for special operations succeeded. Peter and Leni Gillman write about how, later in the war, the British Secret Service were keen to recruit internees to work as spies and saboteurs behind enemy lines – a task many of them would have been eminently suited for. But the training, in the remote and rugged terrain of northern Scotland and Northern Ireland, was arduous and had a high dropout rate. Failure to satis-factorily complete the course carried more than a sense of shame or disappointment. Rather ruthlessly, it was decided that 'enemy aliens' who had been trained in the operating techniques of the Secret Intelligence Service but had failed the course should be placed in isolation. A separate wing in Stafford Prison was cordoned off and sixty prisoners were kept there for the duration of the war.

Many of the refugees who fought during the war wrote of the liberating experience of putting on a British uniform. After their dehumanising treatment in Nazi territory and the humiliation of internment and even deportation in Britain, they felt they were finally being recognised as human beings again.

* * *

Help from refugees also came from a more oblique angle: intelligence, gathered through the mass interrogation of refugees. Artemis Photiadou's article in *Intelligence and National Security*, entitled '"Extremely valuable work": British intelligence and the interrogation of refugees in London, 1941–45', provides fascinating information on this topic. Here she considers the work of the Royal Victoria Patriotic School, an extraordinary gothic edifice in Wandsworth, originally built to house orphans of the Crimean War, which became the focus of British intelligence efforts to interrogate thousands of refugees who fled to Britain after the Second World War began.

Once it was realised that the Nazis were not dropping hundreds of spies into Britain by parachute, the Royal Victoria Patriotic School became the first line of defence against enemy agents arriving with refugees. Efforts were made to make the school appear more like a welcoming holding camp than an interrogation hub – it was even given the innocuous name the London Reception Centre. It is not difficult to imagine the sort of reception the Nazi state, or indeed the Soviet Union, would have given to such arrivals, and Britain's restrained approach towards these potentially dangerous newcomers paid off handsomely. Not all of them were refugees – a few were prisoners of war or deserters – and between all 30,000 of them, processed between 1941 and 1945, they provided much valuable information.

Naturally, there were many among these 30,000 refugees who provided little of value. Reports on each refugee were graded from A for 'completely reliable' through to D for the faintly Fawlty-esque 'ignorant fellows who may have noticed things but cannot be certain of them'. Photiadou writes that only 1.5 per cent made the A grade and 8 per cent the D grade.

But the A information, and some of the 90-odd per cent that fell in between A and D, was extremely useful, not least in the planning of the invasion of Normandy in the summer of 1944. One French hydrology engineer provided detail of coastal pumping stations and how their sabotage could cause flooding to hamper enemy troop movements. Other arrivals passed on information about coastal fortifications, particularly the formidable blockhouses guarding the most likely invasion sites along the French coast. One German deserter told his interrogators at Wandsworth that there were minefields beyond the coast at Cherbourg which could be detonated automatically and provided sketches to show their exact location. He also revealed information about the telephone communication system around this vital Normandy port. A Polish slave labourer who had escaped passed on information about submarine repair pens in the port of Lorient.

Cousins Henry Taymans and Joseph Abts, two refugees from Belgium who travelled for seventy-seven days across France, Spain, Portugal and Gibraltar to reach the Free Belgian forces in Britain, were interrogated by the War Office, Security Service officers and the Secret Intelligence Service at the Royal Victoria Patriotic School. They passed on the useful information that there was an arms dump in Forêt de Soignes, on the edge of Brussels. Tales like this are all too common – with refugees being treated with suspicion as potential enemy spies rather than as sources of great intelligence which would help the British war effort.

Other more nebulous information – such as the quality of rations available, the impact of Allied bombing, feelings about resistance activity and sundry other tell-tale indicators of life under Nazi-occupation – was also passed on to the government propaganda department and the BBC services, which was broadcasting to occupied Europe. Cannily, the wing of the BBC World Service broadcasting to Germany did not use native German speakers as its announcers. Instead, they used German-speaking British announcers with a slight accent, as it was felt that German listeners would react with hostility to 'traitors' from their own homeland, especially if it was discovered that these announcers were Jewish.*

On a darker note, detailed information also began to build up on the number and nature of Nazi concentration camps. Photiadou notes that one Czech engineer, who had escaped from the Natzweiler-Struthof concentration camp, informed his interrogator that he knew of twenty-seven concentration camps. Having been

---

* The penalty for listening to the BBC World Service in Germany, especially for serial offenders, was a trip to the guillotine, the standard method of execution for civilians in many German states. 'Undermining military strength' was the charge.

assigned an A grade when he first arrived, the engineer's information was deemed completely reliable.

Photiadou also reports on the chilling opinion of a German engineer who was interrogated by MI19 – the department in the British Directorate of Military Intelligence responsible for interrogating prisoners of war.

> The only salvation for Europe lies in Great Britain. The Americans will, after all, withdraw after a time to the US but Germany must be occupied for two generations as this Nazi poison has bitten into the bones of the whole people. All Germans from the age of eight to 30, are incurable. Time must elapse for them to die out and in the meantime Great Britain must exercise a rigid control, exterminating the trouble-makers and re-educating the tractable.

Coming from someone who was part of a regime that habitually executed its citizens for expressing doubt over the fact that the war could not be won, this opinion is slightly understandable, but it turned out not to be true. When Hitler killed himself and the war came to an end, the German people became surprisingly biddable in their desire to rub along with their conquerors. Nazi plans for an underground resistance following capitulation came to virtually nothing.

Altogether around fifty spies were discovered, out of the 30,000 refugees interrogated. British intelligence tried to 'turn' such spies – get them to work for them while maintaining the fiction that they were still active and out in the field. Those who refused invariably faced the usual punishment for spies in wartime: hanging.

The stories of Jewish refugees, many of whom had been interned,

fighting alongside the British in the war are extraordinary and illustrate the calibre of the people the British press were so quick to
denounce as dangerous Nazi spies and potential fifth columnists.
As Simon Parkin said in an interview with the *Times of Israel*:

> I think the issue of internment should be faced in some way – be-
> cause if not, then these things can keep happening, from generation
> to generation, if we don't hold up these stories as a warning for what
> can happen when paranoia is allowed to be whipped up in the na-
> tional press and anti-refugee rhetoric left to run riot.

Chapter 10

Other Newcomers to These Shores: GIs and POWs

One underlying theme to this book is how Britain, as a society, reacted to foreigners. During the Second World War, there was a huge influx of foreigners who weren't refugees. What were their experiences, and how did they compare with those of refugees?

Around 3 million American and Canadian military personnel came here during the war. Among them were 150,000 black soldiers, who were often treated with far more respect and dignity than they were in their home country. The attitude of Europeans in the 1930s and '40s towards people of colour is a sometimes unexpected one. In Britain, many people were repelled by the treatment of black American servicemen by their white American allies. And especially curiously, in Nazi Germany, where black people were the subject of repellent Nazi racist propaganda, this prejudice was not shared by all German people at all. The academic Edward Bourgoin, mentioned in Chapter 1, noted that when the African American academic W. E. B. Du Bois visited pre-war Germany, his treatment by the German population was fascinating. While Du Bois was keenly aware of the persecution of Germany's Jews, which he compared to the Spanish Inquisition and the African slave trade, he was also struck by how little rancour he attracted as 'a man of color'. He also noted that he was treated with considerably more courtesy in Nazi Germany than he was in the United States. Correspondingly, it's also notable that the American athlete Jesse Owens, who won four gold medals at the Berlin Olympics, was treated with similar courtesy, even admiration, by many German people, who mobbed him in the street and outside his accommodation. Hitler, on the other hand, refused to shake Owens's hand when he won his gold medals.

The arrival of this 'friendly invasion' of American servicemen, as it was sometimes referred to at the time, was a cause of some anxiety for both the British and the American military authorities. At the start of the war, Nazi propaganda was working full time to create division between Britain and her North American ally, and this was something that needed to be defused.

It was Britain's great good fortune that Churchill's government were able to forge such a close relationship with the United States. As well as soldiers who trained in the UK before they crossed the Channel to fight in France and Germany, the UK also housed over 200 bases for the US Army Air Force.

There were mixed feelings towards these overseas visitors. Alongside gratitude for their being here, there was a grudging resentment towards American servicemen that sometimes resulted in violence. Part of the problem was that American soldiers were paid around three times the wage of their British equivalents, and this wealth gave them quite an advantage when it came to attracting local British girls. Another issue was the blatant racism many white American soldiers displayed towards their black comrades.

David Dimbleby and David Reynolds's book *An Ocean Apart*, and the BBC documentary series of the same title, contains two telling quotes on these matters. In an interview with Dimbleby, Margaret Whiting, a Cambridge teenager during the war, remembers the Americans thus:

> To go to one of their bases was absolutely fantastic because there was no shortage of anything. Each base was a little America, with plenty of food and drink and fantastic great iced cakes. Every night you could, you were out. All the girls were doing it. It was a lovely atmosphere. At the dances they were really friendly. They'd just come up and say: 'Cut a rug?'

Dimbleby also interviewed John Wilson, who was in the RAF, about an incident on a train from Cardiff to York.

> The train was crowded but there was room next to me for another one. There was a coloured soldier outside [in the corridor]. I opened the door and said: 'Hey, Jack, there's a seat here.' The others in the compartment, except two of us, were all American soldiers. As soon as this coloured man sat down this other big chap got up and said: 'Get out, you goddam nigger.' I told him to belt up, and he came for me. My teeth were knocked right through my tongue.

The issue of segregation was a thorny one for the British government. Despite the closeness of their relationship, the Americans were determined that the outcome of the war would not strengthen the British Empire. The issue of India, in particular, irked Americans. How could the Allies be fighting for 'freedom', they felt, when India was essentially controlled entirely in Britain's interest? Churchill, in turn, used the American practice of segregation to bite back.

The experience of black American soldiers in Britain is a heartening one. Many of these men had come from the southern states, where black people were still treated with an extraordinary degree of disdain. Coming to a country where shops, pubs and dance halls paid no attention to 'the color bar' was a wonderful experience. Many British people, in turn, had never seen a black person. Either way, they warmed to these visitors, who were often considerably politer than their white American comrades, who could be what the British considered 'brash'.

But while ordinary people were keen to support these black soldiers, the government had a more difficult path to negotiate. They were keen to keep relations between their fighting services as cordial as possible and were particularly concerned with the thorny matter of black Americans 'dating' British women. This was also an issue that concerned the more conservative-minded British public. The War Office, write Dimbleby and Reynolds, even proposed a special campaign to encourage British troops to adopt the same exclusionary attitude of the American Army towards 'coloured troops'.

This caused great concern in the Colonial Office, which feared it would cause uproar among the subjects of the British Empire. The War Office moderated their approach. The Cabinet agreed instead that British troops should be asked to respect the attitude of their white American comrades and avoid arguments about race relations. A Cabinet memo laid down guidelines thus: 'For a white woman to go about in the company of a Negro American is likely to lead to controversy and ill-feeling.' And while it was 'acceptable for

British people to offer "friendly hospitality", care should be taken not to invite white and coloured troops at the same time'.

Intending to head off potential culture clashes, the United States War Department produced a leaflet entitled 'Over There: Instructions for American Servicemen in Britain, 1942'.* Written in a terse, no-nonsense style, the handbook offers a fascinating glimpse into the cultural differences between Britain and America, and, allowing for the fact that it *is* Allied propaganda, it gives us something of the ability 'to see ourselves as others see us', to quote Robert Burns.

The advice is winningly sensible: 'Look, listen and learn before you start telling the British how much better we do things.' And frank: 'The British don't know how to make a good cup of coffee. You don't know how to make a good cup of tea.' Rather poignantly, the newly arrived soldier is reminded: 'You are coming to Britain from a country where your home is still safe, food is still plentiful, and lights are still burning.'

Right from page one, the American soldier is told that this is 'no time to fight old wars', mentioning especially the colonial struggle in Ireland and the American Revolution. The British 'can be plenty tough', the reader is told.

The soldier is also told to respect British women in uniform, and that there is 'no shame' in obeying orders from a female officer. British women had been putting their lives in danger, not least in their work in air raids and anti-aircraft crews. 'When you see a girl in khaki or air-force blue with a bit of ribbon† on her tunic –

---

* The Bodleian Library – University of Oxford – produced a facsimile pamphlet in 1994 which is still in print.
† For readers unfamiliar with British and American military traditions, men and women who had won medals did not usually wear them on their uniforms – instead they had a small piece of colourful fabric indicating the medal mounted on a metal strip which they attached to their uniform with a pin. Soldiers in the Soviet Union, on the other hand, wore their medals on their chests as they went into combat.

remember she didn't get it for knitting more socks than anyone else in Ipswich.'

The pamphlet was a precursor to the more widely known information film *A Welcome to Britain*. Curiously, 'Over There' contains no mention of the likelihood of friction between the British and Americans caused by white American hostility towards black American soldiers. But *A Welcome to Britain* makes this a central issue.

The film is a wonderful curiosity.* Running for forty minutes, it was produced by the British War Office and Ministry of Information, with help from the US Office of War, to accommodate this massive influx of American military personnel. Here Burgess Meredith† acts as an American in Britain, giving information, often direct to camera, to newly arrived soldiers and airbase personnel about how to behave in this unfamiliar European country. Beginning with a jaunty First World War show tune, George M. Cohan's 'Over There',‡ we are swiftly introduced to two 'top brass' officers, one American, the other British, who announces: 'This picture is a gift from us to you and is an attempt to show you a little of what England is about. We want to make you feel at home here.' The film introduces its audience to that cross-cultural flashpoint, the pub. As a variety of British people sit around with their pints (for the men) and shorts (for the ladies), a brash American soldier strolls in and announces: 'Well, England. Here I am!' After wading into a

---

* The film is available on YouTube, although a section on prostitution and the risk of catching a venereal disease has been deleted. 'There's been a lot of jokes on this subject,' warns Burgess Meredith in the uncensored version. 'Just make sure the joke's not on you.'

† Meredith is probably best remembered for his role as George Milton in the 1939 Hollywood adaptation of John Steinbeck's *Of Mice and Men*. He worked in a variety of roles in cinema and TV almost throughout his life and even played the Penguin in the fondly remembered 1960s *Batman* TV series, as well as Sylvester Stallone's trainer in the *Rocky* films.

‡ Readers with an unhealthy curiosity in high-kitsch might like to track down 'Freedom's Call' by the girl group USA Freedom Kids, on YouTube – a nightmarish electro-pop reworking of the original Cohan song performed at a Trump rally in 2016 and thereafter an internet sensation.

game of darts, he proceeds to throw his money around and teases a couple of Scotsmen who are wearing kilts. Meredith, cringing in the corner, snaps his fingers and the American soldier disappears in a puff of smoke. Do not mock Scottish people, he warns; 'they're tough.' Meredith spends the rest of the film being charmingly courteous to the locals, who respond with a diffident friendliness.

The most telling moment in the film comes when Meredith tries to tackle a British train compartment door as it arrives at a station and is helped by a black soldier. As they stand together on the platform, an old lady leans out of the carriage window and tells them what a pleasure it's been to meet them and how they must come round for tea if they are ever in Birmingham.*

At this point, Meredith addresses his viewer directly, as the black soldier stands awkwardly beside him. While this sort of invitation 'might not happen at home', he says, there are less 'social restrictions for coloured boys' in Britain and he urges Americans to beware of the prejudices they are bringing to this country. Fortuitously, General John C. H. Lee, who oversees the logistical divisions that black soldiers are usually posted to, is there at the station. They walk over to talk to him as Meredith reminds us that Lee comes from Kansas and his family fought for the Confederacy in the American Civil War. Nonetheless, the general tells the viewers that 'America has promised the Negro† real citizenship and a fair chance to make the best of himself ... Everyone's treated the same when it comes to

---

*   I think we can assume the woman chosen to invite them for tea was deliberately cast as an old lady, because using a young woman in this role would have suggested the possibility of 'impropriety' and that ugly word 'miscegenation'. During the Second World War, thirty out of the then forty-eight American states had laws forbidding interracial marriage. (As did, no surprises, the Nazis.) Interracial marriage has never been illegal in Britain, although, until recently, social convention made it a somewhat rare event.
†   Curiously, Lee pronounces this now obsolete term as 'nigra'.

dying, so it wouldn't be true to America if it didn't try to live up to the promises about an equal chance."

But in practice, the problems black servicemen faced in Britain were almost entirely from their fellow countrymen, particularly with regard to black GIs escorting white British women. One pilot from Kentucky, Captain Vernon Gayle Alexander, commented: 'The blacks were dating the white girls and consequently if you went on a date [with] a white girl you didn't know if she'd been out with a coloured boy† the night before or whether she hadn't.' This visceral racist disgust is reminiscent of those incidents where public or hotel swimming pools in America were drained and refilled if black people had swum in them.

But this racism by white Americans towards black GIs some-times led to violence in Britain. The most serious incident occurred in June 1943 at an army supply base outside Preston, Lancashire, called Bamber Bridge. Posted here were the black logistics regi-ment US Eighth Army Quartermaster Truck Company.

American military policemen had called for a ban on black servicemen visiting the three pubs in Bamber Bridge and local publicans had reacted angrily against this by putting up signs outside their premises stating 'Black Troops Only'. The ill feeling this caused between black and white Americans rapidly escalated and fights broke out between black servicemen and white military policemen. On one occasion, shots were exchanged. This turned into a full-scale shooting match, which resulted in one dead black

---

* This was not true at the time. Aside from the famous black fighter squadron the Tuskegee Airmen, who feature in the Hollywood film *Red Tails*, and the soldiers of the 761st Tank Battalion later in the war, most black servicemen were kept away from combat roles. So much so that only a reported 708 black servicemen died in the Second World War. (In comparison, over 7,200 black American servicemen died in Vietnam.)

† The black jazz musician habit of calling each other 'man', adopted by white hippies in the 1960s and '70s on both sides of the Atlantic, comes from the American racist use of 'boy' when addressing any black male.

soldier. Several other soldiers, both black and white, were injured. Courts martial resulted in sentences of hard labour, but the incident prompted General Ira Eaker, commander of the American Eighth Air Force, to introduce mixed black and white military police patrols. The 'Battle of Bamber Bridge', as it became known by the locals, resulted in a minor news report in a local paper, but the incident was hushed up in the national press, as it had a clear propaganda value to the enemy and ominous potential to inflame race relations among American servicemen.

While undoubtedly some black Americans would have faced racist behaviour in Britain by local people, on the whole, they were welcomed and well regarded by their British hosts. One black GI was reported as saying: 'I'm treated so a man don't know he's colored until he looks in the mirror."* The general treatment of these servicemen reflects the way the British like to see themselves – as fair-minded, decent people. Curiously, this jars with the impression gleaned from previous chapters, that Britain could be unwelcoming to Jewish refugees, who were seen as objects of suspicion, especially at the start of the war. It is likely that the black servicemen's status as an Allied force, versus European refugees being potential 'enemy aliens' and fifth columnists, contributed significantly to this difference in treatment.

But British respect and courtesy towards black soldiers went only so far. While 100,000† British women became 'GI brides' at the end of the war, marriage between Brits and black Americans was, in effect, forbidden. American servicemen had to have permission from their commanding officers to marry and, in accordance with American attitudes at the time, this was invariably refused in the

---

* Black American musicians who came to tour Britain in the wake of the '60s 'blues boom' also found that the warm welcome they received contrasted noticeably with how they were often treated in their own country.

† This figure incorporates estimates for both American and Canadian marriages to British women.

case of black soldiers and white British women. But there were some 2,000 'brown babies', as they were known at the time, born to British women during the war and almost all of these 'illegitimate' babies were adopted or placed in children's homes.

This subject was covered with passion and sensitivity by the British TV journalist Sean Fletcher in the Channel 4 documentary *Britain's Secret War Babies*, first broadcast in the UK in August 2022. The programme offered a fascinating glimpse both into official government attitudes and the lives of the women who had relationships with black servicemen and the children who were subsequently born to them. Fletcher calls these 2,000 babies 'the first significant generation to be born black and British'. This is debatable, of course. Britain had had black communities for several centuries, mostly in big city ports such as Liverpool, Cardiff, Bristol and London. But Fletcher reports that these 2,000 'brown babies' increased the black population of Britain by 30 per cent.

Fletcher looked at the lives of two of these children, Mary and John, and examined how being born illegitimate and black had affected them.

Mary was born in South Wales in 1944, to a Welsh mother and a black Medical Corps serviceman from St Louis, Missouri. Brought up by her grandparents, she never actually lived with her own mother and her husband, who married some years after Mary was born. Her story is accompanied by a tragic twist worthy of Thomas Hardy in that her black GI father wrote to her mother asking them both to come and live with him in America. Alas, the letter was intercepted by Mary's grandmother, who never showed it to her daughter. When Mary found out about this, she relates: 'Grandma said, "They're not going over there." And that was the end of it.'

Growing up, Mary had naturally felt different from other Welsh children and divided her contemporaries into those who treated her as a friend and those who were abusive towards her. (She was, she remembers, habitually called 'a nigger bastard'.) This indeed was one of the great problems facing the children of these black servicemen – not only were they illegitimate, not least because their parents were forbidden to marry, but they were also mixed-race at a time when this was unusual.

In 2022, when the programme was made, Mary was a spritely 77-year-old. She lived a comfortable life in Bristol, surrounded by her own three children, but she felt haunted by a sense of isolation and the life that had been denied to her. After her mother and stepfather died, she began to search in earnest for her biological father. She was after, so she told Sean Fletcher, 'closure'. So, aided by the research skills of a television documentary team, Mary discovered that her father was called Herman Askew.

Fletcher unearthed fascinating documents illustrating government attitudes at the time, including a memorandum from the Secretary of State for War. In particular, there was a concern that white American soldiers would lose respect for Britain if they saw 'British people showing no distinction between white and colored troops'.

The memorandum recommended that the British population should be encouraged to adopt the American convention out of respect for their ally. It noted, most especially, that 'from the point of view of the morale of our own troops … it is most undesirable that there should be any unnecessary association between American colored troops and British women'.

Fletcher's other subject was an amiable, lanky 77-year-old called John. His story is a sadder one than Mary's. His mother had an affair with a black American soldier who had been billeted at her guest house in Weymouth. She was already married to Les, a soldier who had been posted to France following the D-Day landings. When he returned, she had given birth to a black baby and, understandably, John was to become a considerable cause of animosity between husband and wife. John remembers his father as a cruel man who often beat him, adding that 'he should have left then, when he saw that little black baby'. To add to this sorry tale, his mother's lover was also married and keen to keep his English child a secret.

Perhaps Les thought he was 'doing the decent thing' staying with his wife, despite her carrying another man's child. It was not a recipe for happiness. John recalls Les beating both himself and his mother, and a childhood where 'the N-word was quite common'. People would often taunt him with the well-worn racist cry 'Go back to your own country.' Unsurprisingly, he grew up feeling out of place. 'Where do I go? Where is my country?'

His mother never discussed the relationship that had brought him into the world. He was thirty-seven before he realised his father must have been a black GI.

Sean Fletcher's documentary clearly demonstrates the pain these illegitimate, mixed-race children endured and the unhappy, dislocated lives they've lived. The chief constable of Oxford wrote to the Home Office during the war to demand that 'every step must be taken to stop British women misconducting themselves with coloured troops – if for no other reason that we do not desire to have a certain proportion of the population semi-coloured in rural districts in the country in the future'.

More often than not, the child of a relationship between a white woman and a black soldier was rapidly despatched to a children's home. Here, if they were lucky, they would be adopted into a loving home or, more than likely, remain in an institution for the rest of their childhood.

In his documentary, Fletcher reported on one such child, Anne, from South Wales. She was sent to the Holnicote House children's home in Somerset six days after she was born. In an interview broadcast in the programme, Anne told Fletcher:

My mother had to get rid of me because she had told her fiancé she was pregnant and he was in France at the time so they flew him home in order to marry her, but of course she didn't know who was the father of the baby she was expecting ... so he flew back from France. Of course, when she had me she knew it wasn't his.

The husband was told his wife had had a stillbirth.

The story gets darker. 'Her mother blackmailed her about it,' says Anne. 'Do this or I'll tell him about the so-called baby you lost.'

Anne discovered that her mother did not keep in touch with her in the children's home because 'her husband was racist and he would never forgive [her]'. The couple went to their deaths without the husband ever knowing his wife had given birth to a black baby. Fortunately, the story has a happy ending. Anne was successfully adopted when she was five.

Britain's Secret War Babies does indeed end on some note of 'closure'. Both Mary and John are reunited with their American side of the family. John's father died in the 1960s and Mary's in 1983. But they are now both in contact with siblings they had hitherto known nothing about.

Perhaps, in an ideal world, these children should have been

allowed to be with their biological parents. Yet in America, mixed-race marriages have been permitted in all states only since 1967 – the 2016 film *Loving* dramatises this state of affairs. In the UK, mixed-race marriages, although unusual until relatively recently, have never been illegal.

'There's always been something missing,' says Mary. 'There's always been a hole.' She spent her life feeling stigmatised. 'Before, I used to shy away from things because I never thought I was good enough.' The programme helped her feel more at ease with the world.

For John, it helped him answer a question that had haunted him. 'I've always had the strange feeling that when I saw an American flag, that was my flag.'

But Sean Fletcher ends his programme with a sad point: 'Most [of these 2,000 children were] unable to trace their fathers. They knew they were different, but they were unable to fully embrace who they were.'

And that is the saddest legacy of the 'brown babies'. They were born into a country where only some people were able to accept them as they were, despite the warm welcome their black GI fathers had received during the war. The result was a lifetime of feeling dislocated and out of place, and a sense that they had been deprived of the natural course of their life. And, of course, an eternity of running a gauntlet of racist taunts. Refugee children, in comparison, were treated with more compassion. I suppose this tells us something highly uncomfortable about our attitude, in the 1940s, to sexual relations between white and black people. Here, at least, there has been a transparent change in public attitudes. Even twenty years after the war, only 3 per cent of marriages were between couples of different racial origins. By 2022, the figure was 20 per cent.

*   *   *

During the Second World War, Britain also became the home of hundreds of thousands of German and Italian prisoners of war – and many more passed through the country en route to prison camps in America and Canada. At the start of the conflict, prisoners of war arrived in specific groups – mainly German U-boat crews or Italian prisoners captured in Africa. When German prisoners arrived in the early years of the war, and defeat still seemed possible for Britain, they were shipped off to Canada, although some also went to South Africa and even India. It was only when the war had turned incontrovertibly against Germany following the Normandy landings in 1944 that German prisoners remained in British camps in any number.

It is a huge credit to this country that only 0.03 per cent of German prisoners of war died in British captivity. A mutual understanding existed between the British and the Germans that they would keep to the Geneva Convention and treat prisoners fairly. Prisoners were expected to work, but their hours were reasonable. In Britain, they worked a six-day week, usually nine to five – the kind of hours an ordinary British labourer would be expected to do. According to the convention, the work was not directly linked to the war effort but included agriculture, forestry, brick-making and general public works.

In comparison, on the Eastern Front, 35 per cent of German prisoners died in Soviet camps. But, then, the Nazis treated their Soviet prisoners with extraordinary cruelty too and an estimated 60 per cent of Russian prisoners died in German captivity.

Hundreds of prisoner-of-war camps sprang up throughout the UK and held an estimated 400,000 German, Italian and other prisoners from countries allied to the Nazis.

Almost as soon as they joined the war, Italian prisoners were regarded differently than German prisoners, although that did not stop some of them being transported abroad as we have seen in Chapter 8. Unlike the Germans who were fellow northern Europeans, the Italians had an element of southern European exoticism and some even formed romantic attachments with British girls, much to the disgust of British soldiers serving overseas who were confronted with photographs of these soldiers working side by side in the fields with British land girls. The Italians, too, were considered to be far friendlier – political indoctrination had had a far greater effect on German prisoners.

Academic Sarah Franklin writes in the *Irish Times* that Italian prisoners were so well liked by locals that some even formed football teams to play in local leagues. Prisoners who were trusted by the British authorities were allowed to work outside the camps in factories and farms and paid the local rate. Staff at Yealand Manor School (see Chapter 6) who taught the children music, gave over 100 concerts for Italian soldiers in a local prisoner-of-war camp. Sometimes, the Italians were even let out of the camp to visit the school. The children greeted these men warmly, shouting St Francis of Assisi's famous dictum '*Fratelli tutti*' ('We are all brothers'). Robin Greaves, who was the daughter of the Yealand Manor headmistress, remembers Italian prisoners being brought by bus from their prison camp at Milnthorpe to do gardening work in local parks and grounds. The children from the school would sit with them and help them learn English. That no one seemed to think it was a poor idea to teach enemy soldiers the language of the country they were held prisoner in speaks volumes about how these Italians were seen by the local population.*

German prisoners were a more tricky proposition. Unlike the Italians, who were often unwilling participants in what they saw as Germany's war, the German prisoners were more likely to continue to embrace their Nazi indoctrination. Those who indicated their zealous adherence to Hitler's regime were required to wear a black armband alongside their standard uniform. Although escapes were few, fifty-six German prisoners of war did get away via a tunnel from a camp in South Wales in March 1945 – their determination an indication of their continued support to the Nazi regime. All of them were recaptured.

Bob Moore, professor of twentieth-century European history at Sheffield University, relates the tale of a German prisoner at a camp on the south coast, at the end of the war, who was considered safe enough to be put to work helping locals with their gardening. After he was relocated, the daffodils he planted sprouted and spelled out the words 'HEIL HITLER'.

Moore writes that there was a clear divide between the younger and older German prisoners. The young ones, especially, seemed particularly reluctant to give up their Nazi beliefs. The non-stop in-doctrination of their childhood and youth would take much longer to wear off. The Americans and Canadians were also perturbed by

---

* Antony Beevor's excellent book *Stalingrad* contains a marvellous description of the Red Army's first contact with Italian troops. The Russians were astonished not to have met any resistance from these soldiers. They asked an Italian sergeant why his men had not fired on them. 'We did not fire back because we thought it would be a mistake,' he replied. As a fully paid-up Italophile, I have every sympathy for him.

the fanaticism of some of their German prisoners. One newspaper article entitled 'German Prisoners Talk Your Ears Off' by Ernest O. Hauser, in the *Saturday Evening Post* of 20 January 1945, mused:

> The mind of a defeated German looks like one of the cities which his own stupendous crime caused to be laid waste. It is, and will remain, a vacuum. Perhaps a new ideal would rush into it with the force and velocity of air rushing into a vacuum – who knows.

But some German prisoners, like the Italians, did make friends with their British captors. The Imperial War Museum website tells us that 25,000 German prisoners of war made such good friendships and were made to feel so welcome in Britain that they decided they wanted to stay in the country rather than return home.

Ultimately, the black American soldiers, despite the perceived issue of them 'dating' white women, and German and Italian prisoners of war were fortunate in their experiences of coming to Britain. But some uncomfortable undercurrents still swirled around with regard to Jewish refugees. And they became even more apparent as the war drew to an end.

Chapter 11

'It Only Makes Me Hate
Them More': Antisemitism
and the Camps

Jewish people have been subjected to a bizarre jumble of conspiracy theories for millennia. Some of these would rival the
nonsense peddled by QAnon – the worldwide collusion, the child
sacrifices, the secret cabal of white slavers...

Other more low-level, everyday prejudices – stereotypes that Jews
are greedy, miserly, evasive – have persisted too. But despite being
ridiculous, these widespread beliefs have undermined empathy or
support for Jews throughout history – just as the 'tree-hugger' taunt
of climate-change deniers in the late twentieth century undermined
sympathy for a more ecologically responsible outlook and the
right-wing taunt of 'woke' demeans anyone with a scintilla of social
concern.

It is difficult for us in the 2020s to imagine the casual antisemitism of the era covered by this book. But in the 1930s and '40s, anti-
Jewish sentiments were ingrained in all levels of society. Indeed, the
amiable humorist P. G. Wodehouse was quoted by his biographer,

Robert McCrum, as saying: 'Aren't the Jews extraordinary people. They seem to infuriate all nations."

For many people in Britain, the war, and the influx of Jewish refugees, only intensified this hostility. And even when presented with the most appalling consequences of antisemitism – the Nazi death camps – some people chose to disbelieve or play down what they were told. For others, it simply increased the resentment they felt against Jews, reasoning strangely that they had brought this calamity upon themselves. In an April 1945 article for the *Contemporary Jewish Record*, George Orwell† wrote that 'there is more antisemitism in England than we care to admit, and the war has accentuated it ... It does not at present lead to open persecution, but it has the effect of making people callous to the sufferings of Jews in other countries.'

In the conclusion of the article, he writes: 'The point is that something, some psychological vitamin, is lacking in modern civilisation, and as a result we are all more or less subject to this lunacy of believing that whole races or nations are mysteriously good or mysteriously evil.'

Even as the war raged, antisemitism remained a tangible part of everyday life and conversation. The Nazi propagandist William Joyce ('Lord Haw-Haw') had an estimated 6 million regular listeners and 18 million occasional listeners for his broadcasts to wartime Britain. In 1943, Oswald Mosley and his wife Diana were released from prison. Perhaps this emboldened their followers. Graffiti declaring

---

* The debate over the extent of Wodehouse's antisemitism rages to this day. Some quote him musing: 'I do not dislike people in the plural.' Others seem to be convinced he was a virulent antisemite. See the website 'Plumtopia' (honoriaplum.com) for further discussions.

† Orwell biographer D. J. Taylor also considers whether his subject had some element of antisemitism in him, quoting from Orwell's diary of 1931 when he was living rough. He writes that he had met 'a little Liverpool Jew of eighteen, a thorough guttersnipe. I do not know when I have seen anyone who disgusted me quite as much as this boy.' Orwell describes 'a face that recalled some low-down carrion-eating bird'. The fact that a renowned humanitarian like Orwell could think like that rather illustrates the all-pervasive quality of antisemitic feeling in his era.

'The Jews caused this War', 'Jews War – they plan it, make it, finance it, and you fight it' and other slogans began to appear on city walls, along with the initials 'P. J.', the Nazi slogan 'Perish Judah'. Snide remarks about the 'Chosen Race' were commonplace, as Orwell pointed out in his article for the *Contemporary Jewish Record*:

> Middle-aged office employee: 'I generally come to work by bus. It takes longer, but I don't care about using the Underground from Golders Green nowadays. There's too many of the Chosen Race travelling on that line.'
>
> Tobacconist (woman): 'No, I've got no matches for you. I should try the lady down the street. She's always got matches. One of the Chosen Race, you see.'

To cite another example of this everyday prejudice, a bomb shelter stampede at Bethnal Green, which killed 173 in March 1943, was widely believed to have been 'caused by panicking Jews'. This was a complete fabrication. Only five Jewish victims of the disaster were identified among the dead. But people wanted to believe that Jews had behaved in a way that was 'un-British'.

Tony Kushner, in his book *The Persistence of Prejudice*, makes the point that, alongside the national press, local newspapers – often owned by right-wing proprietors and shamelessly devoted to pandering to readers' prejudices – could print the most implausible stories about newly arrived refugees. The *Hampstead & Highgate Express*, for instance, persisted in peddling the myth that Jewish refugees were foreign agents who 'should never be allowed at liberty in the country'. Other north London local papers, such as the *Hendon & Finchley Times* and the *Kilburn Times*, also ran similar stories. Such local papers were particularly prone to running these stories as thousands of refugees had settled in these areas of London.

Moreover, some national papers also fed this prejudice. In 1942, for example, *The Grocer* trade magazine reported forty-eight cases of black market activity. Only three involved Jewish perpetrators, yet it was these three cases that received national press attention.[*]

The black market remained a particular focus of antisemitism throughout the war. In the August 1942 newsletter of the Association of Jewish Refugees is a piece entitled 'Jews and Black Market' which notes:

> In view of the often repeated accusation that there is a high percentage of Jewish offenders in the Black Market, our members will be interested in the following publication, which appeared in the *Evening Standard* on the 25th July: 'I am told at the request of some Jewish bodies in this country a member of the Royal Statistical Society is now engaged in preparing complete figures of Black Market prosecutions, showing how many Jews and Gentiles respectively have been convicted. The results should help to kill any incipient anti-semitism in this country, if, indeed, the purveyors of this racial prejudice are amenable to facts. In a recent five-week period for instance, for which figures are available, out of a total of 50 cases only in three were any Jews involved. Even the most devoted followers of Julius Streicher[†] might have some difficulty in drawing up an indictment against a whole people on this slender basis.'

---

[*] There is an echo of this in the current national press obsession with Muslim 'grooming gangs', which the present government has also framed as part of their culture wars. (A Home Office report of 2020 concluded that 'research has found that group-based child sexual exploitation offenders are most commonly white', but you would never guess this if your knowledge of the subject was only headlines in tabloid newspapers.

[†] Streicher was one of the Nazis' most infamous antisemites and was the founder and publisher of *Der Stürmer*, the Nazi propaganda newspaper.

Another baseless claim was quoted in the *Jewish Chronicle* of 24 July 1942.

> In the *Shields Gazette* Mr A. Robinson of 45, Bede Terrace, Hebburn, had used the most virulent language against Jews as black marketers, saying 'Nine times out of ten the offender bears what appears to be a Jewish name. The Jewish gold-worshippers are fast losing public sympathy.' The same letter was also published in the *Northern Echo* of Darlington. On investigating the matter, the Rev. M. Landau of South Shields, found that there was no such street, and therefore no Mr Robinson living there.*

Antisemitism sometimes took on a more opaque shade. The Association of Jewish Refugees newsletter reported that the fur trade periodical *Fur Record*, in an article entitled 'Blots on the Trade', referred to 'people with sinister names' – a euphemism no doubt understood by those who reacted with a shudder to surnames like Metzenbaum or Rabinowitz.

Later in the same issue, in a piece entitled 'The Position of Refugees', the Association of Jewish Refugees implores:

> Our special situation demands that our behaviour should be impeccably correct and beyond reproach. Each individual Jewish refugee bears a heavy responsibility. Whenever he goes wrong, he does not only imperil himself and his own future – he does so to the detriment of the whole refugee community with which his fate and his acts are invariably bound up.†

---

* I looked this up. There is still no Bede Terrace in Hebburn, although there is a Bede Walk, which is full of post-war council houses.
† Curiously, in a *Guardian* article on 1 May 2023, Duwayne Brooks, who was with Stephen Lawrence on the night he was murdered by racist thugs in 1993, said something entirely similar.

Tony Kushner also points out that it was popularly believed that there were no Jews in the army – despite the fact that many erroneously believed that 'the Jews' had started the war. As detailed in Chapter 9, around 10,000 Jewish refugees joined the Pioneer Corps before they were allowed to join combat units in 1943. Kushner also quotes an army sergeant saying to one Jewish soldier: 'You know I hate Jews … but if all Jews were like you, they would be a wonderful people.' (How wearily familiar this would be to black and Asian immigrants – especially in the 1960s and '70s – in their works canteen conversations.)

Perhaps most shocking of all, Orwell, again in his article for the *Contemporary Jewish Record*, considers attitudes to news of the Holocaust: 'Intelligent woman, on being offered a book dealing with antisemitism and German atrocities: "Don't show it to me, please don't show it to me. It'll only make me hate the Jews more than ever."'

Orwell goes on to say: 'I could fill pages with similar remarks, but these will do to go on with.'

But even as the Holocaust raged, antisemitism thrived. Even between fellow refugees it remained a problem. Among the thousands of Polish soldiers who had escaped to Britain and become part of the Polish Army in exile, antisemitism was so strong that 224 of the 800 Jewish soldiers among them actually deserted and tried to join the British Army instead. Jewish soldiers had been taunted with the threat that when they went back to Poland after the war they would be killed. (This, in fact, happened to many returning Jews in the months after the war, especially if Polish people had moved into the houses or apartments they had once occupied. See Chapter 12.)

By the summer of 1942, terrible stories were reaching the UK

– the first that hinted that the Nazis had gone from random murder and sadistic bullying to the infinitely more horrifying mass extermination. At first, these reports were carried in specialist Jewish publications. In August 1942, for example, the newsletter from the Association of Jewish Refugees reported in a news feature headlined 'Stern News' that 'our hearts are filled with grief and sorrow these days. Each day brings sad news to some of our friends, news of unspeakable crimes committed by the Nazis against our brothers and sisters on the Continent, helpless victims of a brutality unheard of since the darkest ages of mankind.'

News of mass extermination was first formally recognised in Parliament and 'made known to the British public' in December 1942. Early in the next year, this occasionally made headlines in the national papers. On 15 February 1943, for example, the *Mirror* ran the headline 'Huns Kill 6,000 Jews a Day in Part of Poland'. On 20 April 1943, the *Mail* reported 'Half of World's Jews in Peril: 2,000,000 Killed by Nazis'. But these stories were so shocking and horrible they were difficult to believe. Even the British Foreign Office was sceptical.

Some historians, such as Keith Lowe, in his magnificent account of the aftermath of the Second World War in Europe *Savage Continent*, believed that the government deliberately played down this terrible news, 'in case they might then be expected to do something about it'.

The whole business of British knowledge and reaction to the camps is a complicated one, not least because the facts pertaining to this industrial-scale murder of a whole race were so unbelievable. This was particularly pertinent as barely twenty years before, the British public had been fed, and largely believed, atrocity propaganda lies about the behaviour of Germany in the First World War,* and this had done much to undermine belief in the worst behaviour of 'the enemy'. But as the evidence for the Holocaust began to mount, the National Council for Civil Liberties became increasingly concerned. In March 1943, they even asked the government if they were waiting until all the Jews in Europe were dead before they were going to act.

Debate continues to this day about why the Allies did not do more to help Europe's beleaguered Jews. Perhaps more visas could have been granted for Jews who had escaped to neutral countries, but this idea was scotched in case Germany smuggled in its own agents and saboteurs among the refugees – a justification that is still reeled out today for refusing to accept desperate people. Another form of action suggested was to turn the RAF and American Eighth Army Air Force against the concentration camps and death camps and the railway lines taking Jews to their deaths. But this too was rejected – possibly because it would involve killing some of the very people it was supposed to be saving but also because it would detract from the main purpose of the Allied bombing campaign: namely, destroying Germany's industrial strength and undermining the morale of the German population. Besides, the casualty rate among British and American airmen was head and shoulders above that of other services. Nearly half of RAF aircrews (46 per cent) died in the war. The American death rate for their airmen was similar.

It is both chilling and illuminating to see how news of the

---

* The most infamous of these First World War propaganda stories concerned the German use of the corpses of their own dead soldiers in a *Kadaververwertungsanstalt* – 'Carcass-Utilisation Factory'. The facilities were supposed to have been designed to produce valuable components from munitions to household detergents from these rendered bodies. The story was originally concocted to appeal to China, which the British hoped to inveigle as an ally, as the Chinese were known to have a particular reverence for their dead relatives. Britain at this time, though, was a society where a fictional story by Arthur Machen in the London *Evening News* and later in the *Illustrated London News*, about ghostly angel bowmen – possibly from Agincourt – coming to the rescue of beleaguered British soldiers during the Battle of Mons, was also widely believed.

Holocaust gradually filtered through to Britain and these following reports show how the Association of Jewish Refugees and the *Jewish Chronicle* gradually pieced together a nightmare jigsaw puzzle of barely believable facts and supposition.

In June 1943, the Association of Jewish Refugees newsletter ran a piece entitled 'A Twelve Point Programme for Immediate Rescue Methods'. The proposals included:

Relaxation of visa requirements.

Encouragement to Neutral States to admit more refugees.

Provision of new Refugee Camps.

Admission to Palestine, especially of those refugees for whom geographical reasons Palestine is the most convenient place of temporary refuge.

Continued pressure on German Satellites to refrain from cruelties and deportations and to let their potential victims go.

Examination of the Possibilities of exchanging Civilian Internees with Axis sympathisers now under British and Allied control for potential victims under enemy control.

Frequent Appeals by Radio and Leaflet to the people of all Enemy and Enemy-occupied countries, making known the facts of the persecution and urging the peoples on grounds of humanity and religion to resist it by succouring the victims.

In the same newsletter, another article appears:

JEWS ON THE CONTINENT

We have tried to compile some information that has reached the country about the present situation on the Continent, though our friends will of course realise that it is very difficult to verify some of the facts referred to.

From all information available it seems that conditions at Theresienstadt are better than in other camps.

Between 60–70,000 Jews in Holland have already been deported or are in concentration camps awaiting deportation.

The Lithuanian Bishop, Mgr Brizgis, has excommunicated Lithuanians taking part in the persecution of Jews and Poles with the help of the Nazis.

The American Institute of Jewish Affairs stated that Jews in Europe receive only 20 per cent of the food which is indispensable to maintain life, whereas the German population receive 94 per cent. Jews get no meat, fish, poultry, milk, butter, cheese, fruit or vegetables. Jewish forced labourers receive none of the added protective foods and fats which are allocated to all other countries. Able-bodied Jews of German and Axis Europe are generally forced to do arduous work in quarries, iron, coal and sulphur mines or road construction gangs, in saw mills and in textile factories turning out uniforms for the army. In the Baltic areas, in Belgium, Greece, Hungary and Romania, Jews never receive more than half the rations which the remainder of the population gets. In the Polish ghettoes the rations consist of 1lb of black bread, 2oz of jam, 1oz of sugar and some potatoes.

The newsletter goes on to report:

It is becoming more and more difficult to find out the whereabouts of people deported by the Nazis who refuse to collaborate in any attempts to do so. The Red Cross are now as always doing their utmost to assist enquirers, but it is very rare now that their investigations are successful. On the other hand, there is always the chance that people who have not written for a long time are in hiding somewhere, and it would be very unwise to draw attention to them by making enquiries.

The Association of Jewish Refugees then goes on to list what they know about specific areas of Nazi-controlled Europe.

POLAND

Everything humanly possible is being done in this connection [discovering the fate of the Jews in Poland] but it should be realised that tremendous difficulties stand in the way of finding out anything in territories that have been a theatre of war for five years.

HUNGARY

At the moment of writing, deportations from Hungary have stopped.

THERESIENSTADT

There is no confirmation of the rumour according to which Theresienstadt camp is being evacuated.

BIRKENAU

Parcels to Birkenau in Upper Silesia may still be sent if a person is known to have been sent there.

HOLLAND

From the information received we gather that most Jewish people in Holland were sent to camps during the last year, and many of them were redeported from these camps.

BERGEN-BELSEN

This camp is situated near Celle, Hanover. People known to have been sent there may be contacted through the Red Cross Message Scheme.

ITALY

Letters and money may be sent to places in Southern Italy liberated by the Allied Armies.

SHANGHAI

Messages through the Red Cross may be sent to Shanghai, other forms of communication are still impossible.

Even as hard evidence of the camps accrued in the final months of the war, the reluctance to believe the news was still evident. When Auschwitz was liberated by the Red Army at the end of January 1945, the reports and photographs made available were dismissed as unreliable communist propaganda. Given the nature of the Soviet regime, and the appalling crimes it perpetrated against its own people, perhaps this is understandable.

But even when they accepted the fact that these camps existed, the British media was still reluctant to believe that they were as bad as reports indicated. The actual death camps – such as Treblinka, Bełżec and Sobibór – were discovered by advancing Soviet troops, and news of them was once again dismissed as Soviet propaganda. The BBC refused to broadcast a story about Majdanek, the first of the death camps to be discovered in late 1944. The American papers took a similar attitude. The *New York Herald Tribune*, writes Keith Lowe, reacted thus: 'Even on top of all we have been taught of the maniacal Nazi ruthlessness, this example sounds inconceivable.'

It was only when British and American soldiers liberated the westerly concentration camps, such as Belsen and Dachau, that the news was taken seriously in the West. For many British people, it is the shocking Movietone News footage of skeletal corpses being bulldozed into mass graves that remains their abiding image of the camps. I certainly remember, more than any other image from my childhood TV watching, this exact footage being used to shocking effect in the majestic *The World at War* documentary series, narrated so brilliantly by Laurence Olivier. There is an oil painting of Belsen in the Imperial War Museum collection by war artist Leslie Cole entitled *One of the Death Pits*. It is not currently on display but can be easily found online. More than anything else it recalls one of Hieronymus Bosch's nightmare paintings, or the skeletal army in Bruegel's *The Triumph of Death*.

The existence of the camps rendered insignificant any moral squeamishness about the way the Allies had conducted the war – not least the wholesale destruction of German cities by the RAF and American Eighth Air Force, although debate on the Allied bombing campaign still continues to this day.*

For British people, it was only when Belsen was liberated by British and Canadian troops in the middle of April 1945 that they finally realised that all the shady rumours were actually true and these hideous monuments to Nazi cruelty sank into public consciousness.

Parochialism affects all nations, of course. As British troops had liberated Belsen, and photographs of the camp's skeletal inhabitants flooded British newspapers, so this became the abiding image and understanding of what the Nazi camps were like. The

---

* As one German teaching student reminded me, when I was giving a talk at her British school: 'History is written by the victors.' She was referring specifically to the Allied bombing campaign, which reduced many German cities to rubble. We didn't agree about this, but I understood her perspective.

distinction between the concentration camps and the death camps became blurred. The number of emaciated corpses and barely alive prisoners were shocking enough, but there were no gas chambers at Belsen.* Alas, much worse could be found in the ruins of camps at Auschwitz, Treblinka, Bełżec, Sobibór and the other eastern camps dedicated to the industrial slaughter of mostly Jewish inmates.

There is an insightful piece in *Belsen 1945: New Historical Perspectives*, edited by Suzanne Bardgett and David Cesarani, which gives an account by Major Dick Williams, one of the first British officers to enter the camp, of his memories of the day. The major was a representative of the Royal Army Service Corps and he came to check the provision of food and water.

17 April 1945 was just another day. That was, until midday ...

A senior German officer had come to our front line under a white flag ... He told the Corps Commander that there was a camp in the direct line that our troops were advancing ...

Inside and obviously waiting for us, with all the SS on parade there, were Commandant Kramer and Irma Grese, the head of the woman's side ...

We had to actually be very careful as we went on, because covering the ground, throughout the camp, were just piles of this horrible striped uniform, the emaciated faces and shaven heads, sunken eyes. Just everywhere, some hanging on the barbed wire, some lying, some trying to stand. As we went through, two tried to come forward to speak to me, but the SS bashed them on one side.

---

* Those fabled historians the Sex Pistols furthered this misunderstanding in 1978 with their fourth and worst single 'Belsen Was a Gas'.

Aside from the nightmare quality of this recollection, it's notable that the SS escort given to Major Williams did not moderate their brutality towards their prisoners, even in front of their new captors.

The famous wartime radio broadcaster Richard Dimbleby arrived soon after and made one of his most memorable reports. 'I've seen many terrible sights in the last five years, but nothing, nothing approaching the dreadful interior of this hut at Belsen. I ... found myself in the world of a nightmare. Dead bodies, some of them in decay, lay strewn about the road.'*

The *Jewish Chronicle*'s leader comment entitled 'The Lessons of the Murder Camps' from 27 April 1945 makes for a sobering read. The outrage and frustration of years of being ignored or contemptuously dismissed is still palpable eighty years later:

The final and irrefutable evidence of the bestial savagery of Nazi Germany, confirming, as it has done, with almost precise exactness the reports which have been leaking out in the past, has sent a shudder through every civilised heart. The reactions these ghastly confirmations have produced in the free countries are, up to a point, commendable. But they raise a grave question, which demands a fair and square answer: Why have we had to wait until now for this widespread revulsion?

As far back as 1939 the British Government published detailed reports of the villainies in the concentration camps ... The disclosures produced hardly a tremor in those who read them. 'For years,' as Mr Hannen Swaffer† said in last Sunday's *People*, 'every week's

---

* Dimbleby, among many other memorable broadcasts, also reported live on air from a Lancaster bomber over Berlin – an extraordinarily brave thing to do, considering the death rate among bomber crews. He was the father of those two stalwarts of BBC broadcasting: David and Jonathan Dimbleby.
† Swaffer was an English journalist.

Jewish Chronicle read like Foxe's Book of Martyrs.' But few, he goes on to remark, seemed to care. When in 1933, he recalls, he seconded the first resolution to be passed in this country denouncing Nazi atrocities, the general press ignored the meeting and he was accused by Fleet Street colleagues of 'falling for Jewish propaganda'.

The ugly truth remains that, despite all their efforts, and despite even this latest spate of unarguable evidence, the doubters, the scoffers, the knaves, and the well-pleased are still in evidence, and not a single one of those who talked and scribbled of 'exaggerations' has, to our knowledge, had the honesty and decency publicly to retract ...

Some people refused to learn the truth, because it sickened them. It is a revolting thought that even now, after all the utterly confirming evidence, we have still such creatures amongst us. Such contemptible moral cowards prefer to live happily in an unreal world of their own. Then there are and have been others ... who shrugged their shoulders when the ghastly reports were published in the past, and dismissed them as *Jewish* propaganda. In one instance reported to this office only the other day – after the revelations of Belsen and Buchenwald – one of these curs continued to describe it all as 'more Jewish angling for sympathy'.

As the war in Europe ended, debate in Parliament turned once again to the refugees who had escaped the Nazis before the war. On 25 May 1945, the *Jewish Chronicle* reported in an article headed 'Mean Revenge on the Refugees' that calls were already being made by MPs to send Jewish refugees back to Germany.

Mr Austin Hopkinson ... was all for the 'immediate' repatriation of all Jewish refugees who had been persecuted in their country, 'in view of the destruction of National Socialism'. Having, with singular lack of observation, assumed the Nazism was already as dead as mutton, he apparently could not see why its victims should not, with similar precipitancy, be carried to its home, perhaps in time for the official funeral.

The *Chronicle* goes on to note that Winston Churchill, then still Prime Minister, dismissed Hopkinson's remarks, not least on the grounds of 'practical considerations'. Churchill also agreed with the point made by a Mr Silverman,* suggesting that it would be 'cruel to compel the Jews to return to the scene of the crimes committed against them'.

Hopkinson appears again in the same edition of the *Jewish Chronicle* in a debate in Parliament on the Family Allowances Bill

to support an anti-alien amendment moved by Mr Manningham-Butler. This is how he did it: 'In certain parts of the country, not least in industrial Lancashire, there is growing up a very dangerous feeling indeed, that aliens, some of enemy origin, are having a much better time during the war than the native-born working population, and have taken privileges to themselves to which they were not entitled ... We have to try to prevent here those scenes of persecution which have disgraced other countries. The trouble is blowing up the whole time ... and that feeling will extend considerably and danger will arise [if] everybody in this country is to be taxed to encourage a lot of foreigners to come and breed here.'

When Mr Hopkinson's disgusting outburst was hotly challenged

---

* There were two Jewish MPs of that name in Parliament at the time – Sydney and Julius. Both represented Labour and both were the children of Jews who had arrived in Britain from Eastern Europe at the end of the nineteenth century.

and aptly described by Mr Driberg as 'typically reptilian', he dropped the pretence of anxiety for the avoidance of 'scenes of persecution' and exclaimed: 'The meanest types of offences against the food regulations are common among foreigners' ...

The remarkable fact remained, however, that a new anti-Jewish technique (cloaked under the guise of anti-refugee) seems to have been patented by the hon. member in question, which consists of spreading anti-Semitism on the pretext of wishing to prevent it ... The serious thing about this latest move is that it should emanate from a member of the British House of Commons, and not only that, but that Parliament should be used as a sounding board for what Mr Aneurin Bevan called Mr Hopkinson's 'barbarous indecencies' ... Fortunately, Mr Hopkinson and his 'nonsense' found little approval, at any rate of the vocal kind, in any part of the House, but plenty of repudiations.

But the way some British people understood the Holocaust was sometimes bewildering. In June 1945, the Association of Jewish Refugees newsletter published this story:

JEWISH REFUGEES AND ATROCITIES

A number of attacks on aliens have recently been published by national and local newspapers following the great outburst of rage and indignation when the horror camps in Germany were discovered. These outbursts unfortunately in many cases did not discriminate between the perpetrators of these crimes and the victims, between German Nationals and Jewish refugees from Germany.

The Association of Jewish Refugees also issued a statement explaining why Jews from Germany did not wish to be repatriated.

To the Jews of Germany, their former country is the graveyard of their families. There are no bonds left between them and Germany. In their overwhelming majority they have no desire to return to the country where these atrocities were committed and be compelled to live among people who perpetrated the murder of the Jews or connived in these crimes. They prefer to live anywhere else in the world rather than Germany.

Despite the appalling news of the Holocaust, it seemed to have had little ameliorative effect on antisemitism throughout Europe, which was achingly apparent in the calls to return Jewish refugees to Germany and Eastern Europe. On 31 August 1945, less than a month after the Japanese surrender that marked the end of the Second World War, the *Jewish Chronicle* ran an editorial entitled 'The Poison Flows On'.

The piece contains heartbreaking information about the continual hostility towards Jews in Poland, not least in the treatment of Jewish children who had survived and wanted to return to their old schools. The *Chronicle* writes of a child who had been sent to several schools to continue his education, returning each day battered and bleeding from attacks by his fellow school children. In the end, he had to register in yet another school as a non-Jew.

Another reported story details anti-Jewish riots in Kraków and Rzeszów following rumours of ritual murders of Christian children. Belgian newspapers blamed black market activity exclusively on 'the Jews'. British soldiers stationed in the country reported no Jews among the black marketers, although you do wonder how they could tell.

As the year rolled on, there were still calls to return Jewish German and Austrian refugees to the shattered countries. On

26 October 1945, the *Jewish Chronicle* in a piece headed 'Alien Scare in Hampstead' reported on a meeting convened by the Left Book Club at Trinity Church Hall, Finchley Road, to protest against a petition for the deportation of the refugees living in the borough. The petition had been supported very vocally by the Women's Guild of Empire – a curious group of right-wing suffragettes. The meeting 'was very lively and there were many interruptions'. In the tradition of refugee scare stories wildly overexaggerating numbers, the petition had stated there were 30,000 refugees in Hampstead, although the true number was 19,000.

> During the meeting Miss Eleanor Rathbone, MP, said she would not like this shocking, ugly, and selfish movement to go on without joining her voice with the protest against the petition. Who were these aliens whom these people wanted to expel? Where did they want them to go?
>
> 'German agents,' yelled someone.
>
> 'Do you want to drive out the Jews because they are Jews' she asked. (Voice: 'They are Germans.')

The protesters were in a minority. The *Chronicle* reports that the vicar of Holy Trinity Church 'said he was against the petition because it was contrary to reason, contrary to decent behaviour, and because, speaking in his capacity, it was contrary to the principles of Christian faith (loud applause)'.

In support of those protesting against the petition, one man declared that '88 per cent of the refugees had been doing useful work throughout the war' – someone else yelled out: 'And black marketing.'

The *Chronicle* ends the report by stating:

> Mr Victor Gollancz* said that they were facing a crisis which might
> lead them either to the reestablishment of humanity and civilisation
> or to the total destruction of civilisation ... There was only one hope
> and that was that in this desperate crisis they should all in their indi-
> vidual lives learn to put the common good before their own narrow
> interests and to put mercy against narrow racialism and nationalism
> which they had fought against (applause).

One common recollection of many of the Jewish refugees who
had come to Britain was how their experience and the fate of their
families became a taboo subject with British people. These days we
might call it compassion fatigue – one of those mealy-mouthed
expressions which give us permission to pathologise ill-behaviour.
British people – who had endured the Blitz, years of rationing and
other wartime difficulties, and for some families, the death of a husband, father or brother,† not to mention loss of other opportunities
such as education and job prospects and a stolen youth – simply
weren't interested in the horror stories every Nazi concentration
camp victim carried in their soul. Tony Kushner and Katharine
Knox quote former Nazi camp survivor Vera Karoly who said:

> Even though I had a burning need to speak about my wartime expe-
> riences with the new acquaintances whom I met in London, nobody
> seemed to want to hear about this. They always changed the subject,

---

* Presumably, this is the famous publisher. He was an early campaigner in the effort to get people to understand what the
  Nazis were doing to the Jews of occupied Europe.
† Less than one in 100 (0.94 per cent) of the UK population, civilian and military, lost their life in the Second World War. For
  those serving in the armed forces, the percentage was 12.5 per cent, or slightly over one in ten. Poland, at the worst end of the
  Nazi regime, lost almost one in five of its pre-war population.

saying things like 'We do not want to know about all the suffering you went through in the war.'

A similar phenomenon was noted by survivors of the First World War. One particularly poignant moment in Vera Brittain's heart-breaking memoir *Testament of Youth* occurs when she finally gains a place at Oxford after the war. She writes about being mocked in an undergraduate theatrical review as a solemn, dreary presence. Her fellow Oxford students, who were too young to have suffered the worst of the Great War, had no sympathy for the fact that she had lost her brother, fiancé and two other close friends in the conflict.

But some survivors of the Holocaust simply refused to think and discuss what had happened to them. *Kindertransport* veteran Martha Blend, née Immerdauer, for example, wrote that in the post-war world she could not bear to think about what her family had gone through. Only many decades later could she bear to revisit Vienna.

In a curious postscript to this chapter, it is interesting to see how parts of the British press reported on the trial of the Belsen camp guards, which occurred before the year was out. The focus was essentially on the camp commandant and one of the female warders rather than the camp's victims. Understandably, the main villain of the piece was Commandant Josef Kramer, whose powerful build, heavy brow and dark staring eyes make him look like a serial killer from a Thomas Harris novel. The other main focus of press attention were the women who had worked at Belsen, to which reports add a queasy sexualised tint. The *Mail* and the *Express* seemed particularly fascinated by Irma Grese, who was said to be in charge of the female guards. On 25 September 1945, the *Express* reported that 'Irma looked around the court and shook her ringlets back into place behind her shoulders' when confronted by the testimony of 'Dora Szafran, a pretty dark haired 21-year-old Jewess from Warsaw'.

Another article in the *Express* from 16 November 1945 asks 'How Did Irma Greese Get Like This?' The typo is the *Express*'s. They habitually spelled her name like this. (I understand it's pronounced Grey-zer.)

Irma Greese, whom some newspapers call the Blonde Beastess of Belsen, faces her judges today ... When she was a little girl Irma Greese cried when she saw that her brother had cut his lip. But within ten years of those tears she was using whip and gun and gas with skill and despatch on the hapless inmates of Belsen concentration camp ... The girl whose record for cruelty probably exceeds that of any woman in history will not be surprised if she is sentenced to die.

The tabloids' treatment of her as an object of sexual interest and revulsion does seem to trivialise the horrors visited on the camp inhabitants. Grese and Kramer were hanged by Albert Pierrepoint in Hamelin Prison, both on the same day – 13 December 1945. Grese was all of twenty-two.

Chapter 12

The Ants' Nest: After the War

The end of the Second World War in Europe resulted in the collapse of one of the most repellent regimes the world had ever known, but it created a plethora of complex problems.

Britain, as one of the three great powers which brought an end to Hitler, once again faced the prospect of a further influx of refugees, now rebranded as 'DPs' – displaced persons, that is, people who had been uprooted from their communities, either involuntarily in the case of slave labourers, or because they were fleeing from fighting. Difficult decisions would have to be made about who the British would welcome and who they would turn away. Two of the greatest mass migrations of refugees at the end of the war – the Poles and the Jews – are considered in the following chapters, but this chapter looks at refugees who are commonly overlooked in histories of the Second World War: the defeated armies who were unable or unwilling to return to their own countries; the former inhabitants of the Nazi concentration camps; and the thousands of Germans who now became refugees in their own country, particularly those who fled to the British zone of occupation.*

---

* After the war, the United States, Soviet Russia and Britain divided Germany into zones of occupation. France, too, took a section. The British zone included Lower Saxony, Schleswig-Holstein, North Rhine-Westphalia and the Ruhr – essentially the upper west of the country.

Although Britain was one of the 'winners' in the war, the conflict had devastated the country's wealth and standing as a great power. Its infrastructure had also been severely weakened by aerial bombardment and now it had to share in the cost of feeding and policing a devastated Europe. All this came on top of its attempts to keep a grasp on its vast and rebellious empire – one of the central reasons many British politicians had wanted to fight the war in the first place.

The Nazis had forcibly imported over 8 million slave workers from the conquered territories to work in their fields and factories – a level of servitude not seen in Europe since the time of the Roman Empire, as Keith Lowe points out in *Savage Continent*. Germany, in the weeks after the fighting ended, now resembled 'one huge ants' nest'* as these millions of people attempted the long walk home. German civilians were especially affected too. As the map of Germany was redrawn, 12 million Germans were expelled from land that had previously belonged to the Third Reich. Four and a quarter million of these refugees came to settle in the British occupation zone in western Germany in a massive logistical exercise known as Operation Swallow.† This feat of human migration required the region to absorb 6,000 new inhabitants every day for an entire year.

There were more complex issues too – many of those fleeing west to avoid capture by Soviet troops were doing so because they feared Russia's vengeance. Some were simply prisoners of war or slave workers who assumed they would be punished for surrendering

---

* This term borrows from the Polish refugee Marilka Ossowska, who had the most extraordinary escape from Poland. She and a group of other displaced persons hitchhiked to Italy and then took a boat to Britain in 1946. She eventually went home in 1960.

† Not to be confused with Operation Swallow the Norwegian commando raid on the German heavy water plant at Telemark in 1943, or Operation Swallow an American prisoner-of-war escape attempt over 1944/45.

– an entirely reasonable concern considering the gross inhumanity of Stalin's regime.* Others had committed atrocities against Russian soldiers and had very real reasons to feel their Soviet captors would treat them with equal savagery.

In all this, it is possible to feel sympathy for Germany's civilian population, not least its children. During the war, the German Army had occupied the eastern territories with extraordinary cruelty and callousness, and their own women and children paid a terrible price when the war turned against them and the brutal, battle-hardened Red Army swept in.† But the Soviets did not set out to let their conquered subjects starve to death – a deliberate strategy of the German Army during the Barbarossa campaign. This inhuman policy was grudgingly revised when the Germans realised they were driving Russian civilians into the hands of the partisans who were, if nothing else, a source of food. The mass starvation that followed Germany's defeat was more often than not a consequence of shortages and the chaos of a completely ruined infrastructure following the Nazi 'scorched-earth' tactics in the final months of the war.

Throughout this all, in the first few months of the peace, British politicians and military commanders had to tiptoe through eggshells to maintain a working relationship with their Soviet allies. It was an almost impossible balancing act. In the final months of the war, Nazi leaders had deluded themselves that 'the West' would come to see Stalin's Russia as the real enemy after all and join forces with the *Wehrmacht* to turn the tide against them. This, of course,

---

* Their fear was entirely realised. As if they hadn't suffered enough, former Soviet prisoners of war and slave workers were habitually sent to Soviet labour camps.
† Antony Beevor's *Berlin: The Downfall 1945* is a heartbreaking read for anyone who admires the heroic resistance of the Soviet people in the 'Great Patriotic War'. Beevor points out that many front-line soldiers were more likely to behave decently with German civilians and those who came after them were more likely to perpetrate the worst atrocities against women and children.

never happened, although the post-1945 Cold War, with its threat to human existence in a nuclear exchange, showed that the Nazis had got their timing wrong rather than the actual course of events.

In keeping with a desire to cooperate with the Russians, the Western Allies' policy was for Axis forces to surrender to the armies they had been fighting. This would have fatal consequences for some soldiers. For example, at the end of the war Nazi collaborators fighting with the Croatian Ustašes* sought sanctuary in British-controlled territory in Austria to avoid surrendering to Josip Broz Tito's Partisans, whom they had treated with great brutality in the vicious guerrilla war in Yugoslavia that had raged throughout the Nazi occupation of Eastern Europe. A myth grew that the British troops had disarmed hundreds of thousands of Ustašes and then handed them over to be murdered by the Partisans. But actual events played out differently. Around 25,000 of these soldiers made it to Austria, while another 175,000 were captured by their Yugoslav opponents as they attempted to reach the border. In another twist in this vicious struggle, between 10,000 and 12,000 Slovenian Home Guard forces reached Austria to surrender to the British forces there. They were disarmed and told they would be shipped to Italy. This also happened to Cossack forces who had fought with the Nazis against the Red Army. Instead, both the Slovenians and Cossacks were handed over to the Partisans and the Soviets, respectively.

From eighty years away, this looks callous, but in 1945 the British Army in Austria was fully occupied in maintaining control of this enemy country. They had few resources to spare in accommodating

---

* A fascist organisation and military force. At the time, Croatia was part of the country of Yugoslavia, created after the First World War.

enemy soldiers who were fleeing the wrath of armies they themselves had treated with appalling cruelty.

So, what did happen to them? The Slovenians and Cossacks did
not face full-scale extermination, as had the Jews under Nazi rule,
and unlike Tito's Partisans, they did not face execution if captured
alive. But they were treated with great cruelty, as they had expected. These soldiers were force-marched to detention centres with
no food and water and were shot if they were unable to continue
walking.

The bitterness and resentment of these war years boiled over
again in the conflicts that engulfed former Yugoslavia in the 1990s,
where historic feuds once again divided communities that had lived
peacefully together in the post-war decades in Tito's communist
regime.

But, as so often happens in tumultuous conflicts, the 'fortunes of
war' can smile on some as well as cast others into unjust or well-
deserved fates. Although the British sent the Slovenians and Cossacks to an uncertain future with their former enemies, a Ukrainian
army known as the 14th Waffen SS 'Galician' Division, who surrendered to British troops in Austria, met a much more agreeable
fate.* Recent Home Office papers from the National Archives have
revealed that 7,100 of these Ukrainian men were allowed to settle in
Britain, which protected them from the Soviet Union.

As is often the case, the detailed circumstances here are more
complicated than the bald facts might suggest. Despite the British agreeing with the Soviets that all enemy forces would have to

---

* German SS troops had their blood group tattooed under their left arm. This form of identification worked very much against
them if they were trying to hide among ordinary *Wehrmacht* soldiers, especially if they were captured by the Russians who
often executed them as soon as they found them.

surrender to the soldiers they had been fighting, there were complications with the Ukrainians.

The Galician Division was formed in April 1943 after most of the
Jews in Ukraine had already been killed by the Nazis, so they could
not be accused of having taken part in *Einsatzgruppen* massacres.
They did, however, fight against Tito's Partisans and committed
atrocities during the course of these actions. But in July 1944, the
majority of the division was wiped out by Soviet forces during the
Battle of Brody on the Ukrainian–Polish border.

In March 1945, the survivors were incorporated into the Ukrainian National Army and were now no longer part of the SS. So,
who had been responsible for any war crimes perpetrated by the
Galician Division now became even more hazy.

To this day, the issue remains a controversial one and sympathy
or contempt for these soldiers is split along political lines. False
claims have been made about the division being made up of con-
scripted soldiers, whereas in fact they were all volunteers. Other
apologists have said they fought only for Ukrainian independence
and that allegations of atrocities are Russian propaganda. The plain
fact though remains that the International Military Tribunal, set
up during the Nuremberg trials, declared the SS to be a criminal
organisation, and this was clearly overlooked. As late as 2003, investigations were showing that this division had also taken part in
massacres of Polish civilians. There is widespread feeling that they
had whitewashed their history and the fact that they had allied
themselves with the Nazi cause had been overlooked.

The issue is still very much a live one in Ukraine today, and as
recently as May 2021, 300 people marched in Kyiv to celebrate the

Galician Division, displaying the heraldic banner of the unit – that of three gold crowns and a lion on a blue background.

Their latter-day supporters now see them as fighters for Ukrainian freedom. Then, as now, this is an especially hot topic. In the war years, the Soviet Union had only recently visited a deliberately engineered famine on the region – the Holodomor – in order to suppress rebellious Ukrainians, and this would have been an understandable motive for Ukrainians wanting to fight against what they saw as their Soviet oppressors.

Nonetheless, this veneration of the SS Galician Division is extremely controversial, not least with Ukraine's Jewish population, numbering among which is President Volodymyr Zelensky.

As the war ended, the Galician Division were fighting in Austria and retreated west to surrender to the British rather than the Soviet Army to their east. The British disregarded the understanding of enemy forces surrendering to the soldiers they had been fighting because many of these men came from Galicia, which had been part of pre-war Poland. So, the division was transferred to Italy and settled in a camp near Rimini. Eventually, in April 1947, when relations between the Soviets and the Western Allies had deteriorated considerably, the British Cabinet decided to transfer the division to Britain as prisoners of war. Most of them were then employed as agricultural labourers. Some were also transferred to Canada.

Some of these soldiers were included in the European Volunteer Workers scheme along with many others from displaced person camps in Germany and Austria. In this programme, homeless Europeans were invited to come to Britain to work in industries where there were labour shortages.

Following several other administrative shenanigans, these soldiers from the Galician Division were given permission to settle in Britain, although many of them subsequently emigrated to other countries.

* * *

As the war ended, the British government was reluctant to take in more Jewish refugees who had survived the Nazi camps. Other countries were equally as unwilling. One Canadian immigration official, when asked about how many Jews the country was prepared to accept, replied: 'None is too many' – this infamous remark is now the title of a book on the subject, by Irving Abella and Harold Troper.

But Jewish refugees who had arrived in Britain before the outbreak of war were allowed to stay and often chose to take British nationality, despite some pressure to have them repatriated (see Chapter 11). Those who had served with the British armed forces now felt a deeper connection with the country that had offered them refuge, and many played an indispensable role in Britain's post-war army of occupation in Germany. Some Jews spoke of being *zwischenmensch* – men in between – but the majority settled into predominantly middle-class lives regaining much of the professional status and prosperity of their pre-Nazi days. In May 1945, the Association of Jewish Refugees announced:

> Many of us have founded a new life for ourselves and our children in this country. We have cut off all ties with a country which is responsible for the wanton destruction of once flourishing Jewish communities. We are certain that Jewish refugees with their skill and

experience will contribute to the welfare of this country in the same way as they played their part in the war effort.

This seems a fair summation of what actually happened.

But Jewish aid organisations did persuade the Home Office to take in child concentration camp survivors. They were reluctant, but just as Kristallnacht had created sympathy for the Jews before the war, so the terrible images of the camps flooding British newspapers and cinemas via newsreels in the summer of 1945 created a groundswell of sympathy which made this generosity politically acceptable.

Academic Rebecca Clifford looks at Britain's treatment of postwar Jewish refugees in her paper 'Britain's response to WWII child refugees puts modern society to shame', published in *The Conversation*, and writes: 'The child refugees who came to Britain after World War II were given a much better welcome than those reaching British shores now.' Accepting such child refugees was, points out Clifford, an act which 'fitted in with Britain's post-war self-image as a right-minded liberator and victor'.

So, officials were despatched to Europe to locate 1,000 child survivors in the displaced persons camps which had sprung up all over the ravaged continent. Strangely, whether from suspicion of officialdom or simply a desire to try to get back home and find lost relatives, only 732 of these children were willing to come to Britain. A reception camp was prepared for 300 of them at Lake Windermere and volunteers placed clothes, dolls and teddy bears on beds to make the children feel welcome.

So, on an August day in 1945, several planes packed with these refugees landed at a nearby airbase and volunteers were shocked to see that almost all of them were teenage boys. Only eighty were girls and only twenty-five were under ten years old. And, to add to the confusion, many of these children looked much older than their stated age. Nonetheless, the reaction of the children is worth savouring. An account from the Jewish Museum in London quotes Icek Alterman, who had survived in both Auschwitz-Birkenau and Dachau, saying: 'We had arrived in paradise.'

The demographic of the consignment revealed some terrible truths about the world they had recently left. Although camps such as Auschwitz contained some young children, most under-tens were despatched to the gas chambers as soon as they arrived. Older girls, too, trying to care for their younger brothers and sisters, were often sent to their deaths alongside them. Boys were less likely to have taken on this protective role in a family. They were also more likely to lie about their age on arrival and thus be deemed suitable for work at the *selektion* which occurred with every trainload, where prisoners were divided into those who would be sent immediately to the gas chambers or those who would be worked to death in the weeks or months ahead.

The fact that many of the children looked far older than their stated age is easily explained. These children had lived through a hellish experience and also suffered from starvation and disease. Their youthful appearance did come back, writes Clifford, but it took a long time.

The children, who had had such a traumatic start to their lives, were regarded with trepidation by the adults who cared for them. Adults feared they would have had no moral training and might even be dangerous. Today, we talk about 'damaged' children and it doesn't take a great deal of imagination to envisage how damaged a child who had survived a year or more in Auschwitz might actually be.

This was a grim fact of life – and even the distinguished Jewish leaders who were behind this transportation of child refugees admitted as much. Sir Leonard Montefiore wrote in 1947 that these children were 'abnormal in some way or another ... To lads who have successfully bamboozled and deceived the SS and the Camp Commandant, to hoodwink a Jewish Committee and its Welfare Office must seem mere child's play.'

But, still, in a video interview for the Yiddish Book Center, Bernie Frydenberg, a Polish Jew and child survivor of Theresienstadt, recalls his experience of arriving in Windermere after the horror of the Nazi camps. 'We got some fresh clothes and we got showers and we got fed a little bit, and life was good.'

The assimilation, care and sympathy offered to these damaged children makes a depressing contrast with the current climate. Clifford writes of refugees today: 'They face a toxic environment, with a suspicious public, an inflammatory, anti-refugee right-wing media, and politicians who are anything but sympathetic.' Child refugees today are often sent to 'detention centres that are effectively prisons'.

*   *   *

Having reluctantly hosted Jewish refugees from Nazi Germany in the years before and during the war, Britain now found itself in the post-war world contending with another massive refugee problem. The British zone of occupation in west Germany was a huge responsibility and an unimaginably difficult task for a country so undone by the war. But Britain had yet to concede that it was no longer the power it had been. The task before the occupying forces was onerous. Quite aside from the destruction wrought by the fighting and Allied aerial bombardment, the Nazis' 'scorched-earth' policy of destroying their own infrastructure as they retreated had left the country in utter ruins. Benjamin Anderson, in his scholarly essay 'British Political Responses to the German Refugee Crisis during Occupation', writes about Victor Gollancz's visit to the area in the autumn of 1946.

One morning he stepped out onto a cold, frosty street in Hamburg. Rubble remained strewn everywhere, the pavement and roads were almost indistinguishable, and the buildings continued to have gaping holes. A teenage boy, dressed in a jumper, shorts and no shoes, shuffled in front of Gollancz and stopped at a row of large tin buckets that were filled to the brim with people's garbage. He shivered as he rustled through the bins in the hope of unearthing some food. For Gollancz, it was a wretched sight, but as one Dusseldorf education officer later suggested, it was all too common.

Alongside Germany's own refugees, there were also over half a million displaced persons in the British zone of occupation, many of whom had been weakened almost to the point of death by their time in Nazi concentration camps. Yet the only solution available to house and feed them was to keep them – in the literal sense of the word – in concentration camps. Of course, they were treated far differently by the camp authorities than they had been by the Nazis, and there were education and training programmes to prepare these residents for the post-war world. They were given a generous cigarette allowance and entertainments such as dances, concerts and films were laid on. But they were still concentrations of Jewish refugees. After the first few months of peace, the idea that they should 'go home' and leave the British zone was not a popular one among them. The Jews from Poland, Romania and Hungary who had survived the war as slave labourers had no desire to return to their previous homeland, which had persecuted them with sometimes as great a savagery as the Nazis.* And now these Eastern European countries were under the control of communist Russia – a country which had its own terrible history of antisemitism.

And there were further complications. The appalling history of Europe's Jews in the Nazi era had one last dreadful chapter, even after Hitler's defeat. For those Jews who had been tough or lucky enough to survive the death camps and the myriad other misfortunes of Nazi rule, in the weeks and months after the war, the prospect of returning home had beckoned. Many of the survivors hoped they would find out who in their extended family remained alive, and some even hoped they would be able to reclaim the homes or apartments that had been theirs before the Nazis arrived. But those who had the strength and determination to walk their way home through 'ants' nest' Germany were often in for a terrible surprise. The Poles, who among all of Europe's Jews suffered the highest casualty rate in the Holocaust,† found that the old hatreds remained very much alive. Even after the Nazis had been defeated, and terrible atrocities had been visited on Poland's non-Jewish population, the country was just as hostile as it ever was. Soon, word got out that Poles were killing Jews who had managed to return from the camps. There were even pogroms, most notoriously in the southern city of Kielce, where forty-two Jews were killed and over forty injured at a Jewish community centre for displaced persons, a full year after the war had ended.

---

* The wartime history of the Eastern European states occupied by, or allied with, the Nazis makes for a deeply unsettling read in relation to the treatment of their Jewish populations. Much of the killing, particularly in the pre-gas-chamber phase of the Holocaust, was carried out by execution squads of volunteers from within these very countries, working hand in hand with the Nazis.

† Of 3,300,000 Jews in pre-war Poland, only around 340,000 survived the Nazi occupation.

Incidents such as this convinced many Jews in the British zone who had survived the Nazi camps that they could never go home.

Hitler's regime had begun by making refugees of its own beleaguered Jewish citizens. With grim irony, when the Third Reich collapsed, huge numbers of Germans became refugees themselves. Over 1946, the situation in west Germany was growing worse by the day. The brutality of the Soviet occupation was driving thousands of German civilians west. Some chose to go, to escape their Soviet conquerors, and some were expelled. The Nazis had encouraged their citizens to colonise the lands they had invaded and those who had made this ill-considered move were now violently unwelcome. Other former citizens of Hitler's Reich now found themselves as despised residents of Poland and other Eastern European territories where borders had been redrawn.

Between February and July 1946, up to 8,000 of these people a day were arriving in the British zone of occupation from the east – including Jews who had tried to resume their lives in their former homelands and were now lucky to return to the relative safety of British-occupied Germany.

The responsibility the British had of administering this unholy upheaval was made considerably worse by the fact that Britain itself had been impoverished by the war. Cities had been ruined by the Luftwaffe, and food was so short that rationing actually became more stringent after the war ended. This created a conflict between a humanitarian desire to help a stricken conquered foe and what became known as 'Vansittartism' – essentially a belief expounded by the British politician and journalist Lord Robert Vansittart that the German people had brought their misfortune upon themselves and deserved to be punished for it.

The food shortage in post-war Germany now bordered on famine. Quite aside from the scorched-earth tactics of the Nazis, an unusually heavy rainfall in the summer of 1945 had resulted in a particularly poor harvest. Benjamin Anderson writes that the British were forced to reduce German rations to 1,000 calories a day – only 200 more calories than those given to Belsen's skeletal inmates. This indeed caused terrible hardship among the German population – all too visible in their gaunt appearance and frequent cases of oedema, a build-up of fluid in particular parts of the body occasioned by starvation.

The need to feed the Germans clashed directly with the need to feed the British people. With sympathy for the Germans already thin on the ground, the British people understandably felt that they and their allies had a higher claim to the little food available to post-war Europe. In the first few days of peace, Lord Vansittart wrote in the *Daily Mail* that 'in Europe in this hungry winter our first duty must be to our Allies, and especially to the Dutch. The Germans must have bottom claim.' At the time, there were few who would have disagreed with him.

But over the next year the question of how to keep the conquered nation alive became a pressing one. Esteemed war correspondent Alexander Clifford wrote a harrowing piece in the *Mail*, published on 22 July 1946, entitled 'Slowly, quietly, hygienically, the Germans are moving towards death'. Clifford begins his piece by evoking Belsen, which is now 'quiet and deserted'. But 'outside its gates you find the new Belsen – the hygienic, slow-motion Belsen – organised by us. Leave aside for the moment the question of whether you care about it – whether it simply serves the Germans right – and concentrate on discovering exactly what the situation is.'

Clifford writes about the uneven distribution of food and how many people look perfectly healthy but then goes on to warn that 'now the people in the big German cities are weakening day by day. The disease and death curves are creeping doggedly up. The old unbearable smell of Belsen is beginning to seep out from the slums of Hamburg and the Ruhr.'

The problem the British have, he admits, is that they control the industrial area of Germany. Other powers, notably the Russians, occupy the farming areas. Clifford's colleague on the *Mail*, Lord Vansittart, replied soon enough. On 29 July, in an article headlined 'The real German story', he writes that 'there is sad suffering, of course. What else could there be after six years of destruction – and who began and begat it? ... The Germans will still blame us for everything. They always blame everyone but themselves.'

Vansittart goes on to repeat Clifford's assertion that the main food-producing districts in Germany are in the Russian zone. But he cannot help being beastly to the Germans,* adding: 'We were always going to have plenty of trouble. The Germans are very troublesome people, and they hate losing wars.'

His piece brought an interesting response in the *Mail*'s letters page a week or so later:

Sir – I arrived here [Germany] loathing the Germans. I had a few ideas, like Lord Vansittart.

These ideas are held by the majority of our troops here; but I am leaving convinced that Alexander Clifford ... has given the most accurate survey yet to appear in print ... That any nation can be

---

* Anyone with a few minutes to kill might like to look up Noël Coward's highly sardonic 'Don't Let's Be Beastly to the Germans' on YouTube.

perverted is admitted by the prosecution at Nuremberg. That millions of good people remain can be verified here by any observant, impartial investigator.

Sergeant, Army Education Corps, BAOR

Curiously, a vocal majority of *Mail* readers seemed to agree. In an early version of the *Mail*'s system that lets readers upvote and downvote comments, there is an editorial comment: 'Stop-press score in the still-seething post-bag controversy: For Clifford 180; For Vansittart 93.'

Another letter in the same mail bag also sheds light on the general absence of food in both victorious and defeated nations.

My son has been in the army eleven months ... [and writes] we are also on very strict rations as far as food is concerned. We get approximately 4oz of bread per day and some old crusts. For breakfast this morning we had a slice of meat roll and a few mouldy potatoes. The other meals are only enough to feed a corner of one's body.

For my generation, it is difficult to imagine that level of hunger. But it persisted to haunt the generation who fought or were born in the war.*

The reluctance to help Germany is understandable – certainly the argument that Britain had to have a healthy population in order to recover was undeniable. There was also concern that helping to put Germany 'back on its feet' could lead to a resurgence in Nazi-like violence which a weakened Britain would be unable to resist. The

---

* The 1960s British sitcom *On the Buses* even featured an episode where bus driver Stan chats up a canteen dinner lady in the hope that she will slip him a couple of sausages to take home. Creating such a plot device would be unthinkable to anyone born in the 1950s and onwards.

situation was even starker, now that a fear of Soviet aggression in Western Europe was growing by the day. But with *that* in mind, was letting Germany grow so weak also a poor strategy? After all, a strong west Germany could be a vital ally in the struggle to keep Soviet Russia from dominating and even overrunning Western Europe.

Furthermore, writes Benjamin Anderson, the aim of the Allies was to rebuild Germany as a democracy – the safest way to prevent a recurrence of the disastrous political extremism that had swept Hitler to power. As one politician wrote in *The Spectator* in September 1946: 'However guilty that country may be, and however much suffering they have inflicted on the world, it does not alter the fact that starving and hopeless people are not going to build a democratic state.'

The British were beginning to realise they needed Germany as an ally against the Soviets, as the uneasy post-war peace settled into the tumultuous Cold War. So, in 1947, to ease the burden of caring for their regions of occupation, the British and Americans fused their zones together. In this way, they could care for the people they oversaw and stand up together to the threat now offered by the Soviets.

Although German displaced persons were often grateful to be away from the vengeful Soviet Army, the Jewish residents were anxious to be on their way. And most of them wanted to go to Palestine.

Meanwhile, the fate of another multitude of people uprooted by the war had to be decided – the Polish refugees who had come to Britain when the Nazis had conquered their country, and the Polish soldiers who had fought side by side with the British in Africa and Europe.

Chapter 13

From Soldiers to Refugees: Poland after the War

A t the end of the war, thousands of Poles, both in Britain and under the control of the British Army overseas, no longer wanted to go back to their own country. Having been an army in exile for the duration of the war, they now became refugees. How did this come about?

The history of Poland in the twentieth century would bring tears from a stone statue. Never has a European country suffered so much from finding itself caught between two powerful neighbours. Ostensibly the reason for Britain's entry into the war, when Chamberlain made the sovereignty of Poland a 'red line' for Hitler, the country had the tragic distinction of possessing the highest percentage of fatalities for any of the Second World War's combatant nations.* Almost one in five Poles died between 1939 and 1945 (17 per cent of the 1939 population), this figure abetted no end by the murder of nine out of ten of its 3.3 million Jews.

---

* Around 25 per cent of Belarus's population died in the war, but this figure is usually subsumed in the overall total for the Soviet Union, which unquestionably sustained the greatest number of fatalities, accounting for 12 per cent of its total population.

Despite the invasion of the country from the west by Nazi Germany, then two weeks later from the east by the Soviet Union, many of Poland's armed forces managed to escape to neighbouring countries. And many of them then managed to reach Britain, where a Polish government in exile had been established. By 1940, around 20,000 soldiers and airmen had arrived, along with 6,000 or so sailors, together with a small number of warships, submarines and cargo vessels. Adding to this total, around 228,000 Polish soldiers who had escaped via other countries would go on to fight in theatres from north Africa, Italy and Western Europe, under the direction of the British Army command.

Members of the Polish Air Force played a substantial role in the Battle of Britain. These pilots became the largest group of foreign nationals fighting in the RAF and filled an essential gap when the British did not have enough trained pilots. The Polish pilots had their own 303 Squadron, also known as the Kościuszko Squadron, and they proved their worth by shooting down more German planes than any other squadron during the Battle of Britain.

Ironically, Air Chief Marshal Sir Hugh Dowding had originally declined the opportunity to replace losses in squadrons with Polish airmen, thinking they would bring a defeatist attitude. This was one reason they were given their own squadron – along with the more practical reason of communication difficulties with airmen who did not speak English. But the pilots who saw them in action were impressed. One RAF pilot is quoted as saying: 'When they go tearing into the enemy bombers and fighters, they go so close you would think they were going to collide.' After the Battle of Britain, Dowding said: 'Had it not been for the magnificent material contributed by the Polish squadrons and their unsurpassed gallantry, I hesitate to say that the outcome of the Battle would have been the same.'

Despite Poland's gallant efforts, the support it received from Britain waned as British reliance on the Soviet Union waxed. Even the appalling discovery in April 1943 of the bodies of between 22,000 and 28,000 Polish officers, executed by the Soviets in the spring of 1940, in a mass grave at Katyn near Smolensk, did not weaken the British determination to preserve their alliance with Russia at all cost. And no matter how hard the Poles pushed the British and American governments, realpolitik dictated that these two allies would do nothing to antagonise their powerful Russian partner. The reason why is all too obvious and can be seen in the casualty figures of the Eastern and Western Fronts. Hitler's defeat was paid for in Russian blood. Nearly 9 million Russian soldiers died fighting the Germans, and their civilian casualties were considerably higher than any other nation – an estimated 21 million. In contrast, American military and civilian casualties reached 418,000 in all theatres, east and west. The British lost around 450,000, again in all theatres, including civilian casualties. In the sullen Cold War peace that followed, Russia's sacrifices were consistently downplayed, so much so that I remember hearing, during Ronald Reagan's presidency, that many American school children thought Russia had fought on the side of Nazi Germany.

But that is not to excuse the malignant behaviour of Russia's rulers. An apocryphal story has grown up around Stalin. 'Death solves all problems – no man, no problem,' he is reputed to have said. The quote actually comes from the novel *Children of the Arbat* by Anatoly Rybakov, which features the Soviet dictator in

ALIENS

a semi-fictional setting. But it so accurately reflects the inhuman ruthlessness of the Soviet tyrant that it seems entirely plausible he would have said it.* But regardless of its veracity, aside from his own people, no country knew the terrible truth of that phrase quite like the Poles. Having already shown his utter contempt for the sovereignty of his western neighbour by annexing half the country in September 1939, following the Nazi–Soviet Pact in August of that year, arguably the dirtiest deal in history, the Russian dictator led a country which visited appalling cruelty on Poland. The afore-mentioned Katyn massacre of 1940 being one example. Further evidence of Russia's intentions towards an independent Poland could be gleaned from the behaviour of the Red Army in the summer and autumn of 1944, when they halted outside Warsaw for several weeks while the German Army systematically destroyed the Polish Home Army who had risen up against them, hoping to present their capital city as a liberated territory to their supposed Soviet allies. Perhaps 200,000 Poles – civilians and members of the armed forces – were killed while the Red Army stood by waiting for the Nazis to wipe out independent Polish resistance for them.

Even the lesser crimes against the Poles are harrowing. Following the invasion of 1939, over 300,000 people were deported to forced labour camps, mostly in Siberia, to chop down trees in the arctic wilderness.

The lot of these Polish prisoners gradually improved when the Nazis crossed the River Bug to invade Soviet Russia in June 1941. The captive Poles were offered an 'amnesty' by the Soviets and their

---

* Another of Stalin's famous phrases, 'The Pope? How many divisions has he got?' said in response to concern that the pontiff would be offended by a particular Soviet policy, has been quoted in one form or another, and in various circumstances, by sources as eminent as Harry S. Truman and Winston Churchill. It seems to suggest that Stalin wheeled the phrase out whenever he wished to indicate he had no respect whatsoever for the concerns of the Pope.

most high-profile military prisoner, General Władysław Anders, was released from captivity to assemble an army in exile of 100,000 men. Anders was a romantic figure, who had trained at the General Staff Academy in St Petersburg when the area of Poland where he was born had been under the control of Russia's ill-fated final monarch Nicholas II. Anders had served as a cavalry officer and had fought bravely in the First World War. When Poland became an independent nation after that war, he became a leading figure in their armed forces. During the invasion of 1939, he was wounded several times and then captured by the Soviets. Despite being tortured by the NKVD and held in the notorious Lubyanka Prison in Moscow, he was considered too valuable to be executed. Once the Nazis invaded, the Soviets restructured their relationship with Poland and made the pragmatic decision to make an ally of the London-based Polish government in exile, at least for the time being. Anders was the obvious candidate to head an army made up of all the Polish soldiers the Soviets had imprisoned rather than murdered.

At first it was hoped these soldiers would fight alongside the Russians, but this proved an unworkable idea. Following a difficult few months, Anders and his army were allowed to leave Soviet Russia via the southern border with Iran. Polish soldiers fled to Red Cross camps in India, Africa and the Middle East, where many made their way to the British mandate of Palestine. The Polish government in exile created a new wing of the Polish armed forces from these exiles – the Second Polish Corps. These men, serving under Anders, fought alongside Allied soldiers, most famously at Monte Cassino, one of the most decisive battles in the campaign to liberate Italy from the Nazis.

Britain had entered the war determined to do everything it could to protect Polish independence. And Polish soldiers who had taken up exile in the UK or fought alongside British soldiers had also understood that their ultimate goal was to return to an independent Poland. But as the war progressed and Soviet Russia began to beat back the Nazi armies, overrunning the eastern countries of Europe on their way to Berlin, it became increasingly obvious that Poland's independence was going to become a thorny issue. When Churchill, Roosevelt and Stalin met at Tehran in November 1943, the balance of power between them had shifted. Roosevelt, in particular, had realised that the Red Army had become a hugely powerful military force and that Soviet Russia would be one of the two greatest powers in the post-war world. The wants and wishes of Britain and her dwindling empire were becoming less important. The Americans, especially, understood the need to accommodate the Soviets in Eastern Europe, which meant, in essence, that they would control the territory between Germany and their own border.

This depressed Churchill immensely, but without American support he could do little about it. In October 1944, as the Red Army approached the borders of Germany, he flew to Moscow to speak to Stalin one to one. In what became known as the 'percentages agreement', the two leaders thrashed out an understanding as to who would dominate the post-war regions of Eastern Europe. Bulgaria and Romania, Churchill understood, were Russia's to control. Stalin, in turn, was happy to trade off Greece, despite the strength of its own communist party, which was likely to be a major presence in any post-war government.

By the time the Allies' three great leaders met again at the Yalta Conference in the Crimea, in February 1945, the Red Army had

already occupied Poland. Churchill realised his hope of an independent Poland after the war was not going to happen. He confided to his private secretary Sir John Colville: 'Make no mistake,
all the Balkans, except Greece, are going to be Bolshevised, and
there is nothing I can do to prevent it. There is nothing I can do for
Poland either.'

But before the war was over, Stalin was still keen to present an
air of compromise and reasonableness. He was not yet prepared
to count his chickens. At Yalta, he reassured Churchill that the
post-war government of Poland would be broader than a Moscow-
backed communist regime and that there would still be 'free and
unfettered elections as soon as possible'.

Churchill was taken in. Historians Simon Berthon and Joanna
Potts, in their book *Warlords: An Extraordinary Re-creation of World
War II Through the Eyes and Minds of Hitler, Churchill, Roosevelt and
Stalin*, write that Churchill confided in Cabinet minister Hugh
Dalton: 'Poor Neville Chamberlain believed he could trust Hitler.
He was wrong. But I don't think I'm wrong about Stalin.' He was.

Poland's fate was sealed at the Yalta Conference of February
1945, where Churchill and Roosevelt agreed with Stalin that after
the war Poland should remain in the Soviet 'sphere of influence'.
Despite talk of free elections, this was a tacit acknowledgement
that Poland would remain under Soviet control. Polish independence and the right to a democratic government was no longer an
option. This outcome led to an outcry, not only from Polish forces
based in Britain and other parts of Europe but also from within the
British political establishment. Even future British Prime Minister
Alec Douglas-Home objected, being part of a group of MPs who
drafted an amendment protesting against the acceptance of this

Yalta ruling. While respecting their opinion, it is difficult to see this as anything other than gesture politics. What could Britain do? The Red Army had occupied Poland in the final months of 1944. Who controlled the country was a fait accompli that Britain and the Polish government in exile could do absolutely nothing about.

Churchill offered Britain's exiled Poles these emollient words: 'His Majesty's Government will never forget the debt they owe to the Polish troops … I earnestly hope it will be possible for them to have citizenship and freedom of the British Empire, if they so desire.'

Following Churchill's fine words, the government procrastinated. The agreement at Yalta had promised 'free elections', but in the months following the war, it wasn't entirely unfeasible that these might still come about and result in a Poland that its scattered citizens would actually want to return to. But as the post-war months rolled by, it became obvious that the country was going to remain in Stalin's iron grip, not least because the Soviets were executing many figures from the Polish underground likely to cause them trouble in the post-war world – as they had done with the Polish officer class at Katyn.

Many exiled Poles were in the UK already, not least the government and military personnel who had fled to France in 1939 then escaped again at Dunkirk in 1940. Others, in Anders's Second Polish Corps, had arrived via a hellish and circuitous route which had seen them spend two years in Soviet labour camps. They, especially, had a very clear motive for not wanting to return to a homeland under the baleful control of Stalin's communists. At the end of the war, a further 21,000 came to the UK following their liberation from German prisoner-of-war camps, and a further 2,000 political prisoners came from Nazi concentration camps. Altogether, in the immediate aftermath of the war, there were between 130,000 and 135,000 Poles living in temporary accommodation in Britain.

Some of the Poles who were living in Britain in 1945 had had the most terrible experiences during the war. Tony Kushner and Katharine Knox quote from one such exiled soldier in their book *Refugees in an Age of Genocide*. His tale is so extraordinary a fiction writer or action movie screenwriter would be wary of pushing their luck by depicting it. Truly the living embodiment of the faux-Chinese curse 'may you live in interesting times'.

> I was just finishing National Service when Hitler invaded Poland. On 17th September I was taken a prisoner of war and imprisoned in Austria. I escaped three times. Twice I was captured. The third time I managed to get to Russia – my home was then under occupation – but they condemned me as a spy. They took me on a train to Siberia. For twenty-two months I laboured in the salt mines. Then General Sikorski* managed to get Polish prisoners out – I was one of the lucky ones. First I went to Persia, then through the Middle East and ended up in Italy. That is where we finished our war. We stayed as an occupation force for two years and then came to England.

Although Churchill in his final weeks as Prime Minister had spoken plainly about his desire to allow Poles to stay in Britain, there was a hope that this residence would be temporary and that the Poles would decide to return home in their tens of thousands. Alas, by the time the euphoria of victory settled into a hostile peace, the case for not returning became more and more persuasive.

---

* Sikorski was the Polish Prime Minister in exile. Anders served under him.

Fortunately for these Polish exiles, the Labour government that succeeded Churchill in July 1945 contained prominent members of the wartime Cabinet who fully supported what had become known as 'Churchill's Pledge'. But this situation put the British government in a dilemma. Why should they let more than 130,000 Poles stay in a devastated post-war country, now considerably more impoverished than the pre-war Britain that had been so reluctant to admit the victims of Nazi Germany?

The solution was a classic political sleight of hand. To avoid controversy over the issue of taking in more refugees, it was decided that these Polish people weren't 'refugees'. They were 'displaced persons' or DPs. Most of the Poles were men. To counteract this gender imbalance, and to ease labour shortages, the government set up schemes to bring workers over from Europe in a manner that also allowed them to be classed as 'European Volunteer Workers', again, rather than 'refugees'. Essentially, European Volunteer Workers were here to do the jobs that British people were reluctant to do. Kushner and Knox point out that these job vacancies could have been filled by members of the Commonwealth, most especially African-Caribbeans or Africans, but the Poles were considered to be more 'racially desirable', even though they lacked the common thread of the English language which Britain's colonial subjects possessed.

The quaintly named Operation Balt Cygnet brought thousands of Baltic women over to work in British hospitals. Another scheme named Operation Westward Ho! brought men and women over from Eastern Europe to work in industry. A further scheme was set up for Ukrainian prisoners of war (Chapter 12).

Some of the Poles who came here after the war were that most cherished class of refugee: the transmigrants. Altogether, over 30,000 stayed in the UK temporarily, before departing to the United States, Canada, Australia and Latin America.

But not everyone in government was keen to see the Poles settle in the country. The Home Secretary, the formidable Herbert Morrison, did not approve of their 'displaced person' or even 'European Volunteer Worker' status. He thought this would open the floodgates to 'all those many aliens who desire to stay here and claim they have rendered assistance to the war effort'.

Morrison offers a fascinating snapshot of the attitudes of the time. A towering figure in the Labour Party, he had come to national prominence as the head of the London County Council, much as Boris Johnson did as London's mayor in the 2010s. Morrison it was who drove the building of so much interwar social housing, and who amalgamated the buses, underground and trams together as the London Passenger Transport Board, more commonly known as London Transport. Being from a humble background (he was a policeman's son from Stockwell, south London), he had an acute understanding of the resentment 'new arrivals' would provoke among the least privileged end of the socio-economic scale. As Home Secretary in 1942, he had looked unfavourably on a scheme to bring 350 Jewish children to England from Vichy France, citing a reluctance to provoke 'anti-foreign and antisemitic feelings which were quite certainly latent in this country'. This possibility was scotched early in its infancy when the Nazis occupied the whole of France and these children were consumed in the Holocaust.

Morrison also had similarly bracing views on black American GIs and the following quote reveals how much social attitudes have changed since the 1940s. 'I am fully conscious that a difficult social problem might be created if there was a substantial number of cases of sex relations between white women and coloured troops and the procreation of half-caste children."

Morrison went on to head the nationalisation of many industries that were a characteristic of the post-war world. He truly was a character from another age. His second marriage was to a prominent conservative businesswoman – again, an alliance that would seem extraordinary in our more divided times.

The British rewarded their Polish allies with a cooperative approach to citizenship. At the end of the war, a Polish Resettlement Corps was established in the British Army and Poles who wished to settle in the UK were invited to enlist. The corps offered them two years' security, where they would have the opportunity to take English lessons and learn a civilian trade. Then they would be able to 'undertake work which is helpful to this country'. It was a practical policy aimed at addressing areas of labour shortage, such as construction, coal mining and agriculture. The Polish Resettlement Act of 1947 – described as Britain's first mass immigration law – went on to formalise this understanding. It meant Poles in Britain would be entitled to employment and unemployment assistance.

In the immediate post-war years, that classic cause of refugee resentment 'they're taking all the housing' was defused by settling the demobbed Polish soldiers in army camps. There were forty Resettlement Corps camps around the country, as well as hostels for other European workers. This neutralised local resentment to some

---

* Although a politician speaking today as Morrison did in this quote would face political opprobrium, race is still a highly divisive issue. As I write, the media is full of stories about a black charity worker at a royal reception who was repeatedly and brusquely asked where she 'came from' by a member of the court who had lifted her hair away to look at her name badge. What was most notable about the story was the complete incredulity displayed in the readers' comments in the *Daily Mail*. They could not understand, in their thousands, why being repeatedly asked 'where they were *really* from' might make someone feel unwelcome.

extent, but it also meant that the Poles continued to spend their time in their own national bubble and hindered their need to learn English. As late as 1959, three of these hostels were still operating.

You certainly had to be pretty hardy to live in the camps. Zosia Biegus (née Hartman) recalled her time at Northwick Park, a Polish displaced persons camp near Chipping Campden, after the war: 'The huts ... had no internal plumbing, water was fetched from strategically placed cold water taps ... Washing and toilet facilities were in separate buildings. Just imagine having to walk that far in all kinds of weather, not to mention every time nature called.'

And, of course, the Polish Resettlement Corps was not suited to everyone. Many Poles were educated professionals in their pre-war lives – military officers, teachers, civil servants, lawyers, doctors – and the kind of future Britain had in mind for them was not one they relished. In a curious parallel with the Jews who had come here before the war, most had to find work as unskilled labourers and pursued employment in heavy industry, mining, hotel and catering and as domestic servants. But unlike their Jewish contemporaries, in the long term, fewer were able to regain their status as white-collar professionals.

The Poles had come to Britain with a distinct disadvantage. Many of them who had fought in the war had done so within their own Polish units. So, many of them spoke little or no English. It was here that Jews who arrived before the war had a distinct advantage when it came to 'getting on'. Their children had been sent to local schools. Austrian *Kindertransport* veteran Ilse Gray, for example, didn't even remember learning to speak English as a youngster; she just picked it up in the playground (see Chapter 5). Children are lucky like that, if they learn a language at an early age. Other Jewish refugees, most from the educated 'professional classes', were often multilingual anyway. The Poles who came here were invariably adults and fish out of water.

At the other end of the social scale, trade union attitudes regarding the employment of Poles were mixed. Tony Kushner and Katharine Knox report that the Trades Union Congress insisted no Poles should be given work in areas where British workers were available. The National Union of Mineworkers refused to allow the employment of Poles, even if they had previous experience, although they did relent in January 1947. Some factory unions claimed Polish employees engaged in piecework produced too much, showing up their British counterparts. Nonetheless, two of the biggest unions, the Transport and General Workers' Union and the General and Municipal Workers' Union, were far more welcoming to Polish exiles.

At first many Poles settled around Swindon, where there was a Polish Army base, but many also settled in London and a substantial number took up the opportunity to emigrate to the Commonwealth territories of Canada and Australia. Clearly, having endured such a terrible war, and having fought fiercely alongside British forces, the Poles who did not want to return home had a special case to remain in Britain. They had also been presented with a final outcome entirely the opposite of what they had fought and hoped for. As one Polish exile reconciled to staying in Britain admitted: 'It wasn't the real Poland after the war. It was not our Poland. It was communist.'

Despite their major contribution to the British war effort, hostility towards the Poles who settled here began almost as soon as the war ended. Polish soldiers were not even permitted to take part in the victory parade at the end of the war, for fear of offending Joseph Stalin following the Yalta settlement. And the ideological straitjacket of left-wing politics at the time led some British trade unionists to regard Poles in Britain as 'fascists' as they had fled from communism. This attitude was also reflected in Britain's left-wing newspapers. The *Daily Worker* and *Tribune*, and even the *Daily Mirror*, resented them as opponents of the Soviet regime and they also labelled them as 'pro-fascist', a bewildering appellation for refugees who had suffered so much in the hands of the Nazis.

Some Poles found the British sense of humour difficult to grasp, too. Looking back from 2009, one Pole reminisced:

> I feel more English than Polish, although I'm never allowed to be English, if you know what I mean, by English people – it's always 'that bloody Pole!' – jokingly. This is my home. I've been here since 1948, sixty-one years now. They say you're almost native if you count in a language, and I count in English.

Barely a year after the war ended, it seemed as if the majority of the country resented the fact that these Polish people were here and having government money spent on their upkeep. A Gallup poll,* taken in June 1946, showed that 56 per cent of those asked disapproved of the government's decision to allow Poles to stay. Naturally, this affected the morale of these refugees. Marie Woodruff, of the charity the Catholic Committee for Relief Abroad, visited the camps and reported:

> Many of these people have had weary years of trekking across Asia, Africa and Europe. Others have had years of concentration camps

---

* This American company began conducting opinion polls in 1935 and still operates all over the world.

and forced labour ... Now that they are here, in all the uncertainties
of a perpetual transit camp, with apparently no future to look forward to, they have lost all courage.*

One anonymous Pole said: 'We knew that Poland was sold to the
Russians. Churchill and Roosevelt, they sold us down the drain. We
knew we couldn't go back. It was painful, very painful.'

Despite government assistance, the experience of Poles in Britain in the immediate aftermath of the war sometimes makes for
a difficult read. They were safe, to be sure, unlike many returnees
to Eastern Europe, but life must have presented a dreary prospect
after the hope and excitement of the war years.

Kushner and Knox quote one R. Marciniak, a Polish woman who
worked for the RAF in Nottingham, who was interviewed in Knox's
book *Credit to the Nation: Study of Refugees in the United Kingdom*:

At the end of the war we were just chucked out on the street. No
money, no home, no family, no help. I went to the headquarters because you were supposed to take all the clothes, coats, uniforms and
gas masks, sheets and blankets, back to the store ... A young lad
there said: 'Where are you going now?' And I said: 'I don't know.
I'm going on the street' ... He said: 'Keep everything you've got and
just give me the gas mask because that's the government's.' He exchanged me a new skirt and I wore that uniform a long, long time. I
had that and two blankets ... and that's how I started my life. I got
eight pounds, sixty coupons, that's all I got.'

---

* Curiously, sixty-six Poles were among the 1,027 passengers aboard the *Windrush*, which arrived in 1948 with the first West
Indian immigrants to settle in Britain. The Poles had been travelling since 1939 and came via Soviet labour camps, then
Central Asia, then Mexico and the United States.

And sometimes even the most deserving men and women had little help. The case of Christine Granville, born into the Polish aristocracy as Maria Krystyna Janina Skarbek, and how she was treated after the war is disheartening. She was inundated with medals when the conflict ended for her work in the Special Operations Executive, but she was still dropped by the British secret service with a month's pay and left to her own devices in Cairo, where she was stationed in 1945. Although she eventually gained British citizenship in 1949, she lived the rest of her short life in cheap accommodation doing the sort of low-status jobs that beggar belief in anyone who knew what she had done in the war. To make ends meet, she worked as a telephonist, a waitress and a salesgirl, before taking a job as a cabin steward on an ocean liner. This was a woman who had had the brass *cojones* to go into a Gestapo holding centre in France and persuade this most feared branch of the Nazi state to release three of her secret service colleagues* who were awaiting execution, by persuading their captors that they would meet a terrible fate when Germany lost the war.† She died in June 1952 when a man who was infatuated with her stabbed her to death in the hallway of her London residence. Her murderer was hanged at Pentonville ten weeks later.

In 1951, the UK census showed that there were 162,339 British residents who listed Poland as their place of birth – up from 44,642 in 1931. Still, the Poles who had found refuge here faced an uncertain future. Kushner and Knox even speculate that they were housed in deliberately uncomfortable camps to deter them from staying. But

---

*   One of these men was legendary secret service operative Francis Cammaerts, uncle of the novelist Michael Morpurgo, who wrote about his life in the book *The Mouth of the Wolf*.

†   Having the face and figure of a catwalk model, and a reputation for derring-do so extraordinary that Ian Fleming is said to have based two 'Bond girls' (Vesper Lynd and Tatiana Romanova) on her, has ensured Christine Granville a rich afterlife at least, with four biographies and an English Heritage plaque outside her final residence.

the social cohesion that had seen them through their exile, despite leaving them at a distinct disadvantage in the English-speaking post-war world, eventually paid off. The Polish community slowly began to make headway in rebuilding their prosperity, supported by their own social clubs and their loyal adherence to the Catholic Church. By the 1960s, say Kushner and Knox, the British people no longer saw them as 'potential scabs, fascists and Casanovas' and instead began to perceive them as 'good workers, solid citizens and family men'.

For all the flaws in their post-war treatment, the Polish community in the UK were handled with understanding and loyalty by their British hosts, not least because they had fought so bravely alongside British military forces.

Poles with a romantic disposition always hoped General Władysław Anders would lead them to victory against their Soviet occupiers. He remained a high-profile figure in the Polish community in Britain, although the Soviets deprived him of his rank and citizenship. But he was out of their clutches. He died in 1970, in London, a whole twenty years before the collapse of the Soviet Union. At his request, he was buried in the vast cemetery at Monte Cassino alongside the soldiers of the Second Polish Corps who had fallen there during their most famous battle.

Chapter 14

Echoes of King Canute: Israel

Britain had a central role in the events surrounding Palestine during and after the Second World War and in the creation of the state of Israel. Not only did British policy have a massive impact on Jewish refugees; it also affected the existing Jewish community in Britain.

Nearly 30,000 Palestinian Jews enlisted to fight alongside Britain in the Second World War. Many had been training with the clandestine Zionist paramilitary force the Haganah. The war also permitted the Zionists to develop their own munitions industry. In their struggle against the Nazis, the British and the Palestinian Jews now had a common enemy, much as the Soviet Union had good reason to strike an alliance with its unnatural bedfellows the Western democracies. And aside from the global aspect of the conflict, there was also the more immediate problem of German and Italian troops pushing along the coast of north Africa and the chilling prospect of the Middle East falling to the Nazis.

But hostility between the British and the Palestinian Jews still remained, exacerbated no end by the dawning realisation of what the Nazis were doing to their captive Jewish populations. The Zionists blamed the British for their failure to rescue Europe's Jews.

As the war drew to a close, it was plain to the Palestinian Jews that their British occupiers were a waning power. America was now the most powerful nation on earth and efforts were made to persuade its politicians to back the Zionist cause. In May 1942, a conference of Zionist leaders at the Biltmore Hotel in New York proposed the establishment of a Jewish state in Palestine, with unrestricted Jewish immigration rights.

In Britain, after the war in Europe came to an end, a new Labour government replaced Churchill's coalition government in July 1945. They were broadly sympathetic to the idea of a Jewish homeland, but once in power, the reality and complexity of the situation was daunting.

But as the full horror of the Nazi Holocaust was revealed to the world, there was a great groundswell of sympathy for the Zionists, in particular, towards refugees wanting to travel to Palestine. In Washington, Congress voted to support unrestricted Jewish immigration there. America's new President Harry S. Truman pressed the British to permit the immediate entry of 100,000 Jewish refugees.

The British prevaricated. Despite the discouraging evidence of twenty years of failed negotiations, Foreign Secretary Ernest Bevin still hoped the issue could be decided around a conference table. Regardless of American pressure, and the fact that post-war Britain was now heavily dependent on the United States for economic support, Bevin still hoped for a negotiated solution. In November 1945, he announced the formation of an Anglo-American Committee of Inquiry to try to find an equitable solution to the deadlock between Jews and Arabs.

Five months later, the committee announced its findings. The British would continue as the principal great power in control of Palestine. Their mandate still held. But they also acquiesced to Truman's demand that 100,000 Jews should be allowed to come to Palestine. The Jews there should be allowed once again to purchase land. The committee also declared that the best hope for Palestine was still a unitary state of Jews and Arabs.

As the debate raged, news arrived regarding the fate of Jews who had tried to go back to their former lives in Eastern Europe. As detailed in Chapter 12, many were murdered and most of those who were not had prudently returned to the relative safety of occupied Germany. From there, a few hoped to reach Britain or America, but for most there was only one place they felt they would feel safe: Palestine.* With this in mind, a people-smuggling organisation known as Brichah – meaning 'flight' in Hebrew – was created.

Even in Western Europe, and in full knowledge of the Holocaust, reaction to returning Jews could be callous. Keith Lowe quotes typical remarks aimed at survivors of the camps: 'What a pity you were not made into soap' and 'They must have forgotten to gas you.' One Dutch camp survivor recalled: 'Where there should have been pity, I encountered the dry, difficult to approach, repellent, amorphous mass known as officialdom.'

In Germany, the former citizens of the Third Reich were shown hard-hitting newsreels about the Holocaust, as part of the process of 'denazification'. Many viewers were moved to tears, but the newsreels did not always produce the right results. Lowe writes of two cinema audiences in Garmisch and Memmingen (both close to

---

* One ten-year-old Jewish girl in Poland named Yehudit Kirzner, who had survived in plain sight because 'she did not look Jewish', was told by her father not to tell anyone in her post-war village school that she was a Jew. Only when the family left for Palestine, her father said, would she be able to be Jewish.

Munich and the Austrian border) where the film was greeted with cries of 'They didn't kill enough of them' and thunderous applause.

So, *quelle surprise*, at the end of the war, 300,000 of Europe's surviving Jews, mainly from Hungary, Czechoslovakia and Poland, attempted to flee the continent. These migrants found that almost everyone wanted to help them on their way. Poland and Hungary, as they had been before the war when they complained that they as well as Nazi Germany had a 'Jewish problem', were especially keen to help them go. Even the Soviet Union, notoriously reluctant to let its citizens escape its communist regime, encouraged this migration. Ports in Italy, France, Romania, Bulgaria and Yugoslavia all allowed Jews to embark to Palestine. America, especially, facilitated this exodus, not by allowing entry to the United States (only 12,849 Jews were permitted entry to America immediately after the war) but by helping to facilitate the journey – not least in their persuasion of their British allies to allow 100,000 Jews to enter Palestine.

Now the only country actively trying to discourage this great flow of people to Palestine were the British, the great power still officially in command of the territory. Many of those who made the journey, the British protested, were not survivors of the camps but Jews who had managed to evade capture or who had sat out the war in the Soviet Union. The British were also reluctant to believe the stories of further Jewish persecution in their former homelands. Keith Lowe writes that they protested that these tales of post-war murders and even massacres in Eastern Europe were a ploy by Zionists to encourage huge numbers to flee to Palestine. Lowe also states that representatives of the British government argued that it was morally wrong for Europe's Jews to leave. A British Foreign Office statement declared it was 'surely a counsel of despair

... to admit that the Nazis were right in holding that there was no place for Jews in Europe'. This is a difficult point to argue against. The Nazis' seething hatred for the Jews had prompted their desire for Europe to be *judenfrei*, and this was an ambition they largely achieved.

Lowe points out that Ernest Bevin even said that 'there had been no point in fighting the Second World War if the Jews could not stay on in Europe where they had a vital role to play in the reconstruction of that continent'. But Bevin was almost certainly being disingenuous. Very few soldiers, apart from Jews themselves, felt they were fighting to protect Jews. Their persecution in the hands of the Nazis, it seemed, was very much a post-war justification for the harsh way the Allies had targeted the Nazi civilian population in their bombing campaign.

Britain was in an unenviable position. Having been the originator of the Balfour Declaration – declaring support for a Jewish homeland – and having taken on responsibility for the territory of Palestine in the post-First World War settlement, a full-scale conflict between Jews and Arabs even greater than the pre-war struggles was now materialising in front of their eyes. So, alone among the victorious nations, Britain continued to try to prevent the exodus of Jews from Europe. Royal Navy ships intercepted the boatloads of refugees heading for Palestine and tens of thousands were interned. While some were kept in camps within Palestine and even Mauritius, most were sent to displaced persons camps in Cyprus, which were run along similar lines to prisoner-of-war camps. 'After all that,' recalled concentration camp survivor Rose Lipszyc, 'we were back behind barbed wire again.' She added: 'The English weren't starving us, and they weren't killing us like the

Germans, but it was so traumatic, that the very same people who had freed me just a short time ago now incarcerated me.'

Over 50,000 of those intercepted en route found themselves under canvas or crowded into squalid huts, behind barbed wire and under constant guard. Medical aid and a reasonable diet were provided, but this must have seemed like an unwelcome interlude for the prisoners, many of whom had survived the Nazi camps. Although 400 or so of these captives died in this further detention in Cyprus, the camps also produced 2,000 babies, and inmates organised training and educational courses for themselves.

For Britain, the Cyprus camps were a failure on several levels. Quite aside from the poor 'optics' of often ragged Jewish refugees being held behind barbed wire, the camps did very little to discourage the boats heading for Palestine. As Keith Lowe points out, in all this there was an element of 'King Canute trying to hold back the tide'.

Beset with its own economic decline and dwindling military power and weighed down by the desire to preserve its rebellious empire, Britain's ability to maintain order in the mandate of Palestine was failing fast. Sensing this, militant Zionist groups in Palestine grew bolder and began an active terrorist campaign against their British guardians. This, in turn, was to spark a rise in antisemitism in the UK.

For me, it is a difficult issue on which to take sides. Who could fail to sympathise with the Jews who had survived the abominable cruelty of the Nazis and had subsequently discovered, post-war, that they could *still* no longer return to their former Eastern European homes and were offered scant welcome by other Western nations. No wonder Palestine was such an attractive destination, and as the opportunity presented itself, no wonder so many Jews took it. But, then, who could argue with the Arabs who found themselves invaded by a rival religion. Lowe quotes the Arab historian Walid Khalidi, who pointed out that his fellow Palestinians 'failed to see why they should be made to pay for the Holocaust'.

The Jews who had settled in Palestine had been quick to realise that they would have to fight for their lives to stay there. Their new promised land was not the refuge from hostile Europe they had wanted. Ever since the 1930s, Jews had been in a constant battle with Palestinian Arabs to stay there, and as more Jews arrived, the greater the hostility they generated. So much so, it is estimated that 10 per cent of the male Arab population of Palestine were killed, injured or exiled in the years before 1945. But the tide was turning against the Palestinians and the population of their country changed in remarkably little time. In 1922, 11 per cent of the country was Jewish. By the end of the Second World War, this had risen to 31 per cent. The Jews in Palestine, hardened by the Holocaust, had become a well-organised, determined and fearsome force.

The British continued to resist Jewish immigration to Palestine and persisted in their attempt to bring order to their mandate. This prompted fierce resistance from Jewish militias, who had their roots in pre-war Palestine as self-defence organisations intent on protecting Jewish settlers from their Arab neighbours. The three most significant were the aforementioned Haganah, the Irgun and the Lehi, and after the war they turned their attention on the British soldiers stationed in Palestine.

As all this seethed away, British attempts to reconcile Jews and Palestinians through diplomatic channels continued to fail. The two sides were completely intransigent. The Palestinian Jews refused to accept any solution that did not involve a Jewish state and suggested a partition of territory between Jews and Arabs. The Palestinian Arabs refused to accept any notion of a Jewish state and were determined that all of Palestine should be controlled by Palestinians.

In June 1946, the conflict escalated when the British cracked down on Jewish opposition with Operation Agatha, arresting known resistance fighters and mounting raids on arms caches. This in turn prompted the bombing of the British Army HQ in Palestine at the King David Hotel, Jerusalem, which caused the death of ninety-one people.

By 1947, the British also decided to send a refugee ship named *Exodus* back to Europe as the Cyprus camps had become so crowded. The ship, acquired by Palestinian Jews, had sailed from France in July 1947 with over 4,500 Jewish refugees, all of whom were displaced persons or survivors from the Nazi camps. In an attempt to make an example of the ship and discourage others wanting to make the journey, *Exodus* was intercepted by British warships off the coast of Palestine. During the interception, the British opened fire on the ship and one Jewish crew member and two refugees were killed, with several others being wounded. Crew member Avi Livney's account shows the ferocity of the British attack:

On our last night, the British ships came in one at a time, rammed us, threw tear gas bombs and stun grenades, and succeeded in getting a large party of club-swinging marines on board. Three people were killed, including our second mate Bill Bernstein. Over a hundred were injured. By daybreak, we surrendered and were towed into Haifa.

At the Palestinian port of Haifa, the passengers were transferred to three smaller vessels and returned to Europe. Back in France, the passengers refused to leave and the French authorities refused to forcibly remove them. As the incident made headlines around the world, the passengers went on hunger strike for twenty-four days. 'The conditions were terrible, we had no sleeping berths, everyone was on the floor,' recalled one fifteen-year-old boy, Yossi Bayor, who was a passenger on the ship.

Eventually, the British government told the ships to sail to Hamburg, and the passengers were interned in camps in the British zone of occupation. The whole episode was a PR disaster for Britain and attracted global attention, triggering much sympathy for the refugees and the idea of a Jewish state.

Meanwhile, the Jewish defence forces continued to wage a clandestine war against their British occupiers who were trying to contain this resistance with increasingly draconian measures. Between 1938 and 1947, twelve members of the Irgun and Lehi underground resistance were sentenced to death by the British, ten of whom were hanged, with two others dying by suicide while awaiting execution.

The goings-on in Palestine provoked outrage among many British people, stirred up no end by hostile newspaper reports. A *Daily Mirror* piece on 4 August 1947, for example, gives a flavour of the tone:

IRGUN GIVES 'EYE FOR AN EYE' ORDER

As the terrorist Zvai Lenmie broadcast: 'We'll follow the Bible Commandment "An eye for an eye,"' Jewish thugs in Palestine yesterday blew up the railway south of Tel Aviv.

In the summer of 1947, the Irgun carried out an attack on a prison in Acre, facilitating the escape of twenty-seven Irgun and Lehi fighters during which British and Palestinian prison warders had been killed. In retaliation, three Irgun guerrillas, captured during the raid, had been sentenced to death following a trial. To try to save these three men from the gallows, the Irgun captured two British soldiers and threatened to kill them if the sentence against their men was carried out.

These events, which became known as the 'Sergeants Affair', came to a tragic end and had a profound impact on the British will to remain in Palestine. At the heart of it were two twenty-year-old lads, with the sort of then fashionable interwar Christian names that bring to mind The Shadows or Larry Parnes's stable of 1950s British Elvis wannabes. Sergeants Clifford Martin and Mervyn Paice stare out of their surviving photographs, pop idol handsome, their young lives cut short in increasingly horrible circumstances which would culminate in their cold-blooded murder.

The whole story makes an uncomfortable read. Martin was the son of an Egyptian Jewish mother and even spoke Hebrew. Paice had every sympathy for the Jewish cause in Palestine. Both of them were passing on useful information to a Haganah contact when they were bludgeoned, chloroformed and bundled away on the night of 11/12 July by the Haganah's rivals, the Irgun. They were held in the basement of a diamond-polishing plant in Netanya, and for three frantic weeks, the British Army tried to find them. The circumstances of their imprisonment are the stuff of nightmares. Held in a tiny cell barely twelve square foot in area, soundproofed and in total darkness, the two men were given a supply of food and drink and a bucket for body waste. They were also supplied with an oxygen cylinder for when the air became too foul to breath. This they endured for seventeen days while the news of their kidnapping became a subject of international interest, with desperate pleas for their safety being made by their parents.

But the British were determined to go ahead with the execution of the three Irgun fighters who had been sentenced to death and they were all hanged at dawn on 29 July. Later that day, the Irgun commander in charge of the operation, Menachem Begin,* decided on immediate retaliation, describing the decision to execute the two sergeants as the most difficult of his life.

The executions were even crueller than the preceding seventeen days in captivity. Hanged by a rope suspended from the ceiling, the two men were made to stand on a chair which was then kicked away, leaving them to be slowly throttled over fifteen minutes. Reports of the execution say the first man to be hanged asked if he could leave a message but was told there was no time. The bodies were then left dangling in a eucalyptus grove near the village of Even Yehuda. Notes were pinned on them reading: 'Two British spies held in underground captivity since July 12 have been tried after the completion of the investigations of their "criminal anti-Hebrew activities" on the following charges.' There followed a list of spurious indictments, including: 'Membership of a British criminal terrorist organisation known as the Army of Occupation.' Perhaps anticipating unfavourable comparisons between the executions of the Irgun fighters, who had been tried in a court and had their cases examined at length, this fake information attempted to give the impression that the two lads had been given a fair and legally justified trial.

'Found guilty of these charges they have been sentenced to hang and their appeal for clemency dismissed.'

---

* The very same Menachem Begin who became the sixth Prime Minister of Israel and won the 1978 Nobel Peace Prize with Egyptian Prime Minister Anwar Sadat following the peace treaty between the two nations.

To add insult to injury, a booby trap was placed under the bodies and a soldier cutting them down was temporarily blinded in the explosion.

The executions were reported all over the world and provoked outrage. Contrary to whatever some people thought 'the Jews' would think, the Association of Jewish ex-Servicemen in Britain placed a wreath on the plinth of the Cenotaph, inscribed with the words: 'In memory of Sergeant Martin and Sergeant Paice, who died doing their duty in Palestine. From the Jewish ex-Service comrades of the British forces.'

In Palestine, British forces unleashed their anger on the Jewish population, in an appalling breakdown of army discipline. Having been under constant strain and fear of being kidnapped themselves, when they heard their comrades had been murdered, British soldiers went on the rampage, killing five random Jews and smashing shopfronts.

The Irgun's bold reprisal provoked considerable ill-feeling among fellow Jews in Palestine, too. A television documentary maker, working in 2012, found few surviving participants in these events willing to speak about what happened and, most importantly, their own participation. A memorial grove was established to honour the two British sergeants and still exists to this day.

Understandably, Jews in Britain feared a backlash and the reaction against the killings offers a telling insight into the nature of racism. In the days that followed the murders, and the international newspaper headlines they provoked, Britain's homegrown Jewish population had to endure the nearest thing to a pogrom since medieval times. In Liverpool, especially, angry crowds rioted for five days and 300 Jewish properties were attacked, including a synagogue which was burned down. There were also riots in Manchester, London and Glasgow. Synagogues were daubed with antisemitic graffiti such as 'Hang All Jews' and 'Destroy Judah', and other properties were defaced with graffiti including 'Hitler was right' and 'Jews – good old Hitler'. Jewish gravestones were desecrated. It is not difficult to imagine the bewilderment of British Jews in response to these attacks. One Manchester shopkeeper, for example, placed a sign in the window of his premises reading: 'As a British sailor I fought for you. This is my reward.'

Many national newspapers downplayed the reports of disorder in British cities, but *The Guardian* covered these incidents in greater detail and they certainly make for disturbing reading – not least in the clear evidence that antisemitism was indeed 'lurking under the pavement'.

The headline 'New Outbursts Against Jews' appeared in *The Guardian* on 4 August 1947:

> The incidents in Manchester began again after darkness fell. Police were called to disturbances in Derby Street, Cheetham Hill Road, to which a crowd of civilians had gone hearing that Jews were meeting in the Assembly Rooms nearby. A crowd of 300 or 400 waited outside the Cheetham Hill Assembly Rooms and people attending a dance and social there were unable to leave for some time ... At Salford a large crowd held up traffic to watch the plate-glass windows of Messrs Montague Burton's shop in Broad Street being broken and there were cheers and cries of 'Down with the Jews!'
>
> Demonstrations occurred in a number of parts of Liverpool last night ... A large store in Wavertree Road was considerably damaged. A large number of plate-glass windows were smashed and, it is understood, that goods were taken from windows.

There were other reports of looting in damaged shops in other areas of the city, including a Jewish cabinet-making factory: 'A hostile crowd damaged N.F.S. hoses and fought firemen as they tried to fix hydrants in position to fight the fire at the cabinet works.'

In another incident, reported *The Guardian*, a small wooden synagogue in a Jewish cemetery was set alight and the staff attacked while they opened the cemetery gates to allow the fire service in.

The article went on to report:

The chief trouble centre was in Lawrence Road, Wavertree, where over a hundred windows belonging to both Jewish and non-Jewish owners were shattered in an outburst of hooliganism lasting over two hours. Five arrests were made in the area, and when the police were escorting the men into Laurence Road police station the crowds demonstrated and the station windows were broken by bricks and bottles.

Birkenhead's Jewish community faces the prospect of going without meat after a week-end resolution passed by fifty public abattoir slaughtermen who refused to handle kosher killings.

On 6 August, *The Guardian* published another article headlined 'Uneasy Calm After Liverpool Riots':

The ugliest aspect of this epidemic of violence is that most of those taking part in it are youths and girls, that children have been among the looters, and that great crowds have watched acts of savagery without any evidence of disapproval, still less any attempts to intervene. How much of what is happening is real anti-Semitism and how much hooliganism, though of unprecedented viciousness, can only be guessed at.

> In Mount Pleasant ... a Gentile woman who had had a stone
> through her window said she thought the disorders were caused by
> 'the scum of Liverpool, mostly after loot'.

There are some curious parallels here with the nationwide riots
that followed the police shooting of Mark Duggan in the summer
of 2011. Quite apart from the high-summer timing there was also
evidence of opportunist looting. *The Guardian* article quoted above
finishes with this observation:

> More disorder broke out at Eccles last night ... Shortly after dusk
> a crowd of 200 to 300 people gathered in the town square ... The
> crowd moved up Church Street where windows were broken at a
> Woolworth's store, a shoe shop, and a music shop ... There is no ev-
> idence that the disorders are in any way connected with anti-Jewish
> feeling.

Having recently watched David Baddiel's autumn 2022 Channel
4 documentary *Jews Don't Count*, I have every sympathy with his
remark that as a Jew he feels as responsible for the events in Israel
as any white Christian should feel about what Putin is doing in
Ukraine. This the rioting people of Liverpool, Manchester, Glasgow and London obviously did not feel in 1947. 'The Jews' were
to blame, just as modern-day racists are happy to believe all 'the
Blacks' are criminals and all 'the Muslims' are terrorists.

The killing of the sergeants in 1947 also provides material for
a debate on the effectiveness of terrorist tactics. In the UK, every
antisemite felt they nursed a justifiable hatred. But following the
outrage, the British stopped executing Jewish resistance fighters

in Palestine. So, for the Irgun, these retaliatory hangings could be justified by the result they produced.

Shmuel Katz, a senior figure in the Irgun high command, said: 'The British understood that after the *Olei Hagardom* [the Jewish term for their "martyred" underground fighters] went to the noose with their heads held high and after the sergeants were hanged, there was no more scope for escalation. The game was over.'

For Britain, the killings were the final straw. The will to remain in what was an obviously intractable situation ebbed away. Even Winston Churchill, now Leader of the Opposition, was happy to denounce the British presence in Palestine as a costly occupation with no tangible benefit.

Among the British people, opinion was divided. Many sympathised with the Zionists and their desire for their own homeland. But every violent incident, especially one that resulted in the death or injury of British soldiers, continued to provoke outrage.

One extraordinary piece appeared in the *Daily Mail*'s comment column on 8 September 1947, in the middle of the sorry saga of the *Exodus*. Entitled 'Have Done With', it is a classic example of having your cake and eating it too. While expressing sympathy for the Jewish passengers of the ship, the writer uses terms that would make any reasonably minded 21st-century reader squirm. 'The lurid drama of the Jew ships is complete,' writes the author of the piece. 'Here were three shiploads of Wandering Jews come to haunt the twentieth century.' He goes on: 'All are to blame, including Jews. For though there were unplumbed depths of misery in those ships, there was also more roguery to the square yard than in almost any other vessel in the world.' He then describes the passengers as 'victims of the propagandists, profiteers, and terrorists of their own and other races'.

Deeply resenting the poor publicity generated by Britain's clumsy handling of the *Exodus* affair, the writer foams:

> To gullible foreigners it seemed to justify all they had been saying about the 'brutal British'. And to make more trouble they swiftly seized the chance to infiltrate agitators among the Jews who sailed to Hamburg under the protection of the British flag.
>
> Britain, rightly or wrongly, is only trying to carry out the terms of the mandate entrusted to her. If the mandate is to be withdrawn – so be it.

He continues in a bate of self-righteous fury:

> The British people will be delighted to lay down a burden which has brought them many kicks … We should hand it over to those wise nations who know so much better than we do how to run it – or better still, to UNO. Britain should get right out of Palestine. It is no use to us morally, materially, economically, or strategically. Let us have done with it.

The last paragraph somewhat undermines the pretence that Britain was in Palestine out of the goodness of its heart.

Following a further futile attempt to bring the warring parties together, the British decided to take their intractable problem to the newly formed United Nations. The UN suggested a partition of Palestine with separate areas for Arabs and Jews but that the territory should remain economically united. The hotly contested city of Jerusalem would belong to neither Jews nor Arabs, and instead would be an international city, separate from either side. This solution seemed equitable enough to the post-war powers that held sway at the United Nations and was adopted on 29 November 1947 by the UN General Assembly – as Resolution 181.

For the Zionists, this was the breakthrough they had been hoping for. For the Arabs, it was a disaster. Further fighting between the two sides broke out immediately and escalated into a full-scale civil war.

As their global power and influence slipped away, the British announced they were giving up their mandate. There was no appetite to remain. They would leave on 15 May 1948. Britain's Zionist opponents in Palestine seized the moment. The Haganah, the Irgun and the Stern Gang, often bitter rivals in the past, now joined forces and were able to seize most of Palestine. Arabs were driven from their villages. Massacres took place. Between 300,000 and 400,000 Palestinians fled in terror to neighbouring Arab countries.

The day the mandate ended, the Zionists proclaimed the Jewish state of Israel. The United States and the Soviet Union, in a now rare show of unity, immediately recognised the new nation. The following day, the land was invaded by the armies of Syria, Transjordan, Iraq and Egypt. This seemed like a daunting prospect, but none of the Arab countries acted with any degree of coordination. And their combined fighting strength was actually less than 22,000 soldiers. They faced a tough and highly effective fighting force of 60,000 well-motivated Israeli soldiers. And most important of all, in the damning words of Peter Mansfield's *A History of the Middle East*, the Arab armies were 'useful only to perform ceremonial parades'. In this way, 600,000 Israelis were able to fight off 40 million neighbouring Arabs.

Fighting ended in January 1949 and temporary borders were

agreed. No peace treaty was signed and hundreds of thousands of Palestinians fled from their homes to adjacent areas where they and their descendants continue to live diminished lives, eking out an existence in refugee camps.* These circumstances are known to Palestinians as the Nakba – the catastrophe. In Israel, 156,000 Arabs remained and became citizens of the new state. Post-establishment of this new nation, Jews continued to flow into Israel and by 1970, around 2.5 million lived there. In 2023, the figure is a little over 7 million. The existence of the state, surrounded as it is by hostile neighbours, remains highly contentious. As does its relationship with the West. In the years since its creation, Israel's existence is still unsettled and a running sore for the Arab world, fuelling a succession of terrorist outrages and the rise of the medieval fascist theology of Islamic State.

Historian Jonathan Schneer, in his book *The Balfour Declaration: The Origins of the Arab-Israeli Conflict*, characterises this seemingly irresolvable situation then, as now, with a poetic reference to Greek mythology: 'During World War I … Britain and her allies slew the Ottoman dragon … By their policies they sowed dragon's teeth. Armed men rose up from the ground. They are rising still.'

But at the heart of this complex story, there are millions of people who felt that the only place where they could feel safe from the malignant disorder of antisemitism was a homeland of their own. One *Kindertransport* refugee, Bertha Leverton, is quoted in Lyn Smith's *Forgotten Voices of the Holocaust*. And regardless of the rights and wrongs of the thorny issue of Israel and the Palestinians who were uprooted, it is difficult not to feel sympathy with her perspective:

---

* The Sabra and Shatila refugee camps, scene of two infamous massacres during the 1982 Lebanese Civil War, had their origins in the diaspora that followed the establishment of the state of Israel.

Everybody in the whole world closed their doors ... If they had opened their doors, they could have saved European Jewry ... That is a guilt that the whole world has to bear, as well as Germany. And if Britain had done what it could have done: opened the gates of what was then Palestine, they could have saved European Jewry. But they did more than any other country in the world in saving Jews, and that record stands.

Conclusion

An 'Ecosystem of Hostility': The Twenty-First Century

Dear Mogg

I need to get on this small boat bandwaggon asap. Suella has
shown how the fate of the NHS, Education, housing, street
safety, teenage health all rest on us stopping them. I'll go and
stand on Dover Beach and wave a flag.

Pro patria in pitta

Boris

MICHAEL ROSEN'S SATIRICAL TWEET IMAGINES
A CORRESPONDENCE BETWEEN BORIS JOHNSON
AND JACOB REES-MOGG. APRIL 2023

This book has been looking back to the 1930s and '40s to consider the treatment of Britain's wartime refugees by the government, the newspapers and the public. So, how do we compare
today? As I write, the newspapers are full of stories about the 'small
boats' crossing the Channel. The furore over migrants is still making
daily headlines and features prominently in political speeches. For
some people, immigrants, refugees and asylum seekers have merged
together into a blob of undesirable foreigners wanting to take an

unfair slice of our rapidly diminishing pie. Then, as now, politicians seek to capitalise on the anxiety this has created to further their own agendas.

Speaking as the man on the Clapham omnibus, I think Michael Rosen is right. The government in power since 2010 has presided over a catalogue of disasters. While I admit that the global pandemic and the war in Ukraine have added to our woes, I'm sure most fair-minded people would acknowledge that the mayhem of Brexit and the economic dogma that public utilities work best when privately operated – see how well that's worked out for the railways, the water companies and Royal Mail – have not benefited us as a country. And all the Tories and their attack dogs in the newspapers and newly emerging partisan TV news stations have to offer are ludicrously over-egged culture war assaults on 'woke' and the 'liberal elite', bound up with a blatant attempt to also blame these troubles on refugees and asylum seekers.

So, is this fear of refugees, and other immigrants, justified? Figures released by the Office for National Statistics show that one in six of the population of England and Wales was born outside the United Kingdom. In London, the figure is four in ten. Net migration for 2022 was over 600,000. Regardless of whether this influx is actually beneficial to the country, the harsh truth is that this is an unfortunate time to be a refugee wanting to come to Britain – and current Conservative rhetoric and hostile newspaper coverage make no exception for people fleeing oppression among the other arrivals who have come to live and work here.

This is also a country with a considerable housing shortage and a social infrastructure left in tatters by a Conservative government which has presided over a huge increase in the wealth of its backers and natural supporters. Unquestionably, a large influx of new arrivals needing housing, educating and the attention of a doctor is adding to this problem.

In Chapter 11, I quoted an article from 1942 concerning Jews and the black market from the Association of Jewish Refugees newsletter. The piece reports in hard facts the small number of Jews actually involved in this activity compared to the perceived notion that 'the Jews' were the major players in this illicit trade. The writer laments: 'The results should help to kill any incipient anti-semitism in this country, if, indeed, the purveyors of this racial prejudice are amenable to facts.'

Alas, being amenable to facts regarding refugees is still a major issue eighty years on. The anger surrounding the subject is fuelled by a perception that asylum seekers tumble off the boats at Dover clutching an English phrase book whose opening sentence is 'Take me to the benefits office'. Such opinions are frequently aired by callers to radio talk shows like LBC and in tabloid readers' comments.

The idea that such people blithely 'rock up' (as one radio phone-in caller put it) on our shores to be aided and abetted by wealthy lawyers keen to fill their pockets by giving them what we as a country are being denied is a potent message, and one the government has been keen to sustain even at the highest ministerial level.

The topic will be a curious one for future historians, especially those who might take an interest in our media. The whole issue has been a tabloid obsession for the entire twenty-first century, and as it was in the 1930s and '40s, it is cloaked in a fog of misinformation. The situation is complicated and ripe for sophistry and many current popular views on the subject are based on distortions, half-truths and even outright lies. A casual glimpse at the British tabloids will tell you that 'soft-touch Britain' is refugees' number one destination and that these people are criminals who don't share our values and are coming here to claim benefits AND to take our jobs. But Home Office statistics, as pointed out to me by journalist Danuta Kean, show that Britain received 56,000 asylum applications in 2021 compared to 191,000 in Germany and 121,000 in France. Figures for 2022 are similarly instructive. Home Office figures reveal 74,751 asylum applications for that year. European Council figures for 2022 say 962,160 asylum applications were made in the EU, with the majority for Germany or France. Kean also points out that asylum seekers can't even claim benefits in Britain and neither are they permitted to work.[*]

Despite some of the tabloids' best efforts to keep their readers ignorant, we no longer hang stray monkeys because we have mistaken them for shipwrecked enemy Frenchmen.[†] But there's no doubt that the tabloids still have an unhealthy ability to shape the opinions of the British people, not least to the advantage of their enormously wealthy proprietors. It is not only their ability to manage news and perceptions to their benefit; they have long known that feeding prejudice – hate-mongering, in essence – is a lucrative endeavour too.[‡]

To pick an article at random to illustrate this point, I want to consider a piece in the *Daily Mail* on 28 October 2022 headlined 'Residents hit out at anti-social behaviour at Holiday Inn housing

---

[*] This, in turn, fuels the market for 'illegal' workers, especially in areas of the labour market formerly filled by migrant EU workers who are no longer allowed to come to Britain since 'free movement' ended.

[†] This apocryphal story was supposed to have happened in Hartlepool during the Napoleonic Wars. Alas, it's probably no more true than the story about former Hartlepool MP Peter Mandelson admiring the mushy peas in a local fish and chip shop and asking for a portion of guacamole.

[‡] I can think of no better example of this than the tabloids' treatment of social workers. If they take away a child from dysfunctional parents, they are 'the town hall Gestapo'. If they don't and the child is killed by the parents, they are dithering hippy do-gooders.

130 asylum seekers...', which complained that the young men who had been placed there, in a budget hotel seven miles from the centre of Rotherham, had been disturbing local people with loud music and football games that went on into the early hours. Looking online, I see that the story was not picked up by any other newspaper and that it had provoked only a couple of tweets and only the far-right organisation Britain First had featured it in their online material.

Regardless of the rights or wrongs of the story, what is especially notable about the *Daily Mail* coverage is how it makes a deliberate attempt to stir up enmity towards the local Labour MP, John Healey, by selectively quoting from his letter to Suella Braverman about the situation. The part of the letter where Healey points out that the backlog dealing with asylum cases, which 'has tripled in the last four years with a total of 109,735 asylum seekers stuck in the system awaiting a decision at the end of March 2022', is not mentioned in the body of the newspaper article.

The readers' comments are also noteworthy. The ones reproduced below are from the 'best rated' and all have thousands of readers ticking the green arrow to demonstrate their approval. For readers unfamiliar with the *Daily Mail* website, each story usually allows readers to leave a comment under the article. These comments can then be rated by other readers, who can click on a green arrow to signify approval and a red arrow to show disapproval. It is then possible to ascertain the popularity of a particular view. These comments are, of course, open to exploitation by pressure groups and that modern-day mythical creature the troll, and it is difficult to know which comments are genuine. The fact that few contributors use their real names is not reassuring. Quite aside from a total lack of sympathy for the migrants at the Holiday Inn, it's especially notable that the same complaints about refugees which come up time and time again are exactly the same ones from eighty years before. For example, 'Hammihamster' writes:

> I wish someone would pay all my bills and feed me for free, unfortunately despite paying taxes all my life I have to wait months for a hospital appointment, and had to spend 10 hours in A&E to get help. Our country is in crisis because we are paying for free loaders who are stretching the capacity of our NHS.

'Surreyresd' comments:

> Stick them all in old army barracks on bread and water until they want to get back in the boats to france

And 'Tudor14' writes:

> And yet thousands of veterans are still living on the streets.

The comments repeat a classic theme of the undeserving 'them' getting far more than the deserving 'us'. The issue of homeless veterans is a complex one often relating to a catalogue of woes known among veteran support groups as the 'eight Ds' – drink, debt, drugs, divorce, depression, domestic violence, dependency culture and 'digs', meaning accommodation. But like most knee-jerk reasoning, the easy explanation is far more understandable. Yet there is no real correlation between help given to refugees and help denied to military veterans.

Perhaps most depressing of all are the remarks of 'Musical Patri-ot', the most popular comment on a follow-up article from the next day by Tory MP Natalie Elphicke, entitled 'When will The Left admit this is no refugee crisis... but simply illegal immigration':

> Why aren't the government taking it seriously? The costs of housing and feeding these folks is bad enough. The real problem is the crime and threat to our physical wellbeing. We have no idea who these people are. Half of them hate our culture and wish to change it. The other half want to operate drug cartels. We are completely ruined by those who are supposed to govern.

So, here we have in a nutshell the twin prejudices faced by refugees: they are here to commit crimes and they hate our culture.

The American writer and philosopher Susan Sontag once said that '10 per cent of any population is cruel, no matter what, and 10 per cent is merciful, no matter what, and the remaining 80 per cent can be moved in either direction'. My money's on most of that cruel 10 per cent being regular contributors to the *Mail* online comments.*

The outrage generated by thousands of refugees and asylum seek-ers 'living at our expense in hotels' is not helped by the extremely slow business of processing asylum applications. In 2021, the average wait was twenty months to receive an initial Home Office decision. A year later, *The Guardian* reported that over 40,000 asylum seek-ers had been waiting between one and three years for a decision. Other European neighbours such as France and Germany manage

---

* Despite the obvious scope for pressure groups and even 'Putin's troll-farms' skewering online opinion, I do think these comments are a broad reflection of the attitudes of the right-wing public. It was notable that when Paul O'Grady, famous for his drag persona Lily Savage, died in 2023, almost all the comments in the *Daily Mail* were generous and positive and a handful only were critical of his 'abhorrent lifestyle', as one contributor put it – a clear indication of how much the country's attitude towards homosexuality has mellowed in my lifetime.

to process such claims faster, although waiting times are growing longer as demand increases.

At the moment, the United Nations 1951 Refugee Convention, established after the war to ensure refugees were given legal protection, is a thorn in the government's side. Not least because it prevents politicians from carrying out some of the more draconian measures the government wishes to enact to deter refugees coming to Britain. For example, the terms 'illegal' or 'bogus' asylum seekers, so widely used by some Conservative politicians and their partisan newspapers, are bogus in themselves. Under international law, anyone has the right to apply for asylum in any country that has signed the 1951 convention and to remain there until the authorities have assessed their claim. This convention also recognises that people fleeing persecution may have to use irregular means in order to escape and to claim asylum in another country. So, at the moment, there is no legal way to travel to the UK for the specific purpose of seeking asylum. A classic catch-22.

In addition, opponents of access for refugees are frequently heard asking why 'they' don't claim asylum in the first country they reach. But there is nothing in international law that obliges a refugee to do this. Besides, many in fact do exactly that. According to statistics amassed by the Refugee Council in mid-2022, Turkey hosts around 3.7 million refugees, Germany 2.2 million and Pakistan 1.5 million, to mention the top three countries hosting refugees. 'Soft-touch Britain' is not even in the top twenty-five countries hosting refugees. Other bodies, such as the California-based World Population Review, put Britain even further down the list at country number thirty-two, in figures from 2023.

But it's not just tabloid newspapers which present their readers with a skewed version of reality here. Many in the current government have been happy to do this too, adding to this increasingly fractious and complex debate with plain untruths. An *Independent* article in April 2022 detailed all the lies Johnson and his ministers had told Parliament to date, provoking the Conservative MP and former Attorney General Dominic Grieve to condemn 'a disregard both for good governance and truth'. In March 2022, for example, Johnson claimed Britain had taken 'more vulnerable people fleeing theatres of conflict since 2015 than any other country in Europe', whereas, as detailed above, other European countries had in fact taken far more than Britain.

Former Home Secretary Priti Patel also added to the obfuscation by claiming in February 2022 that anyone who was not Syrian or Afghan was an 'economic migrant'. When Conservative MP Tim Loughton asked Patel 'what safe and legal routes' were available to asylum seekers who were not Syrian or Afghan, she replied: 'Economic migrants do not need safe and legal routes.'* Railing against 'asylum shopping', she went on to claim in relation to those crossing the Channel in small boats that 'the majority of them are people who are not claiming asylum or fleeing persecution'.

This at a time when her own Home Office released statistics showing that almost all people arriving in small boats were claiming asylum and that two-thirds of these applications were granted on the first decision and a further half of all appeals against a refusal were then successful.

The *Independent* article goes on to reveal that Suella Braverman's claim when she was Attorney General that the Channel crossings

---

* Presumably this remark predated the outbreak of the war in Ukraine, which began in late February 2022.

were 'illegal' was also false. The way the law stands is that the people smugglers are acting illegally, but their passengers are not. You cannot travel to Britain through a legal route without a visa, and Britain does not issue refugee visas. British law also recognises that people have to be present in Britain to claim asylum and that trying to get to the country to do this is not illegal. All of which makes the current policy of attempting to ban refugees 'for life' from applying for asylum if they come here 'illegally' a nonsense and a cruelty.

What is especially disheartening is Braverman's inability when she was appointed Home Secretary to explain how asylum seekers *can* take a safe and legal route into the UK. Speaking at a Home Affairs Select Committee on this very subject in November 2022, the Home Secretary claimed that people 'can put in applications for asylum' and that there are 'safe and legal routes', yet she failed to explain what these were when quizzed by Tory MP Tim Loughton. He said that her 'very weak' responses highlighted 'that there's a shortage of safe and legal routes' into the UK for many migrants. What this plainly suggests is that it is important for the current government to 'look tough' on immigration, even to the extent of making promises they know are legally unlikely to be kept.[*]

So, what *is* our attitude towards refugees in the twenty-first century? Britain is still a popular spot for people fleeing war zones, political and religious oppression and whatever else the twenty-first century visits on its inhabitants. The reasons for this are varied, not least the universality of the English language and family ties for many of the people seeking to come here. And although it's not their fault that we have such a wretched housing problem and

---

[*] This has been a hallmark of this government and their newspaper allies. Sound bites are trumpeted by the Tory press with little or no follow up on whether they have been achieved. For example, Johnson's 'forty new hospitals' pledge in the 2019 election has seen fewer than a quarter of new hospital building projects even getting to planning permission stage by 2023.

ramshackle underinvested public services, it's still unarguable that having people arrive in great numbers is not going to ameliorate these problems.

So, now, more than ever, I think we are ambiguous about refugees. The hugely popular Paddington books and films about Michael Bond's *Kindertransport*-inspired bear present the British as a kind and welcoming people.* It would take a brave soul in the right-wing press to dismiss Paddington as bleeding-heart lefty propaganda. Even Boris Johnson latched on to this feel-good factor in a speech in 2022 declaring:

> For centuries, our United Kingdom has had a proud history of welcoming people from overseas, including many fleeing persecution … From the French Huguenots to the Jewish refugees from Tsarist Russia, to the docking of the Empire Windrush, to the South Asians fleeing East Africa … all have wanted to be here because our United Kingdom is a beacon of openness and generosity.

Such sentiments sit uncomfortably with a man who has been criticised by lawyers who see him as being responsible for attacks on their profession by violent right-wing extremists. Even in the speech above he could not resist having a pop at 'a formidable army of politically motivated lawyers who for years have made it their business to thwart removals and frustrate the government'. Previous speeches of his concerning the law and asylum seekers had castigated 'lefty human rights lawyers and other do-gooders' and

---

* I always liked the title of Barry Turner's account of the *Kindertransport* arrivals: *And the Policeman Smiled*. It's a lovely shorthand picture of an essentially benevolent society.

'left-wing criminal justice lawyers [acting] against the interests of the public'.

The current government's attitudes and actions are undoubtedly popular with some sections of the public, but I wonder how many? I sense disquiet even among some of those in the Tory Party. In April 2023, Home Secretary Suella Braverman denounced refugees trying to come here as criminals who 'possess values which are at odds with our country'. She infamously announced she 'dreams' of sending failed asylum seekers on a one-way flight to Rwanda.* But here she stands at odds with several establishment figures who even her most credulous admirer would find difficult to dismiss as 'woke' bleeding-heart do-gooders.

Richard Dannatt, the former head of the British Army, declared that Rwanda was 'not the sort of environment I would put people from Syria and elsewhere in the world into'.

Former Cabinet minister and party conference darling from the Thatcher era Michael Heseltine told *The Independent* in May 2023: 'This is not the Conservative Party I joined, and there is a very nasty flavour of commentary beginning to develop. I was deeply concerned at the implication that somehow there is a different sort of human being that is seeking refuge in this country.'

Even former Conservative Prime Minister Theresa May described the government's small boats policy as 'a slap in the face to those of us who actually care about the victims of modern slavery'.

Given the forging of links between right-wing conservatives in the UK and the new Trump Republicans, I await with trepidation the arrival of the insult 'CINO' (Conservatives in name only) to go

---

* Braverman has also been happy to use the inflammatory word 'invasion' in reference to refugees and dismissed opponents of her refugee policies as 'an activist blob of left-wing lawyers, civil servants and the Labour Party'.

with the sinister 'RINO' dismissal of anti-Trump Republicans like Liz Cheney.

I like to think that this particular brand of conservatism isn't particularly popular in itself – although I'm happy to admit I could be wrong. The *Daily Mail*, unquestionably the bogeyman of this book, is after all one of the UK's most popular newspapers. How much this has to do with its politics – rather than its celebrity tittle-tattle, its Orwellian 'two minutes hate' for Harry and Meghan and its online photosets of wannabe celebs 'showcasing' their 'pert' bikini-clad bodies – is open to debate. I'm guessing it's a mixture of all these things. I'd like to think that Boris Johnson's huge electoral majority occurred because the Labour Party made the disastrous choice of electing Jeremy Corbyn as their leader rather than because of a widespread admiration for what Johnson and his party stood for. (When I watched Keir Starmer's gracious and dignified tribute to the Queen after she died, I found myself thinking 'What on earth would Corbyn have said?' and more importantly 'What would he have looked like when he said it?')

The Tories, I suspect, would be foolish to think that the majority of the population are right behind them in the divisive culture wars they are creating as a distraction to their failing governance of the country. The laughing-stock quality and miserable viewing figures of those new right-wing TV channels GB News and TalkTV give me hope that people can still see through this particular line of reasoning.* I think the sort of Tory politicians who subscribe to the new National Conservative philosophy know in their hearts that only lies will keep the less-discerning voter on side – after all, that was how

---

* I watched GB News the other day out of curiosity and was immediately confronted by an awkward young man talking about 'the woke mind virus'. If he'd stopped me in the street to say such things, I would have assumed he'd wandered out of a psychiatric hospital.

they achieved their Brexit victory. 'We send the EU £350 million a week – let's fund our NHS instead' is a far more appealing slogan than 'Let's turn the UK into Singapore-on-Thames, so the richest people in society can get considerably richer while the rest of you get poorer and we can get rid of those laws guaranteeing protection of your workplace rights and all those other pesky "red-tape" rules that stop us making even more money."*

The picture in the twenty-first century remains more complex and problematic than that faced by the society which had to decide whether to welcome Jews fleeing Nazi Germany. As I mentioned at the start of this conclusion, the newspapers are full of stories about the 'small boat' asylum seekers. Anyone with a shred of empathy might see many of these people as worthy of our sympathy and support. But even the left-wing and liberal news sources recognise that perhaps a quarter or more of these arrivals come from Albania, a country with no great human rights issues or ongoing war. To add fuel to this particular fire, some of these Albanians, invariably young men, have their crossing funded by, and are thus in hock to, criminal gangs behind UK drug businesses. This uncomfortable fact is un-contested even in *The Guardian*, a newspaper which has been most sympathetic to refugees both now and during the period considered by this book. This in turn prompts classic 'whataboutery', where the 75 per cent of migrants in those boats who have a legitimate reason to flee are deemed unworthy of concern because 25 per cent don't. A quick glance at tabloid online readers' comments demonstrates

---

* Many Conservatives are keen to represent 'red tape' as an intrinsically bad thing. But just as the 1987 *Herald of Free Enterprise* ferry disaster seemed to symbolise the Thatcherite erosion of workplace rights and safety standards in pursuit of profit, so the terrible 2017 Grenfell fire in north Kensington seems a fitting symbol for the current Conservative government's disregard of safety in pursuit of profit, not to mention the demonisation of 'the poor' by the council which ignored resident concerns. These are the things I think of when right-wing libertarians rail against 'red tape'.

that many feel the issue of these migrants can be dismissed because 'they're all Albanian drug dealers'.

Likewise, pity the poor Muslim refugee fleeing medieval tyranny, who faces a hostile reception based on the fact that the perpetrators of some of the ugliest terrorist outrages in Britain since the IRA bombings of the previous century come courtesy of British-based Islamist extremists, several of whom came from families who were refugees themselves.*

Muslim refugees fleeing the Taliban and Islamic State and the internecine horrors of the Syrian Civil War also face prejudice based on an interpretation of their faith by some of their co-religionists which is counter to 21st-century Western values. This is almost certainly connected to the sad fact that even the most deserving refugee cases from Afghanistan do not seem to be getting a fair hearing. In a letter to *The Times* in May 2022, General Sir John McColl, NATO deputy supreme allied commander Europe 2007–11, wrote:

> Nine months after the fall of Kabul, hundreds of Afghans, who risked their lives working for Britain for two decades, remain abandoned … The Government publicly promised to relocate locally employed staff to the UK, but the Afghan resettlement system is broken. Applications are left unanswered, pleas for help are ignored, civil servants are taken away for other tasks, and posts are left vacant.

Nonetheless, any politician would be foolish to ignore the simmering anger generated by the entire migrant debate. These issues spark

---

* While three of the four London transport bombers in the 7 July 2005 attacks were born in Britain, all of their families came to the UK as post-war immigrants. The four main exponents of the failed follow-up attack on 21 July 2005 were all born outside the UK. The suicide bomber behind the 2017 Manchester Arena attack at an Ariana Grande concert, while born in Britain, was the son of Libyan refugees who had settled in Manchester. All of these links to asylum seekers have fuelled anti-refugee prejudice.

intense feeling which feed into a sense of grievance and betrayal that is nurtured by the ugly far-right fringes of British politics. Any responsible political debate on the topic needs to make a concerted effort to address popular misconceptions and counter the effects of the tabloid reporting that's stoking this anger for political capital.

Ultimately, whether you believe that we are being 'swamped by an alien culture' in 'soft-touch Britain' or that the government is looking for scapegoats to distract the population from the failures of Brexit and the fiascos of the Liz Truss and Boris Johnson premierships will most likely depend on the newspaper you read or which TV channel you choose to watch for your news.

Now, the period I have written about is fading from living memory – but not quite. My mum, born a month after Anne Frank, died only a year or so ago. On my last research trip to the Wiener Holocaust Library in April 2023, I found a February 2023 newsletter for the *Dunera* troopship survivors which announced that Bern Brent had just celebrated his 100th birthday in Canberra with his son and daughter and many friends. As I write, he is the last remaining passenger of that voyage who is still alive. Formerly Gerd Bernstein, Bern had left Berlin in December 1938 aged fifteen – on a Quaker-organised *Kindertransport*. Fascinatingly, despite the unpleasant nature of the voyage, the newsletter reports Bern as saying that 'being sent to Australia was the best thing that had happened to him … This was Britain's loss and Australia's gain!'

Anyone writing about the thorny issue of refugees and asylum seekers faces a complex set of facts and opinions. The complexities are consistently passed over in exchange for the simple explanation – it's THEM, coming over here stealing our jobs/homes/educational and healthcare resources. I do want us to calm down a bit and for the Tory Party and their newspapers to stop feeding the anger and bigotry around this issue.* In my plea for sympathy, I am sure to be asked 'What would YOU do then, let EVERYONE in?' I'm inclined to agree with Jack Kessler in the *Evening Standard* in his call for 'a grown-up conversation' on the whole issue of migrants to Britain, of which refugees are now an intrinsic part. We are happy to host European refugees from Ukraine. We like it when people from overseas come here to fill labour shortages and pay university fees, even though a recent poll suggested 57 per cent of British people think immigration is too high. Yet only one in ten think we are taking too many Ukrainians and overseas NHS and care sector workers. The complexity of the issue makes it vulnerable to simple solutions and prejudices. People complain about the cost of keeping asylum seekers yet seem to overlook the fact that they are not allowed to work.

Refugees and asylum seekers have always been treated with fear and suspicion and this has frequently denied them the sympathy they deserve. In the 1930s, the Great Depression and the threat of destitution caused by Britain's decline as a leading manufacturing nation, not to mention the looming likelihood of a further conflict with Germany and the uncomfortable truth that antisemitism lurked under the pavement, made many people believe they had enough of their own troubles to worry about to accommodate the refugees who wanted to escape from Nazi Germany.

In 21st-century Britain, our country is beset with anxiety caused by an explosion of price rises for food, power and mortgage payments. Undoubtedly, these troubles blunt people's reservoir of

---

* I find myself agreeing with the Hope Not Hate advocacy group, which wrote in May 2023 that the 'ecosystem of hostility towards migrants' created by the symbiotic relationship between the Conservative government and the media 'sets the country in a dangerous direction' – and we need to do our best to fix this.

compassion for outsiders fleeing war and persecution. Then, as now, political extremists and mainstream politicians are happy to present the refugee as a scapegoat and a distraction.

There is a cruelty to the current government which echoes those Conservatives I write about in the opening chapters of this book – the ones who talked about Jewish refugees 'scurrying' to Britain in their hundreds of thousands and decrying sympathisers as adopting a 'sloppy sentimental attitude' to Hitler's victims. Is there much between Admiral Barry Domvile saying that 'Jewish ways are not our ways' and Suella Braverman's dismissal of refugees who 'possess values which are at odds with our country'?

In Chapter 7, I quoted Simon Parkin in his book *The Island of Extraordinary Captives*:

> Every government must balance its humanitarian obligations with the need to uphold national security. To categorise refugees from Nazi oppression as 'enemy aliens', however, was to invite populist scorn and hatred upon those in most need of compassion in wartime, and represented a moral failing on a national scale.

In the twenty-first century, we also have a lack of humanitarianism, or as I prefer 'basic common decency', in some of our government representatives and newspaper supporters – not least the sort who would use a word like 'cockroach' to describe a fellow human being and then have an editor who thought this was a suitable thing to print in a family newspaper.

In 1940, the Home Secretary John Anderson wrote a letter to his father saying: 'The newspapers are working up feeling about aliens. I shall have to do something about it or we may be stampeded into an unnecessarily oppressive policy. It is very easy in wartime to start a scare.' These sentiments should resonate with anyone in politics who still has a scrap of decency in their soul.

I am fond of that well-used George Santayana saying: 'Those who do not learn history are doomed to repeat it.' We will always have politicians and newspapers keen to sow division and create distraction to further their interests, and it would be naïve to hope this will not always be the case.

So, do we have a long, proud tradition of helping refugees? I would hope that most of the Jews who came here before and during the war would say that we do. But in our current era, we also have a government and popular press keen to foment a lack of empathy towards extremely vulnerable people for their own political ends.

But critical as this book has been about the way Britain treated its refugees during the war, especially the internment of thousands of Jews who did not deserve such treatment, I still believe we should feel proud of our wartime record. The Poles who stayed here faced upheaval and hostility, but they thrived and assimilated. For Jews such as Ilse Gray, who escaped the Nazis by coming to Britain, there was a happy ending. And those refugees who were given such a hostile reception in the 1930s and '40s went on to make a huge contribution to the country's wealth and culture in the years that followed. And not a single one of them turned out to be a spy or a fifth columnist.

Bibliography

Books

Angell, Norman, and Buxton, Dorothy Frances, *You and the Refugee: The Morals and Economics of the Problem* (Harmondsworth: Penguin, 1939)

Bardgett, Suzanne, and Cesarani, David (eds), *Belsen 1945: New Historical Perspectives* (Elstree: Vallentine Mitchell & Co. Ltd, 2006)

Barr, James, *A Line in the Sand: Britain, France and the Struggle that Shaped the Middle East* (London: Simon & Schuster, 2012)

Bartrop, Paul R., and Eisen, Gabrielle, *The Dunera Affair: A Documentary Resource Book* (Melbourne: Schwartz & Wilkinson and the Jewish Museum of Australia, 1990)

Berthon, Simon, and Potts, Joanna, *Warlords: An Extraordinary Re-creation of World War II Through the Eyes and Minds of Hitler, Churchill, Roosevelt and Stalin* (London: Lume Books, 2020)

Blend, Martha, *A Child Alone* (Elstree: Vallentine Mitchell & Co. Ltd, 1995)

Boyd, Julia, *Travellers in the Third Reich: The Rise of Fascism Through the Eyes of Everyday People* (London: Elliott & Thompson Ltd, 2017)

Brendon, Piers, *The Dark Valley: A Panorama of the 1930s* (London: Pimlico, 2001)

Caestecker, Frank, and Moore, Bob (eds), *Refugees from Nazi Germany and the Liberal European States* (New York: Berghahn Books, 2010)

Dimbleby, David, and Reynolds, David, *An Ocean Apart: The Relationship Between Britain and America in the Twentieth Century* (London: BBC Books/Hodder & Stoughton, 1988)

Friedman, Jonathan C. (ed.), *The Routledge History of the Holocaust* (Abingdon: Routledge, 2011)

Fussell, Paul, *Wartime: Understanding and Behaviour in the Second World War* (Oxford: Oxford University Press, 1989)

Garrett, Leah, *X Troop: The Secret Jewish Commandos Who Helped Defeat the Nazis* (Boston: Mariner Books, 2021)

Gilbert, Martin, *Never Again: A History of the Holocaust* (London: HarperCollins Illustrated, 2000)

Gillman, Peter, and Gillman, Leni, *Collar The Lot! How Britain Interned and Expelled its Wartime Refugees* (London: Quartet Books, 1980)

Grenville, Anthony, *Encounters with Albion: Britain and the British in Texts by Jewish Refugees from Nazism* (Cambridge: Legenda, 2018)

Hartshorne, Susan Vipont, *The Story of Yealand Manor School* (York: William Sessions, 2007)

Kochanski, Halik, *The Eagle Unbowed: Poland and the Poles in the Second World War* (London: Allen Lane, 2012)

Kushner, Tony, and Knox, Katharine, *Refugees in an Age of Genocide* (London: Frank Cass, 1999)

Kushner, Tony, *The Persistence of Prejudice: Antisemitism in British Society During the Second World War* (Manchester: Manchester University Press, 1989)

Laqueur, Walter, *Generation Exodus: The Fate of Young Jewish Refugees from Nazi Germany* (Massachusetts: Brandeis University Press, 2001)

Leighton-Langer, Peter, *The King's Own Loyal Enemy Aliens: German and Austrian Refugees in Britain's Armed Forces, 1939–45* (Elstree: Vallentine Mitchell & Co. Ltd, 2006)

Lethbridge, Lucy, *Servants: A Downstairs View of Twentieth-Century Britain* (London: Bloomsbury, 2013)

London, Louise, *Whitehall and the Jews, 1933–1948: British Immigration Policy, Jewish Refugees and the Holocaust* (Cambridge: Cambridge University Press, 2000)

Longerich, Peter, *Holocaust: The Nazi Persecution and Murder of the Jews* (Oxford: Oxford University Press, 2010)

Lowe, Keith, *Savage Continent: Europe in the Aftermath of World War II* (London: Penguin Books, 2013)

Mansfield, Peter, *A History of the Middle East* (London: Penguin Books, 2010)

Müller, Daniel, *Zionism and the British Mandate* (Munich: GRIN Verlag, 2011)

Olson, Lynne, *Last Hope Island: Britain, Occupied Europe and the Brotherhood That Helped Turn the Tide of War* (New York: Random House, 2017)

Parkin, Simon, *The Island of Extraordinary Captives: A True Story of an Artist, a Spy and a Wartime Scandal* (London: Sceptre, 2022)

Patkin, Benzion, *The Dunera Internees* (Australia: Benmir Books, 1979)

Schmidt, Christine E., *A Bitter Road: Britain and the Refugee Crisis of the 1930s and 1940s* (London: CreateSpace Independent Publishing Platform, 2016)

Schneer, Jonathan, *The Balfour Declaration: The Origins of the Arab-Israeli Conflict* (London: Bloomsbury, 2010)

Segal, Lore, *Other People's Houses: A Refugee in England 1938–48* (London: Gollancz, 1964)

Semmens, Kristin, *Seeing Hitler's Germany: Tourism in the Third Reich* (Basingstoke: Palgrave Macmillan, 2005)

Sherman, A. J., *Island Refuge: Britain and Refugees from the Third Reich 1933–1939* (London: Routledge, 1994)

Smith, Lyn, *Heroes of the Holocaust: Ordinary Britons Who Risked Their Lives to Make a Difference* (London: Ebury Press, 2013)

Taylor, D. J., *Orwell: The Life* (London: Vintage Books, 2004)

Ungerson, Clare, *Four Thousand Lives: The Rescue of German Jewish Men to Britain, 1939* (Stroud: History Press, 2014)

Ward, Ken, *And Then the Music Stopped Playing* (Felixstowe: Braiswick, 2006)

Williams, Bill, *Jews and Other Foreigners: Manchester and the Rescue of the Victims of European Fascism, 1933–40* (Manchester: Manchester University Press, 2011)

Articles and Papers

Anderson, Benjamin, 'British Political Responses to the German Refugee Crisis during Occupation', Institute for Research of Expelled Germans (undated)

Berry-Waite, Lisa, 'Policing migration: researching the lives of foreign nationals in a government archive', National Archives (2023)

Clifford, Rebecca, 'Britain's response to WWII child refugees puts modern society to shame', *The Conversation* (2017)

Cohen, Nick, 'Russian spies? No wonder we recoil from this demonisation of refugees', *The Guardian* (2022)

Franklin, Sarah, 'The untold story of Britain's POW camps', *Irish Times* (2017)

Gillman, Peter, and Gillman, Leni, 'An internee ship and a U-boat captain at sea', *The Guardian* (2022)

Goldman, Aaron, 'The Resurgence of Antisemitism in Britain During World War II', *Jewish Social Studies*, vol. 46, no. 1 (1984)

Green, Geoffrey, 'England Expects...: British Jews under the white ensign from HMS *Victory* to the loss of HMS *Hood* in 1941', *Jewish Historical Studies*, vol. 41 (2007)

Karpf, Anne, 'We've been here before', *The Guardian* (2002)

Kershaw, Roger, 'Collar the lot! Britain's policy of internment during the Second World War', National Archives (2015)

Mayblin, Lucy, 'On the Frontline: A Long and Welcoming Tradition?', Discover Society (2018)

Orwell, George, 'Antisemitism in Britain', *Contemporary Jewish Record* (1945)

Philpot, Robert, 'Does Britain's focus on the Kindertransport hide a guilty conscience?', *Times of Israel* (2018)

Photiadou, Artemis Joanna, '"Extremely valuable work": British intelligence and the interrogation of refugees in London, 1941–45', *Intelligence and National Security*, vol. 36, issue 1 (2021)

Pistol, Rachel, 'Refugees from National Socialism Arriving in Great Britain 1933–1945', Gale (2020)

Rosenberg, Stephen Gabriel, '"HMT *Dunera*", the scandal and the salvation', *Jerusalem Post* (2015)

Smyth, Richard, and Moore, Bob, 'Prisoners of War in Britain during WW2: where were they held?', *BBC History Magazine* (2021)

Staufenberg, Jess, 'Amid post-Brexit hatred, remember the Polish soldiers who fought alongside UK soldiers in the Second World War', *The Independent* (2016)

Swallow, Douglas Muir, 'Transitions in British Editorial Germano-phobia, 1899–1924', PhD thesis, McMaster University (1980)

Taylor, Becky, and Ferguson, Kate, 'Refugee History: The 1930s Crisis and Today', Refugee History (2017)

Uncredited, 'The battle of Bamber Bridge', *The Week* (2022)

Uncredited, 'The Heritage and Contributions of Refugees to the UK – a Credit to the Nation', Refugee Week (2015)

Uncredited, 'Over There: Instructions for American Servicemen in Britain, 1942', United States War Department (1942)

Venturini, George, 'The HMT *Dunera* scandal', Australian Independent Media Network (2019)

I also made use of the National Archives website and the United States Holocaust Memorial Museum, the Orwell Foundation and the Refugee Council.

Newspapers and Newsletters

Material from British newspapers came from the British Newspaper Archive at the British Library, London:

——, *Daily Express*

——, *Daily Mail*

——, *Daily Mirror*

——, *Daily Telegraph*

——, *Manchester Guardian*

——, *The Times*

The Wiener Holocaust Library, London, gave me access to:

——, Association of Jewish Refugees newsletters, 1941–45

——, *Jewish Chronicle*

Date of publication for pieces I've cited are given alongside their use in the chapters.

Television Documentaries and Other Material

Britain's Secret War Babies, Channel 4, Wall to Wall (2022)

The US and the Holocaust, BBC Four (2023)

A Welcome to Britain, Ministry of Information (1943)

Acknowledgements

Material for this book came from hundreds of sources both online and in actual old-fashioned libraries and archives. I am especially grateful to the following people for giving me permission to quote from their work: Artemis Photiadou, Danuta Kean, David Reynolds, D. J. Taylor, Jonathan Schneer, Keith Lowe, Leah Garrett, Lucy Lethbridge, Michael Rosen, Rebecca Clifford, Simon Parkin and Tony Kushner.

I would also like to thank: Nicola Sutton and Sonia Bacca at the Wiener Holocaust Library, for their help and kindness; the staff at the British Library's British Newspaper Archive, for their patience in helping me locate material; Torsten Jugl, photo archivist at the Wiener Holocaust Library, for his help in unearthing material; Sally Fricker and Fiona Dunbar, for kindly having me to stay when I needed to visit London to research this book; Gill Offley, for feedback; Daniel Gans and Aviva Gans Rosenberg, for further information and photographs concerning their father Manfred Gans, whose extraordinary exploits appear in Chapter 9; my friend Ilse Gray, who kindly provided me with material from her own records and also from her sister Eva, a fellow *Kindertransport* veteran

who died in 1977; Keren David at the *Jewish Chronicle*; Gemma
Blane at the Association of Jewish Refugees; Deborah Mulqueen
of Vallentine Mitchell & Co. Ltd, for permission to quote from
Martha Blend's book *A Child Alone*, first published in 1995; Mary
Greenham of News Presenters Ltd, for permission to use material
from Sean Fletcher's magnificent Channel 4 documentary *Britain's
Secret War Babies*, made by Wall to Wall; Peter and Leni Gillman,
who were especially generous with their time and advice when I
contacted them to ask permission to quote from their excellent
book *Collar the Lot!*; Robin Greaves, for kindly giving her time
to speak to me at length about her memories of Yealand Manor
School and her mother's book *The Story of Yealand Manor School*; the
Society of Authors, for their generous assistance with a grant from
the Authors' Foundation fund; and finally, my agent Charlie Viney,
Olivia Beattie at Biteback who commissioned this book and also
my editor Ella Boardman, whose eagle eye and helpful suggestions
have proved invaluable.

Most especially, I am indebted to my dear wife Jenny, for her
generous support and kindness while I was writing this book.

Index